English, Solitaire, Cowboy, Cuckoo...

English, Solitaire, Cowboy, Cuckoo...

Real Life Tales of Travel Troubles and Madcap Misadventures

MIKE LEAVER

The Book Guild Ltd

First published in Great Britain in 2024 by
The Book Guild Ltd
Unit E2 Airfield Business Park,
Harrison Road, Market Harborough,
Leicestershire. LE16 7UL
Tel: 0116 2792299
www.bookguild.co.uk
Email: info@bookguild.co.uk
X: @bookguild

Copyright © 2024 Mike Leaver

The right of Mike Leaver to be identified as the author of this
work has been asserted by them in accordance with the
Copyright, Design and Patents Act 1988.

All rights reserved. No part of this publication may be
reproduced, transmitted, or stored in a retrieval system, in any form or by any means,
without permission in writing from the publisher, nor be otherwise circulated in
any form of binding or cover other than that in which it is published and without
a similar condition being imposed on the subsequent purchaser.

Typeset in 12pt Minion Pro

Printed and bound by CPI Group (UK) Ltd, Croydon, CR0 4YY

ISBN 978 1835740 293

British Library Cataloguing in Publication Data.
A catalogue record for this book is available from the British Library.

To Helen, whose obsessional desire to spend a night on the top of Ben Nevis changed my life… and ultimately led me to write this book.

Chapter One

Half a mile from my childhood home stood a building so tall, a small boy could reasonably believe it to be an ancient fortress, now occupied by witches who flew up its great circular stairways on broomsticks. Though a less imaginative infant might simply be shoved towards its terrifying entrance, howling that he did not want to go to school.

In my case, the person doing the pushing was known within the family as Funkle Trumpet. Five years earlier, on the 27th December 1952, she had gone to a special baby shop to see what was available. I imagined this shop to be quite small with a lady sitting behind a counter doing her knitting, until a customer walked in from the street. Just like our corner shop, in fact. Anyway, on entering the baby shop, Funkle Trumpet had taken a particular liking to me, sitting quietly on a shelf. So she had brought me home. But now she had changed her mind and wanted to abandon me at the frightening building, which I had previously only seen from the outside.

By the year of my abandonment, the building had lost some of its original grandeur, now being mostly encircled by a brewery and a sauce factory. This made everything very smelly – sort of tomatoey; tainted by a pong which a small child, unaccustomed to pubs, could not identify. But most mornings, the imposing entrance still gobbled up children, the heavy wooden doors banging shut behind the last straggler, so it was still very frightening.

After pushing me into the terrifying building for five days, Funkle Trumpet gave up trying to abandon me – but only until the following Monday. This time, however, she only took me as far as the lollipop lady who waited on the pavement opposite the school entrance. I believed her only interest in life was waiting for a car to approach, then walking into the road to make it stop. Because I lived in an area called the slums, this did not happen very often. But the lady had the instincts of a power-crazy shepherdess, so gathered her flock of children and waited to wave her magic lollipop wand at any driver who approached. I became her favourite child because I was the best at dragging my feet, knowing that on reaching the far pavement, I would have to go to school.

After a year of being handed over to the lollipop lady, I began to question the routine. In the beginning, I had noticed that most children were taken to school by a grown-up but, after twelve months, only I was still being escorted. I found this most embarrassing. It identified me as a sissy, unable to cope without a hand to hold. So, one morning, I announced that I was going to school and walked out of the door. It caught Funkle Trumpet off guard, because she was still drinking her morning cup of tea. But it was what she had been trying to achieve all along, so I expect she was quite happy with the idea. And so my independent existence began.

I found my first day of freedom quite exciting. From my home I first walked through a narrow entry to reach the street. Here I turned right by a continuous row of houses, until I came to the corner shop. This was the furthest I had been on my own. But this time I crossed the road and headed onwards, all the way to the lollipop lady. It made me feel very brave.

By the time of this adventure, I had already begun to wonder why most yards were completely surrounded by houses, while ours had a gap at the end facing the entry. The houses on either side of this space were joined by a new wall, the smooth bricks making it difficult to climb. I asked Funkle Trumpet about this, which caused her to look very sad.

"It's a bomb site," she replied. "The people who once lived there were all killed."

I did not understand the implications of the last bit. But a previously unknown bomb site – wow! Within the week I had learnt to climb the wall and set about exploring the vast open space. And sometimes I chose that way to come home from school, because walking along a pavement had become boring.

Happy childhood memories are like flimsy play dinghies – used briefly in shallow paddling pools, then disappearing on the winds of time to a place unknown. But traumatic childhood memories have an anchor to hold them firm. There are good reasons for having this selective long-term memory. If something hurts you – say, picking up a piece of red coal from a hearth – you need to remember not to do it again. It is less important to recall the first time you found a hot-water bottle in your bed. In fact my first 'anchored' happy memory did not happen until I was twelve, and this I will come to presently.

So, where to begin with traumatic memories? Well, I can visualise every detail of a particularly horrible event which happened when I was six. It concerned a school lesson in which the girls were taught how to curtsy, and the boys the correct way to bow. During this unnatural activity, the girls had to pull their skirts sideways to make themselves look wider and therefore more scary. The knobbly-kneed boys, wearing short trousers, had no such defence. Surprisingly, this deranged practice did not take place in dark corners, unknown to local child welfare officers. On the contrary, it happened in a classroom with everybody watching; including a lady teacher, who clapped her hands in delight whenever a boy did what was expected. Not me. I deliberately put my arms in the wrong place and walked backwards to increase the distance between myself and the girl.

"No, no," screamed the teacher, "do it nicely."

But the girl, who had previously displayed a silly grin, was now trying to make her face look like that of a snuffling pig in a picture book. How could that be nice?

From this basic information, you might correctly assume that the infants were governed entirely by lady teachers. However, to maintain discipline they terrified us younger boys by saying that the senior school, which was situated in the same building, only had man teachers. These, we were told, caned all naughty boys on stage during every morning assembly. (I am not certain what happened to the girls, because they all disappeared somewhere else on reaching the age of eleven.)

"So," said the deranged lady teacher who thought my bow fell below her high standards, "you must practise being nice to girls before it is too late. Now let us try again – Tina, come here…"

Tina (the Tank) was the most frightening girl in our class. But on this occasion she proved to be my saviour, because she pulled her skirt not only sideways but also upwards to display her underpants. This actually caused the teacher to scream.

Given all this education, I am unable to explain why we did not have useful lessons like how to climb trees. Okay, in the slums any sort of plant life was hard to find, but we had plenty of bomb sites, where mountaineering skills might be developed. And what did the lady teachers do? Flap their hands in delight at the sight of girls chanting silly rhymes as they jumped over a skipping rope in the school playground. The teachers never once came to watch me learning to climb. Though, on reflection, I think ascending crumbling walls without a rope ultimately made me a more careful climber.

At the age of eight I finally completed the desperate climbing manoeuvre which took me from my bedroom window to a steeply slanting slate roof. Two delicate upward steps, aided by a pinch-grip on the windowsill, allowed me to make the long reach needed to curl my fingers over the crest. The far side of this was a vertical wall so, to avoid the off-balance move of sitting astride a ridge, I leant back on my arms. This put inward pressure on my feet, which made my shoes less slippery on the slate. From here, by alternately moving hands and feet sideways, I eventually reached a place from where I could dangle my legs down to a toilet-shed roof. Crossing this took me to within three feet of a gas lamp post. Just below the glass panels surrounding the mantle were two metal arms, which I could reach out and grab. (These arms were also used by lamplighters, who preferred using a ladder.) Anyway, I could hold the arms to swing across and encircle the post with my legs. Lower down, the post had a bulbous middle, together with ornate castings. Descending these took me to the yard. Once I had done the route a few times, I could come and go as I pleased through my bedroom window, without having to trouble my parents to open the front door. And even if I arrived home after dark, I had a gently hissing lamp to see me safely back across the kitchen roof.

HEALTH AND SAFETY ALERT: When I first attempted the kitchen-roof traverse I weighed about twenty kilograms. Crossing a slate roof as a heavier grown-up introduces the term climbers call 'loose'. That is to say, a hold might give way without warning. This could also apply to a child, if the supporting rafters are rotten or the nails rusted away. Sliding off a roof into a brick yard could easily result in injury or death.

Returning to the sticky-out arms on the lamp posts, these offered boys three technical grades or levels of difficulty. The first of these, which I will call 'easy', simply involved hanging from them to swing back and forth. The second, which I shall call 'moderate', required using your tummy muscles to curl up and hook your knees over the arm. But only the extremely brave had the courage to overcome the 'wall' of fear encountered on the third grade, which I will call 'severe'. This meant letting go with your hands to hang fully upside down, like a bat casually resting in a cave roof. However, once you overcame the initial fear, this 'severe' manoeuvre was just something you did if you wanted a break on the walk home from school.

Hanging upside down is a strange experience because the world is above your head. I never once saw a girl hanging upside down from a lamp post, which I considered a good thing. Can you imagine how frightening it would be for a boy if, say, he was sitting on a pavement, totally focused on playing a complex game of marbles, and then he glanced up and saw a girl apparently hanging from the sky? He would leap up in terror and flee, which, I suppose, is where our phrase for insanity – to lose one's marbles – comes from.

This frivolity does hide, though, what I later realised was a scandalous social issue: a sexist education system based on absurd Victorian ideas. For girls to be taught how to curtsy correctly, they had to wear skirts so that they could submissively bend their knees to an assumed dominant male. But I believe all females should be allowed to wear the clothes *they* consider best suit their needs. While at infant school, I had no idea what the distant future had in store for me. Only with hindsight can I say that it was the sexist education system of the 1960s which meant that, in later life, I was going to struggle to find a girlfriend; one who understood that living in an igloo on Ben Nevis was a perfect way to spend a Christmas holiday. But even as a child, I knew there was something wrong with a world which taught girls to do different things to me.

This led to another traumatic experience when I was eight. On this occasion, I was walking home from school when Tina the Tank stepped out in front of me. Because she was very large indeed, I was forced to stop. Then, rather than trying to sneak around her, I retreated until one of her 'assistants' tripped me up. A second assistant quickly pinned me to the pavement with her bony knee. Before I knew what was happening, the Tank had grabbed hold of one foot, an assistant taking the other. I was then dragged down a back entry, while the second assistant blocked any escape. I wish to make it clear that I was heavily outnumbered and not simply kidnapped by one girl. Also, in fairness to Tina, I have to say that she was slightly smaller than a military tank, but I have psychological issues when it comes to admitting that I was frightened by a girl from my class. The far end of the entry was blocked by a high wall, beyond which lay a bomb site. On reaching this wall, the three girls surrounded me.

"We only want to watch you do a wet," said Tina.

Having no sisters, I just assumed doing a wet was the same for girls and boys. In any event, given my terrifying situation, I was able to water the paving bricks without much effort. This generated squeals of excitement. Then the Tank dropped her underpants, lifted her skirt, and – panic! She did not have a winkle. This creature could only be a space alien who could not do a wet, which explained why she had wanted to watch me.

I ran to a corner, which must have confused them, because I was trapped like a timid mouse. But my studies of difficult climbing problems meant I knew that a corner gave me a 'bridging position'. With a gargantuan leap to get my hands to the top of the wall, I ascended, even though the rough brick had no specific holds. Okay, I was also propelled by fear, so my shoes skidded up like those of a fleeing cartoon character. Before the girls realised what was happening, I was lying on a 'summit ridge'. I knew the area well, so continued my escape across two bomb sites and various slate roofs.

This incident proves that climbing, as well as being good fun, aids survival. Indeed, in our evolutionary past, those who retained their 'happy monkey gene' were more likely to gain the advantage of not being eaten by a wolf. Climbing makes us happy because it is closely associated with escaping from animals who have big teeth – or, in this case, from Tina.

During the 1950s and '60s, virtually every house, train and factory burnt coal to obtain warmth and power. This caused much inner-city smog (smoke plus fog), which resulted in thousands of deaths. Older people might reminisce about the times when, as children, they had to get off a bus and walk in front of it, because the driver could not see the kerb. But my strongest memory of the smog is trying to find the toilet shed by using my hands like insect feelers.

Anyway, because of the smog, a doctor said my asthma had become so bad that I qualified for a place at an 'open-air', boys-only state boarding school. These had been set up in the countryside as a solution to the high number of deaths among vulnerable children. So, at the age of ten, I was plonked on a coach and taken to a place which, to me, looked like a secret army training camp. In any event, it was well hidden from the rest of the world and still had a central parade ground where children could be gathered and inspected.

The best thing about the school was the out-of-bounds fence. It gave the establishment the feel of a prison camp, and so made escaping really interesting. The masters played their part in this game by patrolling the nearby out-of-bounds area while carrying walking sticks or canes. This meant us boys could view them as fearsome guards who were liable to beat us if captured. But in the mysterious wilderness beyond the fence, I quickly learnt to avoid capture by going even further afield. This, of course, illustrates the imagination of a ten-year-old boy who had a particular liking for exploring 'foreign' lands. In practice we had head counts at every mealtime, so no adventure could last more than four hours – unless it was done at night. Then, after lights out, I could climb from a dormitory window to experience eight hours of freedom. This was a very important part of my early development: learning to cross rugged countryside in the dark without being seen. By the age of eleven my night vision would, I believe, have matched that of an SAS officer on a special mission.

Having said all this, there was one foreign country I was never brave enough to explore. Across the lane was the girls' open-air school, and it was widely believed that the surrounding territory was controlled by the inmates. Having once been kidnapped by Tina the Tank, I had a mortal fear of being taken prisoner by hundreds of similar 'space aliens'. Attempting to escape from their many clutching hands would surely have been futile.

In addition to exploring outwards, I naturally improved my climbing skills by using the only things available – that is to say, trees. And at this I was better than the big boys because, being lighter, I could venture into the thinner branches at the very top, then sway in the breeze, rather than hearing a loud crack of breaking wood before crashing to the ground.

When not climbing upwards or exploring outwards, we could dare each other to test the boundaries of what was possible within the prison camp, and so gain respect. Due to our limited resources, this often required using great initiative. I remember one amazing dare which involved nothing more than an old earthenware bottle; the sort apothecaries once used to keep medicines. In our case, every classroom had such a bottle to store ink. Every Monday morning the teacher's pet had the important task of taking the bottle around the classroom to fill the individual desk inkwells. Anyway, a boy was once dared to sneak into the history classroom and 'borrow' the bottle, emptying most of the ink outside. He then did a wet in it. Once he had done it, his gang members had to compete, effectively refilling the bottle with black urine. Returning the bottle to the top of the classroom cupboard did not make the room smell, because the cork stopper allowed the liquid to ferment – surprisingly, without actually exploding. The following Monday, the teacher's pet took down the bottle, causing five boys to start giggling. The master noted this, but was obviously in a good mood, so his cane remained lying harmlessly on his desk. And so the ink monitor set about filling the inkwells. Fortunately, in those days we still used nibs on a wooden stick to write – the consequences of doing the urine prank when more modern fountain pens became available would have been catastrophic. Anyway, by the time the ink monitor had filled ten inkwells, he was holding his nose, while the other boys were trying not to laugh. Then the smell reached the master. It was obvious from his expression that he could not understand what was happening. He sniffed, walked between the aisles, then sniffed some more. Finally, he decided to smell the ink bottle, which appeared to remind him of his time in the First World War trenches. Gas! Gas! Gas! In any event, he panicked and tried to push the bottle away. He seemed surprised when its contents splashed far and wide. (In those days, the long trousers worn by grown-ups had turn-ups to catch any liquid which ran down their legs.) But, full credit to the master: after restoring order, he only caned the boys who had giggled before the stopper had been removed, thereby indicating their guilty knowledge of the conspiracy.

Another good character-building exercise at the school was potato-picking lessons. For these, the PE teacher would lead fifty or so boys on a long military-style march to some muddy field or other. We then learnt four subjects simultaneously: firstly, what it was like to be a peasant in the Middle Ages (history lesson); secondly, where potatoes come from – thousands of them – as we worked the field, loading them into baskets, which we then carried to a tractor trailer (farming lesson); thirdly, how work relates to obtaining food, which keeps us alive, and how grown-up employment is a lot harder than having a paper round (life lesson); and finally, how to carry heavy things for hour after hour, and so develop endurance skills (mountaineering lesson). Of particular value to my later life was the PE lesson; strong muscles and mental endurance being essential for carrying a heavy rucksack on long-distance expeditions. I reckon that by the age of twelve my survival skills were equal to those of the average fourteen-year-old boy who had not been hardened by a state boarding school. However, my educational knowledge was equal to that of an average ten-year-old.

From the point of view of a trainee mountaineer, the most important aspect of the school's regime was its zero tolerance of sissiness. I soon learnt that crying was a pointless display of weakness which left you dehydrated and without friends. Knowing how to handle yourself in a boxing ring, and acquiring the ability to hold back tears while being publicly caned, were skills a proper boy needed to learn. Before I reached the age of eleven, my disability of being a crybaby in response to physical pain had been completely cured. This is an essential skill for a mountaineer. If injured in a remote place, it is no use crying because you want your mummy. Survival in such circumstances depends on pretending that it only hurts a bit and getting on with it. Mountaineering is about undertaking a challenge and sometimes putting a little effort into staying alive.

We now come to my first truly enjoyable childhood memory. Strictly speaking, this began when I first experimented with the challenge of running away when I was eleven. But it took a further year before I got really good at it. All my running-away studies took place in the middle of the night, after climbing out from the back window of the toilets. Once beyond the immediate area, the next challenge was to cross a range of hills which, back then, I considered mountains. As well as the physical challenge, I knew I had to dodge the enemy: any grown-up who wanted to capture me. Then, on one particular occasion when I was twelve, I also had to battle against a snow blizzard, which I found really exciting. When the police finally caught me at four o'clock in the morning, they seemed astonished at my appearance: wearing short trousers and generally covered in snow. Without doubt, the whole adventure was the happiest moment of my childhood. It also proved to the authorities that my ability to run away now exceeded their ability to prevent it. So Funkle Trumpet removed me from the school – result!

Having brought some common sense into my life, Funkle Trumpet moved us to live in a caravan by the seaside. Here, at Brean Sands in Somerset, a rocky headland projected a mile and a half into the Bristol Channel. I gazed at the towering cliffs of adventure, knowing that I had finally discovered the place where the grown-ups came to play. On the negative side, my new school also contained twelve-year-old girls, with whom I had to share a classroom. These frightening creatures knew about things of which I had no knowledge. One casual mention of the special baby shop I had come from reduced them to hysterical laughter.

"I bet your father had an awful shock when your mother brought you home," shrieked one.

Why all the girls thought this remark so funny I had no idea. Equally, they seemed confused by the fact that one of my parents was called Funkle Trumpet; the other Fred. I had never really thought about it before; it was just how it had always been in our family.

Chapter Two

Climbing sea cliffs, where falling into the waves replaces the safety offered by a rope, is called deep-water soloing. This is a specialist branch of climbing, generally done by experienced climbers in hot weather, wearing only shorts and lightweight rock boots – or, in my case, school gym pumps. The ability to swim is an integral part of the fun. But when has a pre-teenage boy, presented with towering cliffs above a vast 'swimming pool', ever separated his *actual* abilities from those of his fantasy life? And sea cliffs, he might reason, are only a grown-up version of tree climbing.

Well, not exactly. If you get stuck up a tree – given the need to appear brave at all times – it is normally possible to descend by simply hugging the trunk and slithering down to a convenient branch. On a cliff face, you are on a surface, like a fly, fully exposed to the elements. However, when on the Brean Down headland I only seriously miscalculated the difficulty of a climb on two occasions. On one of these I remember seeing the tips of my pumps tottering precariously on a one-inch ledge; the sea crashing into boulders far below. The steep wall above offered a random selection of finger-holds. In such circumstances it is difficult to be a superhero. But, with hindsight, because falling would have resulted in death, the intricate climbing moves appeared harder than they actually turned out to be.

The second miscalculation was more serious, because the rock ended at a steep bank of mud and grass. There was no skill involved in clawing my way up this; it was purely a game of Russian roulette: if the mud held my weight, I would survive; if I found myself holding a loose clump of grass, then it would be similar to taking a bunch of flowers to my own funeral.

So, when looking up a cliff face to work out a possible line of ascent, pay particular attention to any vegetation above the rock which might make reaching safe ground difficult.

After living in Somerset for six months, my idyllic childhood came to an abrupt end when my parents decided that a caravan was no place to spend a winter. Why their insane retreat to Birmingham needed to include me, I had no idea. So I said I would stay in Somerset by myself. But grown-ups can be very stubborn when they want to be. Naturally, faced with the forced departure from paradise, I ran away to hide in the sand dunes until hunger forced me to hand myself in and allow my parents to fulfil their ridiculous plan.

On returning to the slum dwelling of my infancy, the education authorities once again got involved in my welfare. Apparently, I was on their records as a 'delicate child' who needed to be treated with extreme care. Hence, they decided that the school I had attended as an infant/junior was too rough for my frail body. So, they gave me a place in a special delicate unit set up in a remote corner of a modern comprehensive in the suburbs.

After spending the winter in the city, Funkle Trumpet returned to the caravan at Brean – forgetting to take me with her. (I did not believe her excuse that I was now in a good school, and seasonal moves between Birmingham and Somerset would disrupt my education.) As a thirteen-year-old, I thought a more realistic explanation for her move was that she needed to put some distance between herself and Fred's banjo playing, which was extremely painful on our ears. When it was happening, I would go upstairs and hide my head under a pillow, but in those days bedrooms had bare wooden floorboards, so little sound insulation, and I could still hear it. Also, dividing walls between council houses were only a single brick thick, so the noise could go next door, then return to my bedroom from the side.

Because I was an only child, my parents were relatively rich – at least compared to those who had large families, which kept them in post-war poverty. And because we lived down a back entry, the rent was less than one pound a week. So I now found myself with two parents living far apart, and both earning money in their respective jobs. This led to circumstances which might, in the 1960s, be considered unusual.

On one occasion, after I had cycled 120 miles to Somerset on an ancient bicycle which had been found somewhere, I told Funkle Trumpet that it made my legs ache. On returning to Birmingham the following day, I said the same thing to Fred. Result! I was given a proper second-hand man's bike, which had cost three pounds. This amazing machine had twenty-seven-inch wheels, drop handlebars, and a fixed wheel sprocket with a ratio of four to one, but no gears. For the uninitiated, this meant that one revolution of the pedals gave four turns of the back wheel, resulting in nine yards of travel. So, ideal for any boy who liked overtaking mopeds on level roads, but it required the rider to get off and push the bike up steep hills. Another aspect of the fixed sprocket is that the pedals always whizz around four times faster than the wheels (which is why some old photographs show the downhill rider with their legs sticking out sideways to keep the feet clear of the pedals).

Anyway, with this proper man's bike, I was able to explore far and wide. So, the following year when Funkle Trumpet went back to the seaside after her now-routine winter retreat to Birmingham, I paid it little regard. Cycling between my parents was just something I did. This also had the great advantage that, if I disappeared for any length of time, either parent could think that I was with the other. Complete freedom! Few fourteen-year-old boys experienced such an idyllic childhood.

Travelling to and from places is an integral part of mountaineering. Typically, half the challenge of getting to a summit is the difficulty of reaching base camp. In the Himalayas, there are often many days of trekking through remote foothills before you encounter any difficult climbing. So, proper mountaineers need to learn how to travel, often in circumstances where they cannot simply give up and jump on the next bus which happens to be passing. Well, as a teenager I did not have a permit to enter Nepal, nor a yak to carry my load, but I did have a bicycle. So, after riding back and forth between Birmingham and Somerset for two years, I decided to set myself a greater challenge. This involved leaving the caravan early one morning and, rather than going directly north to Birmingham, heading south-west. On reaching Glastonbury I intended to go across the Mendip Hills to Bath, then to the Severn Bridge, via Bristol. From the far side of the bridge I would head north-east to Gloucester following the northern bank of the river (or any road that was close to it), all using only my own pedal power. My theory for this expedition was that if I could cycle 120 miles without difficulty, then a journey of two hundred miles would only be 66% more difficult. After all, I imagined that those who raced in the Tour de France did this sort of distance all the time.

Everything began well. In fact I have a particularly fond memory of pushing my bike along the footpath attached to the side of the Severn Bridge. The view across the sea was ever so pretty, and knowing that I was about to enter my first foreign country – Wales – was very exciting.

Apparently, in sport, the brain has the ability to balance pleasure and discomfort together with predicted outcomes. If, for example, my leg muscles start to ache after one hundred miles of cycling, and there are only twenty miles to go, the brain overrides the signal until a safe shelter is reached. If, however, after one hundred miles the task is only half completed, the brain – which has a greater understanding of the wider world – decides to agree with the legs that the excessive activity should stop immediately. In the specific instance of riding to Birmingham via Wales, after 121 miles neither my brain nor my legs could understand why I was still sitting on a bike. It is very important that those who undertake adventurous challenges understand this correlation between psychology and physiology. Doing something twice as hard does not necessarily mean it is simply going to take twice as long. In this instance, after walking across the Severn Bridge, when I returned to cycling my brain failed to understand what I was doing in a foreign country, eighty miles from my nearest bed. So, after pushing my bike up a hill, on seeing a signpost pointing to the village of Quay, I paused to consider my options. The village – which I reasoned would be pronounced 'Kway', as in 'Queen' – would have a shop where I could buy a bottle of pop and a chocolate bar. The two-shilling coin in my pocket would just cover this expense, and so stop me feeling thirsty, hungry and slightly miserable. Of equal importance, the signpost was pointing down a hill in the general direction of the River Severn. Maybe I could follow a less hilly road closer to its banks, and so reach Gloucester by a flatter route.

It was a very steep hill, which meant gravity did all the work. Then, on rounding a blind bend, my brain struggled to understand why it was suddenly seeing a lot of water – which was getting closer, very quickly. Instinctively, I risked the tightest turn imaginable, after which I found myself hurtling alongside a harbour wall with the water on my left. This was quite dangerous because, like most fixed-wheel bikes, my bike did not have a rear brake, and replacing my feet in the toe clips to slow down was impossible. Fortunately, after the cobbled surface came to an end there was a strip of rough vegetation, which brought me to a slightly entangled halt. *Uh?* In my first state of panic I had only seen water. Now I saw a wide river, with no obvious way to the other side. I became confused. Where had the village of Quay gone? I was certain I had not passed it. And even here, on the flat, there was no evidence of any recently demolished buildings. It seemed the village had completely disappeared!

Given the steepness of the hill, I had no choice but to push my bike back up what now felt like the side of a mountain. When finally returning to the main road, I realised my bike had a puncture –

presumably because of the recent ride through the tangled vegetation. I could normally repair punctures quite easily, but this one took three attempts, after which I gave in and used the old-fashioned method of packing the tyre with grass. (This idea probably originated when tyres were wider and five miles per hour considered a reckless speed.) When, about ten miles from Gloucester, I came to a late-night garage, I abandoned the grass idea. The money I had saved for my chocolate and pop went on a new puncture repair kit. This solved the problem with the bike, but meant I had not eaten for sixteen hours. Also, I had repaired the puncture using light from the garage window. When I returned to the lane, I realised that it was dark and my cycle-lamp batteries were flat. This meant riding only a little above walking speed and jumping from the bike onto a verge when I heard a car approaching.

As the hours of darkness passed slowly by, I came to understand a lot more about human physiology. First you hit what is known as 'the wall'. In a normal PE lesson this is the point where you fall to your knees and tell the teacher you can do no more. In later life, I was to discover that, if you apply the literal meaning of this statement when mountaineering, the result is generally death from hypothermia – so it is not an option. In this cycling adventure, it was much the same because I was forty miles from home and only wearing a PE kit. Basically, in an age when no one in the slums had a telephone, you had to work things out for yourself. Beyond 'the wall' the body can go on for a remarkable length of time, but only slowly, which is not very good when riding a bike, because it is only the centrifugal spin of the wheels which keeps you upright. When my speed reduced to about one mile per hour, I could do nothing but start walking while leaning on the handlebars, using the bike like a wheeled Zimmer frame – the equivalent of crawling on all fours when mountaineering. On this occasion I got home at six in the morning, twenty-four hours after leaving the caravan. Sissy or what? That's an average of 8.3 miles per hour. However, it was rather more interesting than the fate suffered by rich people, who simply travelled on a boring train.

With regards to the lost village of Quay, over the following six months I spent a lot of time wondering how an entire settlement could simply disappear. Then my geography teacher told the class about the lost villages of Somerset, all of which had apparently disappeared into the bog. I put up my hand to tell him about the lost village of Quay. At first he thought I was making it up. Then, after a few moments, he asked about the river, and if it was a place where a boat might tie up. I had no idea why he put his head into his hands: everyone knows a place where boats tie up is called a 'key'.

A year before my two-hundred-mile cycle ride, my asthma had again intervened in my life. The education authorities decided to use me as an experimental guinea pig. Their idea was to transfer me to the main part of the comprehensive school, where I would be able to take my O levels. (Those remaining in the delicate unit would be expected to leave school at fifteen, presumably to work in a flower shop or something.) The problem the school had was my officially recorded delicate status. "Well," I assume some bumbling academic must have said, "his school largely divides into girl and boy classes. We could always put him in with the girls, because they are gentle creatures who will want to play nicely. Perhaps the boy could do cookery instead of metalwork, where you have to hit things with heavy hammers..."

You can only take imaginary conversations so far. Suffice to say, I became surrounded by a lot of girls who knew I had been transferred from a special unit for weird kids. But as I walked into their classroom for the first time, only I knew of the terrible, dark secret which had come to haunt me: I was starting to like them. This brain malfunction had no rational basis nor practical use, because they had already collectively established my weirdness, so there was no way any individual girl could admit to liking me. However, on the positive side, becoming an honorary girl did mean I learnt how to bake cakes and feed myself from basic ingredients. And because eating is fundamental to survival, I now passionately believe that cookery is one of the most useful things a child can learn, irrespective of gender. This aspect of my life was greatly helped by my parents, who both agreed to my request to stop feeding me and instead give me five pounds a week to fend for myself. In the context of mountaineering, this self-reliance was to become another essential skill.

So I had now reached the age of fifteen, with all the basics of being a mountaineer instilled in my psychology. That is to say, travel, climbing, and a religion based on the idea that it is fun to gain height using anything available – be it a rock, a tree, or a half-demolished building. And now I had the resources to feed myself, I was ready to progress into the world of proper grown-up adventures.

Chapter Three

Earlier, I mentioned that girls thought me weird because I had appeared in their midst from a special unit for delicate children. This is what I wanted to believe at the time. But in truth, my social skills had faltered since going to a boys-only boarding school aged ten. My emotional development had likewise stalled in the same year when I had learnt never to cry, irrespective of physical pain. So my weirdness actually existed – and the girls knew it. But I was exceptionally good at table tennis, a skill learnt at the Young Men's Christian Association; an organisation which, back then, did not allow girls to join. I also played chess well enough to represent a club in the Birmingham league – which, to the best of my knowledge, had no female players. But the girls in my class knew nothing of this secret life; only that I had arrived from a place where the weird kids were kept.

Then, when I was fifteen, a school geology field course took fifty pupils on a week-long trip to Somerset. This exposed boys without sisters to possibly their first experience of girls existing continuously between breakfast and teatime. In such a chaotic environment, the victim either learns to swim – or sinks.

Shortly after reaching Somerset, the coach turned from a narrow road to park on a patch of gravel set aside for picnics. We had an hour to eat our sandwiches or, in the case of an athletic classmate named Charlotte, gracefully climb a nearby slab of rock to admire the view. I was both astonished and halfway to being in love. But what to do about it? Well, the girls were soon to witness my transformation to a superhero. *He's not weird*, I could imagine them saying, *just the hunkiest boy I have ever seen.*

Naturally, I had to climb higher than Charlotte. I was too shy to say hello as I passed her, but she knew I was there, and now it was her turn to gaze skywards at me. Obviously this meant I had to battle with the hardest moves I could find. Achieving this led me to a narrow ledge… where I stayed until, down below, I heard the teacher trying to do a head count.

"Twenty-four… twenty-four… right, who's missing?"

I was not actually missing; more clinging to a bit of rock sixty feet up. I had no idea why being so close to death induced leg-shake. It's a bit like crying, I suppose: completely counterproductive. Anyway, in this instance the girls below were getting really excited about calling the fire brigade. For me, the question of mortality now came down to one straightforward consideration. Was it better to be a weakling rescued by heroic firemen, or risk death as I tried to reverse what I had so bravely ascended?

Knowing that the girls were all watching me, I decided it was better to die in battle than to appear foolish. So I swung my legs over a ledge in the hope my feet would find the foothold I had used on the way up. After completing this death-defying move, I got the impression the girls quickly lost interest in my descent. This soon turned to annoyance: no firemen would be racing into action to give them a thrill – and it was all my fault. On reaching the ground, I stood before the rock, instinctively running a hand along the gentle surface. Then, a little to the left, my fingers squeezed into a tiny pocket. Using this, I pulled myself up and, by edging a shoe sideways, managed to secure a bridging position between two tiny bumps. Very slowly, I straightened my legs until the next hold came to my fingertips. With every muscle at full stretch, I held the position on what at first sight had appeared to be a blank face. This was the moment I realised that I understood rock a lot better than I did girls. It was more predictable.

I jumped back down to the car park; the memory stored in my brain for later use.

Sadly, within a few days of increasing my reputation for being weird by getting stuck on a rock face, I had come to realise Charlotte was the most perfect girl in the whole world. This was to change the entire course of my life, though not in a way I had expected. But more of that later.

More relevant to the topic of mountaineering is how I came to get stuck on a rock face. It was not the difficulty of the moves, because I had done harder things on the cliffs of Brean Down. The problem, I came to understand, was the girls. If you are on a sea cliff, the ocean looks pretty much the same however far above it you happen to be; whereas a load of hysterical girls jumping up and down makes the ground seem more real – and dangerous. Another difficulty was my footwear. For pre-planned rock climbing, I always wore gym pumps. School shoes are not suited to giving the wearer a sense of security when placed on a one-inch ledge.

Those who have not yet climbed anything more interesting than a ladder might think that failure to descend using the same route is entirely due to the consequences of looking down; of freezing in fear at what you ignored coming up. Okay, this is true when the hazard happens to be a group of girls getting all excited about calling the fire brigade, but besides this, surely it is always possible to descend what you have just climbed? The answer is no. For one thing, your eyes are nowhere near your feet, so, while ascending, it is easy to study the ledges on which your feet will shortly be arriving. For a descent, especially if a small overhang is involved, the next foothold is often hidden from sight and needs to be felt through a shoe, hoping you have the right one. Then there are the dynamics of arm strength. You can try to pull up on a trial-and-error basis. If the move is too difficult to complete, relaxing the arms should, theoretically, take you back down to where you started. But in descent you have to ask yourself the question: *Do I really have the strength to pull myself back up if I fail to locate the foothold?* Also, there is the 'lunge move'. Say, for instance, the next handhold is ten inches beyond your fingertips. If you are standing on a good ledge, then jumping upwards is a normal manoeuvre. After the height gain, hopefully gravity brings your hand to a halt in roughly the right place. But going back down, gravity accelerates your body the instant the handhold is lost, and you only have one chance to locate the foothold as it approaches.

There are many more complex dynamics than those mentioned above. I merely point out that just because you can climb up something, that does not mean you can safely reverse it.

Following the geology field course, all my romantic dreams, day and night, became totally focused on Charlotte. This was completely unrequited, because she came from a middle-class world and everything she did ended in success. She was obviously destined for university, which I considered to be my only hope of winning her affections. I finally got down to serious O level study in the hope of entering the same university as her. In this I failed, but it did mean that I spent three years with my head buried in various books. Hence I reached my twenties without going through a pub-and-nightclub phase, and so avoided any romantic complications which might otherwise have got in the way of mountaineering.

At the age of twenty-four, it happened: the catalyst to propel me forwards to the next level of climbing happiness. Strangely, this good fortune began when I left a college building knowing that I had failed what I considered to be a vital exam. My dreams of becoming successful and winning Charlotte lay in ruins. (She, meanwhile, was frequently mentioned in newspapers under such headlines as 'Sports Megastar'.) On one occasion, when she was doing something amazing for charity, I sent a cheque to the fundraising committee, together with a brief note of congratulations. Rather clumsily, I included my address. But, as could be expected, she never replied.

But before returning to the world I understood, I want to introduce you to my partner, Ethel the moped. A few months earlier, Funkle Trumpet had inadvertently ridden her onto the pavement, forcing pedestrians to leap out of the way – after which traumatic event, Ethel was given to me. She was the sort of moped you might get if you bolted a lawn-mower engine onto a sit-up-and-beg bicycle. She had pedals and, in front of the handlebars, a shopping basket. Anyway, after my exam I walked out of the college building for what I knew would be the last time and wandered miserably over to Ethel, who was waiting for me outside the building. After sitting astride her, I pedalled furiously around the car park, which was how you started the engine. After it sparked into life, I took her to the college gates, where I halted. Now what? Go home a failure or…? Some deep instinct made me rev up the engine like a Hells Angel displaying his angry outlaw image. Then I became aware of some younger students looking at me and laughing. Caring nothing for the consequences, I released the clutch and hit the road. Where I went was unimportant, just so long as it was far away from reality.

Three hours later I reached the border of Wales. Given the moped could only maintain twenty miles per hour on level road, I lost all track of distance. Soon – that is to say, after four hours – I reached the Elan Valley. Here a great reservoir is surrounded by mountains. For a child brought up in Birmingham, what I now beheld could easily have been imagined as the Himalayas. I brought Ethel to a halt and gazed upwards, hardly able to believe the scale of everything. I dismounted from Ethel and, without a footpath in sight, marched relentlessly upwards; my ambition being to ascend the highest summit I could see. Eventually I could climb no higher for, in every direction, the rough grassy slopes went downwards. *Next*, I thought, *I will try to conquer Snowdon*, which I knew to be the highest mountain in Wales. At the time, I thought this decision might occupy three curious days of adventure. I tramped back to Ethel, completely unaware that I had just changed the rest of my life.

Chapter Four

In order to conquer Snowdon, I ruthlessly replaced Ethel with a Honda 90cc scooter. This made travelling to the mountain more realistic and exciting. And so, with all this power throbbing between my legs, I roared up the A5 in search of adventure. Sadly the scooter – or, as I preferred to think of it, motorbike – lacked a carrying rack. I had therefore strapped a suitcase containing blankets and a pillow to my back. Camping gear was tied around my tummy.

Sometime around midnight, I reached the Snowdonia National Park, where I pulled into a roadside clearing and prepared to make camp. I had specially purchased the tent for the expedition from Woolworths. This was a discount store founded with the motto that no item they sold cost more than a shilling (five pence in decimal money). By the time I became aware of the world that exact slogan had slipped somewhat, but they were still the place to go if, like me, you were not excessively rich. The tent was ninety-nine pence. To get around the Trade Descriptions Act, it was called a 'children's play tent'. Essentially it was a length of cotton sheet and two flimsy sticks; maximum height about two feet, length five feet. But because I wore wellingtons for both motorcycling and then sleeping, it made little difference if my feet stuck out of the bottom of the tent. I only include this detail because people often remarked on it as they walked by.

According to my road atlas, the triangle representing Snowdon was about half an inch away from the nearest road to its right. So the following morning I left base camp and rode towards the wiggly line on the map which represented the nearest road to this place. This proved to be an amazingly steep hill, at the top of which was a car park. Ahead, the road went steeply down into the next valley, so the car park seemed a logical place to begin my adventure on foot. Snowdon was the only nearby mountain marked on my map. I felt certain that if I kept walking in the general direction, I would come across it sooner or later, due to its size. Also heading in the same direction was a cart track. And so my first proper mountaineering expedition began – though an experienced mountaineer would question the use of the words 'proper' and 'expedition'.

My idea of Snowdon was largely governed by childhood fantasies of Himalayan adventure stories. I therefore tramped unhappily upwards for perhaps two miles. I wanted adventure, not cart tracks up which a farmer could drive a Land Rover. Eventually the track turned to the right, which took me to the shore of a lake. Rocky crags now towered upwards on three sides until they disappeared into a ceiling of cloud. There was no clue as to which bit of mountain might be the highest. Eventually I noticed a group of proper mountaineers approaching along the track which followed the lakeshore.

"Excuse me," I said as they were about to walk by. "Can you tell me the way to the top of Snowdon, please?"

They looked at me suspiciously. I was wearing an old fireman's trench coat to keep warm, while on my head I had a motorcycle crash helmet to protect me from stone fall. On my feet I was wearing my old school gym pumps – for the technical climbing I was expecting to find higher up.

"Pardon?" said one of the proper mountaineers.

"Can you tell me the way to the top of Snowdon, please?" I repeated.

"It's up there," they said, pointing to a patch of cloud. "Just keep following the path." Then they walked on, shaking their heads vaguely.

Sometime later, I was walking through the clouds when a bright orange anorak materialised.

"Excuse me," I shouted. "Can you tell me the way to the top of Snowdon, please?"

The anorak turned around. From beneath the hood peeped one of the prettiest faces I had ever seen. She was about nineteen, and I was still only twenty-four. When she smiled, my knees went all wobbly.

"Of course," she said. "I'm going that way myself. Follow if you like."

"Really?" I gasped in undying admiration. "All the way to the top?"

"Certainly hope so."

"Have you ever climbed Snowdon before?" I asked.

"Seven or eight times, but I'm mainly into rock climbing."

The difference between mountaineering and rock climbing was lost on me. I only knew that before me stood a goddess who had climbed the highest mountain in Wales eight times. I watched her leap from boulder to boulder, thankfully heading away from the boring path. I gave chase, but the trench coat weighed me down, and eventually she waited for me to catch up. She was standing close to a ravine which might have been an entrance to an abandoned mineshaft.

"I'm going that way," she said, pointing skywards. "Follow if you like." She then pointed to her left, while lowering her arm to forty-five degrees. "But it's easier that way," she added.

In the next instant, she leapt over the ravine to land precisely on a slab of rock at the far side. I watched her ascend angelically into the clouds… and that was the end of our relationship. Taking the forty-five-degree option, I plodded upwards, a solo mountaineer heading towards an unknown future of adventure… But not today. The summit of Snowdon can best be described as a place where many footpaths meet. There is also a cafe, so those who have plodded to the top can have a nice cup of tea. Even worse, there is a train service which terminates twenty feet from the cafe entrance. Essentially, I had spent twenty-four hours getting to a railway station!

I have taken the previous account of my first Snowdon ascent largely from my general autobiography, *Yeti Seeks Mate*. This is because that ascent proved to be such a life-changing event; it became fundamental to my future existence. What I did not cover in the *Yeti* book was the descent, which turned out to be slightly unusual. Essentially, being fed up with footpaths, I headed from the summit in the opposite direction to that of my approach. I cannot remember what the plan was, but in any event, it did not work. After wandering about, trying to avoid trouser-clinging vegetation and unstable rocky slopes, I eventually clambered over a drystone wall to reach a road. Because I believed my descent had taken me close to sea level, I headed up a hill to the left. After a few miles, I met some hikers and asked how to get to… well, my description was a lot more complicated than trying to find the top of Snowdon. But I was able to tell them about a high pass with a car park. Further descriptions allowed us to agree that I had left my motorbike at the top of the Llanberis Pass.

"And," enquired one of the hikers doubtfully, "that is where you need to go now?"

"Yes," I replied.

He looked me up and down and seemed to pay particular attention to my pumps; now very tatty. With hindsight, I can say he was thinking, *Shall I send him the only practical way – back over Snowdon's summit – or the way he is less likely to end up dead?* "Well," said the man, "you keep walking along this road until you come to Beddgelert. Then turn left and walk towards Capel Curig. When you come to the Pen-y-Gwryd Hotel, turn left again. This takes you to the top of the Llanberis Pass."

"Is it a long way?" I asked.

He looked at me vaguely. "It is safe," he responded.

It sounded as if I was going to circumnavigate the entire Snowdon range of mountains. The fact he would not tell me the distance made me suspicious. "Eight miles?" I asked.

He did not answer directly. I imagine his mission was to stop me going back into the wilderness so late in the day.

After continuing up the hill for some time, I came to the village of Rhyd Ddu. It was very pretty, but small and completely surrounded by mountains. It did, however, have a signpost pointing towards Beddgelert. I gazed at this for some time. My legs, meanwhile, simply pleaded with my brain to make all the walking stop, just like the time I had visited the lost village of Quay. So now, aged twenty-four, I was familiar with the concept of being lost a long way from home. It's just one of those things you have to work out for yourself.

Turning from the sign, I happened to look in the vague direction of Snowdon. I saw a broad sweep of mountains disappearing into a continuous ceiling of cloud – except for one minuscule gap just visible beneath the lower wisps of swirling mist. A dip in a ridge is known as a col. Did this col have a clear descent path on the other side? Should I take it as a shortcut? Did I really want to walk all the way to a village I had never previously heard of? How many miles could I actually walk before my legs stopped working?

After some thought, and an equal amount of time sitting on the ground, I returned to the wild mountains, initially by plodding up a track. It was not particularly steep and looked as if it had been designed a long time ago for horses' hooves. And so, without any great drama, I reached an abandoned mining settlement. Shortly after this, I came to the col, beyond which a steep, rocky path descended into the next valley. Eventually this joined a well-maintained track which led me deeper into the valley; obviously destined to take me back down to sea level. This induced a feeling of despair which was not helped when, after walking through a forest, I emerged onto a lane with no signpost telling me where to go next. But logically, I reasoned, the village of Capel Curig must be somewhere to the left, so I continued plodding onwards, at least until I came to a big lake. Here the lane veered to the right, which was completely the wrong direction.

After thoughtfully scratching my chin, I looked to the left bank of the lake, which I imagined to be in the same direction as the Pen-y-Pass car park. The only problem was that from that shore, the side of a mountain rose upwards until it disappeared into the clouds. So the question I had asked myself earlier returned: should I now go over the top of this 'in-the-way mountain' which I believed might offer a more direct route to where my motorbike was parked? I did not really know, but suspected that both this and the road option really needed to begin with a cafe which offered a settee onto which a forlorn tourist could collapse and continue their journey the following day. Anyway, I was really fed up with all the road walking, so headed up the in-the-way mountain just to see where I ended up – which happened to be a bog. Besides squelching about in mud, there was a lot of spiky vegetation and rock scrambling.

But all these hazards became less visible when it started to get dark – thereby introducing an element of surprise. Though I knew it was a big mountain, because it kept going upwards 'forever'. Then, on reaching a darker void, I crawled on all fours to look down a horrendous cliff. There was just enough light to see my approach track far below – but no obvious way to reach it. Only after walking along the cliff edge for some distance did I find a descent path to the valley. It was dark by the time I staggered onto the 'Land Rover track' along which I had gaily plodded what seemed like a lifetime before. Now my wasted leg muscles only allowed me to stumble slowly forwards; every step requiring a great deal of thought. Also, my pumps were pretty much dead, allowing me to feel the track with my blistered feet. I returned to my motorbike around midnight, knowing that I had successfully completed my first 'mountaineering expedition'.

I wish to point out that many great mountaineers began their climbing adventures in the area surrounding Snowdon. Most of them already had the psychology which took them away from established footpaths into wilder and more varied places. Eric Jones, who went on to solo-climb the north face of the Eiger, ascended Snowdon as a boy. Like me, it was his first mountain, done on a random impulse. Because he had spent the morning at Sunday school, he arrived on the summit wearing his best church clothes and highly polished shoes. Given that it was the Lord's Day, he thought it inappropriate to remove his tie. For his next explorations he climbed in wellingtons until, like me, he could afford proper boots. Alison Hargreaves, who was to become a goddess of the climbing world, got so lost during her first attempt to climb Snowdon that she accidentally traversed the Crib Goch ridge – though she was eight at the time, so such an extreme diversion might be expected. And she was wearing wellingtons. Was I – who also took a 'creative' approach to footwear, and who had no idea where I was going – destined to follow her path to glory? Well, we all have to start somewhere, and those who dislike footpaths are likely to develop better-than-average survival skills.

Given that so many would-be British adventurers are drawn to Snowdon, I need to deal with some issues associated with my first ascent. These notes are informed by a great deal of hindsight. Let me begin with the name 'Snowdon'. This is an English invention which, locally, is seen to represent the colonial oppression of centuries past. (There was a time when speaking Welsh could result in the 'guilty' party receiving a death sentence; though, in the Victorian age, this had been reduced to mouth-washing with soap and water, merely mimicking death by drowning.) In the light of this, the local desire to call their highest mountain by its original name, Yr Wyddfa, can be better understood. This is increasingly likely to appear on all signposts, possibly without the English equivalent. Some locals drop the 'Yr', which simply means 'the' in Welsh. I will now only refer to it by its original, local name.

For my first ascent, I left the Pen-y-Pass car park at the top of the Llanberis Pass and ascended the Miners' Track, with a deviation to get as close to the north face as possible without actually climbing anything dangerous. This could be described as a bit boring, but with plenty of scope for admiring spectacular scenery or, depending on the weather, walking through clouds. However, the Miners' Track is well marked and it is pretty much impossible to get lost on your way up to the cafe at the summit. Heading from the cafe, directly away from the north face, is ideal for masochists who like to wander around without ever achieving anything significant in their life. I have absolutely no idea how I got to a road or where my final climb over a wall to reach it occurred.

Later, when I was looking up the mountains from Rhyd Ddu, the ridge on the left of the col went up Wyddfa via a scrappy path with a tiny amount of very easy scrambling. The ridge on the right goes up to a separate mountain known as Yr Aran (2,450 feet). Those in search of solitude might enjoy this lower mountain better because it is rarely climbed.

My descent from the previously mentioned col eventually joined the Watkin Path, which is generally considered to be the most arduous walking (with some very easy scrambling) route to the top of Wyddfa. I believe all healthy, sensible people should try this route once – but only a lunatic would do it twice.

My second shortcut across the mountains, which ultimately led to the Pen-y-Pass car park, would make a pleasant 'wilderness' day out – but is best started after a healthy breakfast, because the in-the-way mountain I had climbed was Lliwedd (2,946 feet).

Chapter Five

I have many firsts in the world of mountaineering. Most of these fall into the same category as being the first person to play Beethoven's Fifth Symphony on a mouth organ; in short, achievements so silly that no one else has ever thought to attempt them. (Obviously I have never tried to play any Beethoven on a mouth organ; it is merely a metaphor.) Of these firsts, I achieved a fair number using my Woolworths tent.

On my second visit to Wyddfa, I ignored my sea-level camp in the woods and pitched on the Pen-y-Pass car park. Next morning I went to pay the attendant for my motorbike but, to my astonishment, he charged me for a car.

"No," I protested, "I've only got a motorbike – over there."

"A motorbike and a tent," he replied, "take up as much space as a car."

I am probably the very first person to be charged for parking a Woolworths tent.

That night, after I returned from the day's rigours, I discovered that only a moderate gale had flattened my tent. Further observation revealed the tent poles had snapped like matchsticks. I solved this problem by tying one end of the tent to the handlebars of my motorbike and supporting the other end with my knees. Hence, I spent the night hunched up by the front wheel of my Honda 90, and the attendant still charged me for a car, which I thought rather mean.

On my return to Birmingham, I cut a broomstick in two and shaved the ends. With these home-made tent poles I began my early mountaineering. The only disadvantage was that the poles often obstructed other walkers along narrow mountain paths. Nonetheless, I began a phase where I could camp in the most inhospitable place available.

My first real epic adventure was on my fourth visit to Wyddfa. I left the office at 5.30 on a Friday night and by ten o'clock was tramping into the mountains with all my belongings. I had packed them into a normal suitcase as I did not own a rucksack. By two o'clock I had found a suitably inhospitable pitch just below Wyddfa's north face.

In the morning it was raining. I ate a soggy cheese sandwich and began to tackle the face. High winds created a storm, so I abandoned the direct attempt after fifty feet and arrived on the north ridge by an easier route. I encountered my first real mountain gale and made the summit by a combination of leaning into the wind and grovelling around on all fours.

I entered the cafe very wet and most disillusioned with mountaineering. The man behind the counter also looked pretty miserable. He had recently cut hundreds of sandwiches, only to be told that the train had been cancelled due to the gale. Because I was the only lunatic customer at the time, he offered me four at half price. Eventually two ladies, faces drained of all colour, entered the cafe and sat in the corner. The younger, aged about twenty, made fumbling gestures to try to light a soggy cigarette. The elder, who I assumed to be her mother, seemed to be praying. Then the younger came over to me. She was shaking so much that she struggled to remove the still-unlit cigarette from her mouth.

"Excuse me," she said. "Could you help us? We've never done anything adventurous before – we just thought we'd like to climb Snowdon – but the wind… I don't know if we can get back down."

Despite my misery at being cold and wet, I felt better knowing that the train had been cancelled due to the harsh conditions, and that I was being asked to rescue two ladies in distress. But while I was thinking all this, the lady stepped back to look me up and down. My ultra-warm clothing included three pairs of old office trousers, sewn together at the waist and again at the turn-ups. Quite warm in dry weather, but exceedingly soggy in a storm. Also, because my pumps had been destroyed on my first visit, I was now wearing my old school football boots. And I was sitting in a big pool of water.

Unfortunately, before I could begin guiding the ladies down, two members of the mountain rescue team came in, one with a rope coiled around his shoulders. Sensing help was needed, they offered the women their assistance. I suppose my attire suggested to the damsels in distress that their descent would be more straightforward with the official rescuers than with me. Abandoned, I finished my coffee and began the long slog back to my tent.

As I descended, I became increasingly fascinated by Wyddfa's north face, which came to tower above me. It was now one great waterfall nearly a thousand feet high. The wind held free-falling streams in mid-air before swirling them around like a scene from a Wagnerian tempest. Immediately below the face, two rivers had formed. I had to wade knee-deep through one of them; quite an epic struggle. But then I saw an even deeper river... which had submersed my tent. At that moment the fact I had obtained another first – sub-aqua camping – seemed largely unimportant.

I sat on a boulder to meditate on my total isolation from the rest of the world. After a few minutes, I placed a waterlogged cheese sandwich in the palm of my hand, and proceeded to pick bits up with my fingers. *Made with real Welsh mineral water*, I thought. *Delicious.* Presently, a mouse emerged from beneath the next boulder. We looked at each other curiously for a while. Then the mouse twitched his nose as if to say, *Feed me – please*. Never had I met such a brave little fellow; though, I suppose, living in the mountains, he had little to fear from the nature-loving humans he encountered. Most, I suspect, stopped to feed him. I handed him a chunk of cheese, which he clasped in his paws and dragged back to his shelter. Then we both sat munching our dinner: me in the rain; the mouse less bedraggled. (I am quite aware that mice have a preference for chocolate, but cheese was all I had, so that is what we ate.)

Turning away, I stood in the river to recover my tent. Once out of the water, the canvas blew like a boat sail. It took ages to fold and push everything into the suitcase. The blankets, meanwhile, had been washed into the lake a little way below. Nonetheless, I eventually packed all my gear and stood up to leave. But my soggy suitcase fell apart at the seams. Using the canvas and guide ropes to make a sack, I packed my gear inside and retreated to 1,500 feet. Up went the broomsticks, over went the canvas, and I crept inside. I lay there all night, shivering. At this stage it had become a challenge. The mountain had clearly shown that it did not want me to embarrass it with a Woolworths tent; whereas I was determined to prove that I could survive thirty-six hours on its lower slopes, no matter what. Such is the spirit of mountaineering.

On returning to Birmingham, I did what any normal man would do after suffering such a traumatic event on Wyddfa: I brought a climbing rope to carry over my shoulder. Next time I came across a damsel in distress, she would choose me rather than the mountain rescue service. More usefully, I also taught myself to abseil; initially from road bridges with a handrail around which I could double the rope. But abseiling really needs a harness and a few other bits and bobs, so, to carry all this, I also had to buy a rucksack. The age of having a bank overdraft had begun.

Chapter Six

During my first winter season on Wyddfa, I climbed near-vertical snow by punching it, then opening my hand to dovetail it in place. By trial and error, I discovered this technique only worked on the right kind of snow: compact, yet loosely bound with ice. For soft powder, wet, or excessively iced snow, it needed tools – which was why I requested an ice axe for Christmas. Because my birthday falls on the 27th December, it was standard practice for both presents to be considered as a single higher-value item. Anyway, at the age of twenty-five, I was given a long-shafted walker's ice axe. For obvious reasons, I received this on the 23rd December: after finishing work on Christmas Eve, I rode my motorbike north towards Great Langdale in the Lake District. I now had a Honda 175cc, so probably arrived before midnight. Then, proudly holding my shiny axe, I tramped into the mountains and made camp on a vast snowfield about two miles from the road.

The next morning I emerged from my tent and stood to take a good look around. The most interesting thing was a cliff broken by snow-filled gullies. (I was later told that these were the Langdale Pikes.) They were quite high, but I was certain that with my magic axe they would present no technical difficulty – which proved to be the case. After spending some time playing on the Pikes, I wandered hither and thither, looking for short ice-climbing problems with which to take my axe experiments to the limit. I especially liked falling off into the soft embrace of snow: a bit like deep-water soloing, but without the inconvenience of swimming.

When it got dark, I descended to the lower slopes, motivated by the knowledge that, due to my second-hand paraffin stove, I would soon be having a sophisticated porridge supper by candlelight, in my tent... but the problem with my tent was that its sheeting was the same colour as snow. I spent about two hours zigzagging back and forth before reaching the inevitable conclusion that some horrible person must have stolen it.

I had now come to believe, possibly unreasonably, that I was a proper mountaineer who could deal with survival situations like a Hollywood superhero. I therefore carried a plastic bivvy bag at all times. These are large enough to get inside and pull the top over your head, should it start to rain. This was the first time I had needed to use it, but I knew it would be fine because it was how all mountaineers spent their nights on Mount Everest and the like. In addition, I had the luxury of a motorcycle helmet to reduce the heat loss from my head and ears. After removing the bag from its packaging, I put my legs into my rucksack to increase insulation and wriggled inside the bag while sitting on the snow. Then I slid my arms from my sleeves and hugged myself with fingers on my tummy. Next I pulled my knees up to my chest to trap any heat within my curled-up body. Then I just gazed across the snowy darkness and relaxed.

This phase did not last long. The alternative name for a bivvy bag is a survival bag; the clue is in the name. They are bright orange and so can be seen by rescue teams. In reality, simply sitting on an open mountainside in a sub-zero temperature only remains relaxing for an hour or so. This took me to about eight o'clock, after which I got up and walked down the mountain to find a more sheltered spot near my motorbike. Here, looking at the thermometer on the handlebars, I was horrified to see that it was a relatively mild minus five degrees. I had previously imagined it to be about minus twenty. Having resettled myself on a grass verge, using a drystone wall as a backrest, I prepared myself for the night ahead.

Being sheltered from the slight wind made the position better than the snowfield, but I was still shivering after an hour or so. I wish to point out that I was wearing what I considered to be proper mountain clothes – the three pairs of office trousers I had sewn into one garment, a vest, an office shirt, a jumper and an anorak – so maybe I was halfway to the full survival attire of posh people. Yet I sensed my core body temperature was dropping, which, given that there was no blizzard, made me feel very sissy. I reacted by standing, then walking along the road, back and forth over the same half-mile stretch, for hour after hour. This kept me warm until the first light came into the sky.

Given all the wisdom I had acquired in the two and a half years since my first ascent of Wyddfa, I began to doubt my theory about my tent being stolen. I mean, a Woolworths tent – you could buy a new one for ninety-nine pence! So, I retraced my first ascent path, plodding back into the mountains. This probably led me to a different bit of the vast snowfield because, in daylight, I pretty much walked directly to the tent. Soon after I was having a breakfast of hot porridge; my first food in twenty-four hours.

Within one week of this ascent, I bought a second, short-shafted ice axe and a bigger motorbike. Both were essential due to my winter climbing addiction; especially the need to ride up to North Wales after leaving the office on Friday nights. My only fall was to my bank balance: it quickly descended into overdraft and the bank manager calling me in for "a little chat". But mountaineering is like that. You live to climb and realise that having a grumpy bank manager is better than being cold because you failed to go clothes shopping for thermal underwear.

In this chapter I have covered many issues arising from my night spent in the mountains in less-than-favourable conditions. My main conclusion is: in winter, never wander far into a wilderness without a sleeping bag and a cagoule. The latter is like a long, wide plastic waterproof dress with a hood, which you can pull over the top edge a bivvy bag, and use your head as a central tent pole. This improvised 'human tepee' provides a dry and pleasant sleeping arrangement to around freezing point.

Chapter Seven

Mountaineers do not normally rate wellingtons very highly. I beg to differ. They allow you to arrive on a motorbike and walk directly to a wild campsite without having to hop around in the dark while changing into boots. (Essentially, the wellingtons are being carried on the feet, so leaving more room in the rucksack for the little luxuries in life, like carpet slippers.) Also, as mentioned earlier, if your tent is only five feet long, wearing wellingtons lets you stick your feet out of the bottom, even if it is raining.

My first six months in the mountains destroyed all my previously available footwear. Then, as I tackled increasingly difficult terrain, I had to face the truth. The time had come to go further into debt and buy a proper pair of ex-army boots. Nobody told me these had to be 'walked in' to mould them to the foot shape of any given individual. But I knew nothing of this as, on their first use, I tramped happily around the Snowdon Horseshoe. As this English name implies, this is a continuous ridge in the shape of a horseshoe, which includes four summits, one being Wyddfa itself. In summer it is classed as an arduous scramble. In winter, when the rock is coated with ice and the wider sections covered with snow, the increased difficulty means that most people consider it to be a mountaineering route. But whatever it is called, it should *never* be attempted in boots still to be correctly walked in. Fortunately, I had pitched my tent beneath Lliwedd which, given my direction of travel, meant it was the final mountain of the 'horseshoe'. Thus I could hobble down directly to base camp, where I had a pair of slippers waiting for me. Once inside the tent, I inspected my feet, which revealed blisters that were oozing pus. But a few plasters and the slippers allowed me to prepare supper in relative comfort.

The following morning, I realised that wearing ex-army boots was out of the question for at least a week. But wellingtons with thick socks allowed me to go out for a gentle walk in a fair degree of comfort. At two thousand feet it got very icy, so I strapped on my crampons. Seeing the spikes on my feet caused my confidence to rise. Then I noticed a nice little buttress which rose to a wide snow ledge after about five hundred feet. From this feature, an escape gully came back down to the valley.

> *HEALTH AND SAFETY ALERT: This observation is complete nonsense. Do not venture onto any steep buttress in wellingtons, however magical they might seem.*

Anyway, I was standing in the valley admiring a spectacular sunrise throwing flames of red into the pale blue sky. It was February, probably minus ten degrees centigrade, and everything was sparkling with Arctic beauty. Towering up to my right was Wyddfa's north face, streaked with ice and plastered with snow. Inspired by this dramatic setting, I casually returned my attention to the buttress beneath the snow ledge. *Interesting*, I thought. I only had a walker's axe with me, having left my pure ice-climbing tools in the tent. I was, after all, only out for a gentle walk. However, I decided to have a play on the buttress before heading back to base camp for breakfast.

Things began well, and I passed a very pleasant hour or so weaving my way across the buttress without actually noticing how much height I was gaining. When I looked down, I was surprised to discover that I had zigzagged up something deceptively steep. I changed to careful mode; this being better suited to a situation where there was no particular reason to fall but, if I did so, I would be bouncing down three hundred feet of icy rock. Time passed, with each sequence of moves becoming harder. Then I seriously began to look for the escape route which had appeared so obvious when viewed from the valley. But from my fly-on-the-wall perspective it seemed not to exist. Indeed, I could see no easy line to the left or right, and climbing down looked even harder. The wellingtons and crampons were doing quite well but, limited to one axe in a world dominated by ice, I only had one fully functioning arm with the necessary claws.

Eventually, I came to stand on a narrow ledge with a mantelshelf at waist height. Springing up would have been easy, but retreating extremely difficult. Nothing about this situation was actually dangerous – with the exception of having to use fingers on ice-covered holds. (That's not dangerous in the context of mountaineering, but has a high death potential compared to walking along a pavement.) I looked up and estimated the difficulties to be constant, with only two hundred feet to the top. I did the mantelshelf and was soon engrossed in a climb of total commitment. One ledge led to one crack, without any other options. It was like going up a one-way street and not knowing if the end was blocked off. For one or two moves it was easy to be rational and think that if I made a mistake, I would be dead. But maintaining this attitude for any length of time became increasingly difficult. I wanted it to end; my moves became quicker, and I took less precautions. The adrenaline and nervous strain began to produce undesirable actions. No longer did they tune my body up for a challenge; rather, they made me impatient. Death was still in the abstract.

Eventually I edged around a bulging wall to find a relatively wide shelf of about nine inches. I was so relieved to see something on which I could stand that I swung my leg towards it. Only as an afterthought did I simultaneously tap the surface with my axe. The snow fell away to reveal a few sprigs of heather growing from a horizontal crack in an otherwise blank wall. I was already making the move, so walking off the mountain into nothing. I threw a hand blindly above my head. Miraculously, it seized on something, and then, on one toe placement,

I swung across the abyss past the point of balance, unable to stop myself. I came to hover, hanging mainly from one handhold, my leading foot swinging in empty space. Then I looked up to the hold which just happened to be there. It was only a clump of frozen grass growing from a thin crack. Somehow the vegetation held, and I pulled back to my previous stance. My heart was racing and I was shaking with fear. Death was no longer in the abstract. For one eternal moment I had waited for the fall and the nothingness which lay beyond.

After my heart rate had stabilised, I began to look at the situation realistically. My life was going to end on this mountain; if not now, then in a few minutes. Having accepted this, I felt strangely calm, which I believe is a fairly common reaction. Then, more strangely, my mind began to drift to the world beyond the mountains. I thought about how it would be at the office the next morning. First they would moan about me being late, and then wonder where I was. Perhaps somebody would go to check the boat on which I lived, but more probably they would be annoyed the accounts had not been submitted on time. One of the ladies in the office was very nice, and I wished I had been braver about sending her a Valentine's card. Then I thought about the mountain rescue team who would come across this anonymous body in a few weeks' time. I could imagine the headlines in the newspaper: 'Climber Found Dead in Wellingtons'. I just knew they would pick up on the wellingtons, followed by a paragraph of condemnation. That was all the nice young lady in the office would know, which annoyed me intensely, because with the exception of this one careless moment, my learning curve had been well managed. Next I thought about Charlotte from my schooldays, and wondered if she would even remember my name. Or perhaps she would think, *Oh, he did something like that on our field course.*

Eventually I began to think sensibly about the remaining few minutes of my life. The beautiful sky of early morning had changed to heavy cloud, and a chill wind was racing up the face to lift flurries of powder snow from the ledges. So, I had two choices: stay put until weakness overcame me and I died of exposure – but that might take a long time. It also seemed particularly pathetic, as did sliding off in a vain attempt to retreat. The second choice was to continue upwards; for now I had nothing to lose, attempting the 'impossible' was less silly.

For the next thirty feet I climbed to my absolute limit. Then, with no escape route, I came to stand on a narrow ledge beneath an eight-foot wall which was both vertical and devoid of holds. Annoyingly, above that I could see no more mountain, which could only mean the steepness had eased. With my arm extended, I was able to hook the spike of my axe over the ledge – and it seemed to catch on something. It was a suicidal move which could only fail but, in my present circumstances, the normal rules of survival did not apply. I climbed hand over hand up the shaft, while my crampon points scraped down the rock to reduce some of my body weight. The axe swayed, and I expected it to unhook from whatever was keeping it in place. But the downwards force kept it in place until I was holding the curved top. With my other hand, I felt blindly along the ledge until I found a horizontal crack in the back wall. It was wide enough to take my fingers, and inside it opened out, allowing me to clench my fist. I rotated my wrist by forty-five degrees until it dovetailed perfectly into the rock. Ungracefully, I swung my legs up to the higher shelf. Inch by inch I wriggled along it until it became wide enough for me to stand. Three seconds later it was all over, and I wandered onto easy angled snow which offered many escape routes.

It is a weird experience, accepting that you are going to die – and then looking vaguely around to find that you have not. My entire descent was an 'out-of-body' experience in which I seemed to be floating above the surface. For a moment it even crossed my mind that I might have died and was now merely a spirit, set free to float around the sky. Then my mind drifted back to the valley, where I imagined my crumpled body smashed across the boulders. With morbid curiosity, I traced the likely lines of fall, together with their subsequent landing places. But for the two miracles of frozen grass clumps, and the perfect hold being in precisely the right place, it would have happened. I wandered back for breakfast, very aware that the rest of my life could now be considered a bonus.

All my weekends away began when I left my warm office at 5.30 on a Friday evening. On one particular occasion, by the time I reached the summit of Wyddfa, it was well past midnight. It was nearly Easter and I was not expecting a blizzard. Indeed, lower down the weather had been quite pleasant, but once above three thousand feet there was snow, hail, and winds gusting at around eighty miles per hour. I spent ages trying to erect my faithful Woolworths tent, after which my fingers were covered with ice and my torch fading. But broomsticks are very strong, so I eventually crawled beneath the canvas to find shelter and sleep.

I awoke as the ferocious storm whipped the tent from above me. I managed to open my eyes just in time to see a ghostly image of white canvas flying away from the mountain and into oblivion over the north face. I thought it a very sad end for such a brave little tent. A moment later I realised the benefit of not having a sewn-in groundsheet. Then, waking up completely, I got out of my sleeping bag, without considering that this had the general shape of a parachute. As it filled with wind, I was forced to let go, allowing it to take the same flight path as my tent.

To survive in such conditions with limited equipment requires initiative – but it can be done. First you look for a natural windbreak. In this instance, it was a big, rusty cast-iron pipe left over from the railway workings. I clawed the surrounding snow from one side to make a trench. I suppose it was a bit like sleeping in a bath filled with ice cubes. But I was protected from the wind. Importantly, it also meant that I had most probably achieved another mountaineering first: sleeping on the summit of Wyddfa in a Woolworths play tent – albeit for only half a night.

HEALTH AND SAFETY ALERT: The cafe and railway only operate throughout the tourist season in good weather. So, spending a winter's night on the summit means surviving without help if things go wrong. If you start shivering, the heat generated in your muscles might be keeping you alive – so stay awake and keep shivering. Falling asleep can be the transition into death. Be aware that the mountain rescue service is operated by volunteers who find no pleasure in recovering dead bodies from inhospitable locations.

Please note, wild camping anywhere in Wales is illegal. I leave my readers to judge what I think about this!

Shortly after my return to Birmingham, I bought a Scout Mark II tent and a better-quality sleeping bag. As a result, my bank overdraft became more typical of a proper mountaineer – that is to say, I was generally skint. In my case, I also had a hire purchase agreement on a bigger motorbike, which was necessary as my attention increasingly turned to Ben Nevis.

So, by now we have considered the joy of mountaineering and the interesting situations you might encounter without warning. The lesson from Lliwedd is obviously the most important: in dangerous situations remain calm, focus on every move, and don't bother looking down; it makes no difference to the laws of gravity if you fall off. Next we will consider what happens when things go wrong.

Chapter Eight

By the age of twenty-six – a year before the sad loss of my Woolworths tent – I had climbed the highest mountains in both Wales and Scotland. The obvious omission from the list was the highest in England. Initially, I had ignored this because it was rather small and somewhere near the place where Wordsworth had once wandered around looking at daffodils. But it was still a mountain which needed to be ticked off my list of things to do. The question then became, how could I make it harder?

As it happened, the aristocracy had long since pondered the problem of working-class people finding it too easy to stand on the roof of all England. (Wordsworth had tried to stop the railways coming to 'his' Lake District for that very reason.) Politicians had merely spread false rumours about the mountain's name. So, if you are one of the many who climbed Scafell, believing it to be the highest, you are in for a terrible shock. It's lies, all of it – part of a conspiracy instigated by the upper classes, who want to keep the mountain for themselves. In truth, Scafell is a diminutive peak to the south of the higher summit of Scafell Pike (3,204 feet). But I didn't care if the government considered me an anti-establishment rebel on a mission to educate the masses. I had an AA road atlas with separate triangles for both summits and their heights, so it was easy for me to do the maths. But this did not solve the problem that I still wanted to make it more of a challenge.

After much thought, I decided to locate a road on my atlas a long way from Scafell Pike, then calculate the compass bearing to its summit. My assignment was to follow that bearing without any significant deviation, regardless of anything which might block my progress. If there were rivers to cross or massive boulders to climb over, then bring it on! But not wishing to waste a weekend on such a trivial endeavour, I only left Birmingham on Saturday afternoon, arriving at my selected start point at about six in the evening.

I now (foolishly) carried the sort of equipment you might use to establish a base camp on Everest. So, I walked into the wilderness carrying a large rucksack on my back, plus a second strapped to my chest. Among other paraphernalia these contained a sleeping bag, an airbed, cooking equipment, and carpet slippers. There was some merit in this if I had been intending to establish a base camp near the road, to which I might return after a day's rigours. But because I intended to tackle this challenge as a backpacking trek, my thinking was somewhat dubious.

As I plodded along, wearing a bright yellow motorcycle crash helmet, it is perhaps amusing to consider how Wordsworth might have viewed me from a distant peak: *That yellow thing*, he muses, *reminds me of something but I can't quite think what. And now I see a great fog drifting lonely towards it. Ah – the swamp is sending forth its misty fingers to embrace the yellow thing. Fog and bog, that sort of rhymes. As does boots becoming roots, I like that. Oh! I see it all now: a great yellow dandelion, like a roadside beacon, warning others that nature abhors straight lines...*

> HELPFUL ADVICE: *When crossing a bog, you sink a lot deeper if you are carrying thirty kilograms of stuff. However, the mud gets washed away when you walk through a stream which, without heavy rucksacks, you would otherwise jump.*

Anyway, after dark I squelched my way upwards until I reached firmer ground on the lower slopes of Scafell Pike. Here, the fog reflecting from my torchlight reduced visibility to less than six feet, so I made camp.

Given all my equipment, I spent a very comfortable night, and in the morning enjoyed a fine breakfast of porridge. Then I spent some time standing outside the tent in thick fog, wondering what to do next. Following my compass bearing would take me downhill, probably to another bog. Veering off to the left meant going uphill which, from an altitude perspective, must be closer to the summit. So, after breaking camp, I headed upwards. I found this ascent quite interesting with plenty of rock challenges which, due to the rucksack on my chest, I had to climb slightly sideways. I staggered onto the summit feeling really pleased with myself, because it had been harder than I had imagined. I made this point to a group of people who were already there.

"It's not Scafell," replied one. "And why did you come from that direction? There is a footpath on this side."

Eventually I bowed to their wisdom and accepted that I was actually standing on the top of a mountain called Great Gable. Then someone else in the group gave me directions to Scafell, which involved descending to cross a valley—

"Scafell Pike," I interrupted.

"I am directing you to the correct mountain range," he said, in a hoity-toity voice. Then he seemed to take an unnatural interest in the broomsticks projecting from my rucksack. Finally he shrugged, and the whole group took a collective decision to walk away.

From what the man had told me, it was obvious that my compass bearing had been correct; I had just vastly overestimated how far I had travelled. So in the fog, I had climbed the wrong mountain range. To correct this, I walked down the footpath mentioned. This turned out to be a long circular descent to the base of a valley – which most probably returned me to my original compass bearing, perhaps half a mile further on from where I had recently camped. I then began to climb up the far side of the valley; an ascent I thought hard and dangerous. I had now completely changed my mind about Scafell being an insignificant peak. When I finally reached the summit, I told a group of climbers already there about my epic adventure. They got really cross with me, saying that I should not come into the mountains without a map. When I told them I had an AA road atlas, they actually snorted. Then, very grumpily, they pointed into the fog and told me that I was now on Great End, and Scafell Pike was over there. I headed in that direction for maybe a mile before becoming so disorientated, I decided to lose height. My new plan was to get below the fog so that I could see further than ten feet.

After a few hundred feet of descent, I found myself on a spacious mountainside. My legs were really aching, so I realised my attempt on Scafell had failed. I headed back on a reverse compass bearing – well, sort of, because my earlier circular-descent footpath had confused me. In reality, my small error had taken me into a completely different valley. After a very long walk, I came to an isolated building without road access. A sign outside told me it was a youth hostel. Entering, I staggered to a chair and collapsed. A number of visitors, wearing posh clothes, stared at me. Explaining where I needed to get to required me telling my audience of my recent odyssey, so they could calculate my starting point. They looked at me vaguely, but without expressing sympathy.

Here we come to another useful lesson: after 'the wall' of extreme muscle fatigue, a different sort of pain begins. This is telling your body to stop whatever it is doing and rest, unless that would lead to greater damage, like being eaten by a wolf. Okay, when I was fifteen, after I had finished my two-hundred-mile cycle ride, my body rebuilt itself quite quickly. But now, a little older, the growing phase had stopped. Then pain, if excessive or prolonged, is doing damage to cartilage, tendons and ligaments. So any idea that you *must* get back to work on Monday morning should be ignored. Being dismissed for being unreliable is unimportant when compared to permanently damaging your body.

In my specific Lake District dilemma, I should have begged the hostel to give me a warm place to sleep. What I actually did was follow the directions given to me by the residents, which involved heading up the steep, vegetated hillside behind the building. This, apparently, would take me to a sharp ridge, beyond which was another valley containing the road where my motorbike was parked. The bit of their information I was less happy about was the existence of a lake between the ridge and that road. Eventually I staggered onto the crest and looked down to discover that their directions were largely correct. Indeed, I estimated the road to be within two miles – assuming I could walk across water. I did not recall the hostel group mentioning the word 'big' before 'lake'; probably because I was in the Lake District, where generally all lakes can be considered big. Getting the road atlas from my rucksack, I realised where I was. The lake below was called Crummock Water, and the two rivers feeding it from the right had no road crossings. (Nor, I presumed, a footbridge.) This would explain why the hostel group had said that I must follow the lakeside path north-west – even though it was in the opposite direction to my motorbike. At the bottom of the lake was a river flowing outwards towards the sea. The first bridge to cross this was outside the Lake District altogether. I had no precise idea where I had parked my motorbike but, after crossing the river, common sense told me I had to head back into the mountains.

My steps now took the form of a zigzag stagger, adding to the distance I needed to travel. A little later, when the road began ascending a hill, my journey sometimes involved staggering, other times crawling, but mostly sitting on the verge to rest. I soon adapted my haphazard approach to a more regulated routine of counting ten steps, then squatting by the roadside until my leg muscles allowed me to stand. Eventually, a pickup vehicle with a canvas-covered back stopped by my side. A lady sitting in the passenger seat stuck her head out of the window and looked down at me, now lying on the grass. She asked where I was going. I told her that my motorbike was parked somewhere along this road.

"If you want a lift," she said, "jump in the back. Don't mind the pigs; they are quite used to people. Just squat between them."

Jumping anywhere was clearly out of the question, but I managed to crawl into the back and say hello to my new friends. They nuzzled me inquisitively, while I thought them a little casual with their toilet habits.

I guessed it was around midnight when the pickup let me out near my motorbike. While the immediate legwork was over, I still had to ride home for work a few hours later. Another piece of helpful advice: it is best to arrive in remote places with a good supply of petrol. In this instance, I only had a quarter-tank, and guessed all the local fuel stations would be closed until the morning. But I made it to the motorway – which I soon discovered had been designed with a most unusual feature. It only had a service station on the northbound carriageway, so I had to continue down to the next junction, then come back up, finally getting fuel at two in the morning. Then I had to go up north to the next junction, and turn back – which was where all the lights on my bike suddenly went out, causing me to brake dangerously before locating the hard shoulder using starlight. I messed with the fuses without success; then I gave in, climbed up the bank, and lay down beneath a hedge. At first light, I continued my journey, knowing that I had to be at work in four hours.

All of this was essentially a grown-up version of what I had once experienced on a bicycle riding back from Somerset, by an artificially difficult route. But that had ultimately been successful, whereas my attempt on Scafell Pike had failed to achieve its fundamental objective of reaching the summit. Also, my knees never completely recovered, and in later years were to add an unwelcome level of difficulty to my adventures.

For my actual, successful later attempt on Scafell, I took the easiest public footpath to the top. (This starts from Wasdale Head and is a gentle walk.)

Chapter Nine

It's 1979, I am twenty-seven years old, and heading up the M6 on a manly Honda 550/4 motorcycle called Fred. I now have my Scout Mark II tent, a better sleeping bag, and four ice axes to cover all eventualities. Also, proper mountain boots with projections front and back over which crampons can be secured. For steep ice, I have a pair of FootFangs, which give me the claws of an eagle. My bank manager is unlikely to be aware of any of this because I have recently acquired a credit card to buy such things, and bought Fred the motorcycle on hire purchase.

My initial plan was to spend a second Christmas in the Lake District. However, a little devil inside my head kept telling me that with a powerful beast like Fred between my legs, the extra two hundred miles to Ben Nevis was just a formality. Shortly before, I had read a book about mountaineering in Scotland, and the author seemed to think that in winter its environment is tougher than the European Alps in summer. Of course, the Alps sometimes had wind speeds in excess of 150 miles per hour, combined with temperatures below minus twenty degrees centigrade, but Ben Nevis offered all this, plus very long nights. Because of this exciting challenge, the devil voice kept insisting I miss the turning for the Lake District, due to it being a bit boring. I was still considering this dilemma as I accidentally passed the exit, so continued my northward journey without further ado.

One hundred miles later, I parked Fred on a roadside verge and settled myself beneath a nearby hedge. With my improved sleeping bag, and a lowland temperature around freezing point, this proved most comfortable. And so I slept peacefully until I was awoken by a lot of noise and a sudden surge of light. I panicked, pulled the bivvy bag down to my waist, and waved my arms to frighten away whatever was about to attack me. After a few seconds I perceived that the commotion included a police car and two officers, who had both jumped back in alarm at my sudden surge of activity. It was some unearthly hour in the morning! What on earth had made them stop for a chat? Not wishing to get involved, I pulled the bivvy bag back over my head and waited for something to happen. I could hear two Scottish voices speaking outside. Then everything went silent and, a minute later, darkness returned. I peeped outside the bag to find myself alone. I went back to sleep, and the following morning got up refreshed to continue my journey north.

I arrived at the *small* parking area near the start of the *only* tourist footpath to the summit of Ben Nevis at just gone midday on Christmas Eve. This path is physically demanding but technically easy, with narrow bridges spanning all the fast-flowing streams. (As a variation, a steep, scrappy track leads directly up from the Glen Nevis road to join the main path at about one thousand feet. This approach is rarely used by tourists, so I shall call it the Yeti Path.)

Carrying all the equipment needed for a comfortable base camp, I plodded up the main tourist route, which begins by circling up the side of a neighbouring mountain. At about two thousand feet, the path reaches a col, with the previously mentioned lower mountain on the left and the great flank of Ben Nevis on the right. In summer, this flank has a zigzag track all the way to the summit. In winter the track disappears beneath one vast snowfield. I pitched my tent at the edge of the snow line, which happened to be near the col. Initially the weather treated me kindly, so I settled into my sleeping bag while listening to the wind making playful tugs on the tent canvas. And so I drifted into a sound sleep, until…

Where am I? Why am I wrapped in a shroud of flapping canvas? Ah – a severe gale had collapsed my tent and, because it had a sewn-in groundsheet, I was now being rolled over inside. Eventually I battled my way free from the canvas to see the first traces of daylight creeping over the horizon. Hurriedly, I threw convenient boulders onto the tent, then thought about breakfast. That is to say, I thought about a breakfast I could not have, because all my cooking equipment and my bag of porridge were squashed inside the tent. I fought my way back inside, but only to recover my boots, crampons and axes. Then I plodded up the flank in a strong wind which I realised could hardly be classed as a gale. Scout Mark II tents, I decided, were clearly designed for boys who wished to sing songs around a lowland campfire. In cols, however, *all* wind is channelled at increased force. Once on the flank, I reckoned it was less than forty miles per hour. My old Woolworths tent was lower, with solid broomsticks, and so would have coped with that, had it not blown off the summit of Wyddfa earlier in the year.

Halfway up the flank I discovered that *really* proper mountain boots – with knobbles front and back for securing crampons – needed a lot more walking in than ex-army boots. I got the impression that my blisters acquired on the initial walk-in had now become a gooey mess of blood. These blisters mainly affected my right foot so, taking off that boot, I experimented with placing the outer thick woolly sock on the snow. The slightly sweaty material immediately bonded with the icy surface. I had invented a temporary glue; an idea later employed by the manufacturers of Blu Tack. As I continued upwards, a thick coating of ice quickly clung to the outer sock which, no longer compressed by a boot, meant the inner sock developed the properties of air-filled insulating foam. The downside of my twin inventions was that I needed to continuously monitor my feet, one of which had fangs; the other a sock. I visualised an accident whereby metal teeth landed on bone, forcing me to hop back down to civilisation, shouting for help. Initially, I overcame this problem by swinging my legs outwards like a cowboy wearing spurs after dismounting from a horse. This created parallel tracks; the spiky one apparently disconnected from the sock-print. While quite safe, this walk was only generally used by those who lacked knee joints. I believe the action is also performed in ballroom dancing. Not wishing to be associated with the latter, I did the obvious thing and removed my left boot as well.

The summit is sort of domed, but the great north face presents the ascending walker with an abrupt two-thousand-foot drop on the left. Though I had seen it in summer, now, plastered with snow and ice, it was far more impressive. In particular, I liked the way the windblown snow, called a cornice, overhung the face. These cornices also occur in North Wales, but they are generally quite small. On Ben Nevis they can be many feet thick and extend far beyond the actual mountain. After climbing up the face it is normal to tunnel through them, magically appearing like a mole some way back from the apparent edge.

Strangely, on arriving at the summit, I discovered that no one else was there to appreciate this magical winter wonderland. However, a solitary figure did eventually appear through the slight mist. After saying hello, he commented that it was a strange place to be walking around in my socks. Having been reminded of this, I took off a sock to check for blisters. There was no serious damage. Also, climbing downhill would lead to different pressure points, so the blister issue went away. I put on my boots, while my new companion stared at me, frowning. He then offered to take my photograph using his camera. My first mountain photograph – fame at last!

Presently, my unexpected partner said he thought the snowfield was a bit boring, so I suggested we did the Ben Nevis Horseshoe. According to my *Mountaineering in Scotland* book, this consisted of three main summits connected by alpine ridges, making up the shape of a horseshoe. However, due to a slight navigation error, I inadvertently took an even more interesting descent route. When our steep, snow-filled gully came to an abyss, my partner used a very rude word. After clawing our way back up a little way, we traversed left, then found a way to climb down by a less challenging route. And so we came to an isolated valley somewhere in the foothills. I cannot be more precise without making things up.

A few hours later, we were trekking down the Glen Nevis road which led to Fort William. For some reason, my companion kept talking about death. Probably because it was a dark night, and throughout the day we had seen no one else to ask directions. However, on reaching the start of the Yeti Path, we parted as friends; he walking to Fort William, me returning to the mountains to rescue my tent.

Even though there was little wind in the glen, after one thousand feet of ascent it was trying to blow me off my feet. When I reached the col the wind caught my back; a reflex action sending my arms out to soften the forward dive. From that point on, I remained on all fours, with the wind reversing my cagoule to form a flapping tunnel in front of my face. To add interest, hailstones literally the size of acorns were shot-blasting my bottom. On reaching the raging tent canvas, all I could do was use the guide ropes to tie it into a bundle, leaving the equipment inside. I then pulled it along the surface, the 'ball-bearing-like' hailstones helping it to slide. I could not turn around because the hail made it impossible to face the wind. So, sometimes I managed to crawl backwards a few feet; other times I was blown forwards to become wrapped in the canvas. Getting the bundle over the crest of the col felt like wrestling with a parachute, and it took most of the night. Only as I approached the Yeti Path did the wind drop enough to let me use the guide ropes to package the tent into a neater canvas roll which I could hold in my arms. When I finally reached the small forest at the start of the track, I found a convenient tree against which to rest my back, and waited for daylight. What an amazing way to spend Christmas Day and night. I felt so sorry for those forced to spend it watching television while eating mince pies and trying not to get bored.

When dawn made its first gloomy presence known, I stood up and gazed down at the ice-covered bundle of torn canvas near my feet. Mangled tent poles poked out of various places, and the tangle of guide ropes did little to disguise the fact that the tent was, in fact, 'deceased'. Somewhere in the middle of all this stuff was my cooking equipment, my soggy sleeping bag, and a *once*-dry change of underwear. So I decided that, after leaving the forest, my first port of call would be a cafe for a fry-up breakfast. Or at least it would have been, were it not the 26th December, when almost everything in Scotland remains closed until after the New Year.

It is obvious to me that everyone who hears about my amazing Christmas break on Ben Nevis will want to experience something similar for themselves. Before doing this, there are three things you need to be aware of. Firstly, there is the danger of falling hopelessly in love with the mountain and so believing it to be a friend – or, in my case, my only friend. At this advanced stage in our 'relationship', I ignored his formal name of Ben Nevis. Those who know him intimately generally refer to him as 'the Ben', or just 'Ben'. Secondly, Ben has a way of telling people that he wants to be left alone – the human equivalent of being grumpy – by having temperamental weather moods. With hindsight I can say that during my first Christmas on the Ben, he was very nice to me. Two years later, though, when climbing up a gully on the north face on a windy day, a sudden upward gust out-powered the force of gravity, lifting me from the mountain. There was nothing I could do when floating, except hope that I landed in a safe place. In this particular instance I was surrounded by two ice walls and so was limited to flying up or down, which conveniently dropped me in much the same spot. However, had I been on an exposed buttress, I would most likely have flown sideways, with a far less desirable outcome. So, do not assume that any survival skills you may have learnt in North Wales will be adequate for winter climbing in Scotland. If the Ben is in a bad mood, try to retreat or find shelter. If you achieve neither, the most likely result is death. Thirdly, another way to die is during a phenomenon known as 'white-out'. This is when the snow and sky look exactly the same. The first time I encountered the condition, I was unaware of it. So, to my extreme embarrassment, I will now confess what happened.

One moment I was happily plodding along what I believed to be a wide ridge; the next, the snow beneath my feet appeared to vanish. An instant later a feeling in my tummy told me I was accelerating downwards. Then there was a loud crack and a great whooshing noise to my right. Within the space of a heartbeat, I was again standing on snow, feeling somewhat bewildered by events. Then, thinking logically, I realised that I was standing on a cornice, which my extra weight had caused to collapse. The loud crack had represented the outer edge breaking away, allowing the remaining inner section to support both itself and me. I took three steps left, but fell sideways, failing to realise that the dropping cornice had left a step. Sitting up, I looked to my right but, however hard I peered, could not tell where the snow ended and the sky began. Like I said, all very embarrassing. My double-breaking cornice was lucky because normally when they collapse they do so completely. Anyway, after I clambered onto the true ridge, I took a good look around. White-out, I decided, was an inappropriate word for the conditions. It was more ghostly in appearance, with just a hint of grey. Also, the air was completely still, so there was no swirling wind to pluck visible holes in the smothering 'blanket'. After I was certain that I would recognise white-out the next time it surrounded me, I continued very slowly, occasionally lobbing snowballs around. Hopefully these 'sploshed' onto snow rather than disappearing silently into space; an echolocation technique which got me safely down to the glen.

Chapter Ten

I have always considered going to the picture house a solitary activity, and remain totally baffled as to why people put so much effort into sitting next to each other just to watch the same film. It obviously makes more sense to go as the impulse takes you, then hurry to the middle of three unoccupied seats on the front row, and stick out elbows and legs to claim the surrounding territory. Of course, if the two people next to each other are in love, their lives have become as one, so they need to share experiences in order to have something to remember in their old age.

Anyway, one day at work, a lady called Maggie stopped me in a corridor, then looked away to avoid eye contact. "My friends thought they saw you in the cinema the other night," she said, "sitting on your own – for the entire film."

So this was why people sat together at the pictures: to survey the rest of the audience! After Maggie had told me about this astonishing practice, she wanted to know what films I had seen recently. My viewing preferences were romantic in nature. This did not fit well with the belief within the company that I was a mad motorcycling outlaw. Maggie seemed puzzled by the contradiction.

"I don't have a television," I explained. "I imagine they are horrible things to have in your living room. So when I feel like seeing a film, I go to the pictures."

"On your own – always?"

I did not explain the obvious logic of my behaviour, so merely nodded.

"And you live on that boat of yours, also alone?"

I explained something of my living arrangements; notably that it was a proper houseboat with a brick-built fireplace and gas lamps. So, I had no use for electricity, nor any other newfangled inventions. In response, and for no apparent reason, she then asked if we might go to the cinema together. Because she had a car and offered to take me, I said okay. *Just as long as you do not try to pinch all my popcorn*, I thought.

I remember nothing about the film but, after it was over, we walked outside, where I asked her to come behind the building because I had something amazing to show her. She looked at me oddly.

"No," I said, "you will really like it."

She looked around, as if she expected to see somebody secretly filming us. Then she turned back to me, gave a nervous smile and nodded her consent.

Once behind the building, I pointed to the corner where several of the bricks had worn away. After seeing a film I generally climbed this route on dark evenings because it was near the only lamp. (Other routes, further along the building, were available, but needed daylight.) Anyway, I knew this corner-climbing problem well, so ascended confidently without grunting. After eighteen feet I came to an enormous overhang; that is to say, the underneath of a fire escape.

"You get a good hold on the inside gap," I called down, "then you walk up the wall, lean out, and grab the outer edge. It's a really good hold, so it's nowhere near so difficult as it looks." I then swung out to get both hands on the outer edge. Without using a clumsy knee, I neatly placed my foot lower down the stairway. This gave me a bridging position, allowing me to grab the middle pole of the handrail. "Don't let it intimidate you," I said, "because even though it looks a long way to the ground, your feet are lower than your eyes, and in any event, you are highly unlikely to fall off."

I then did the final swing over the handrail to stand triumphantly by the fire-exit door. Looking down, I realised that Maggie had gone. I assumed that she had needed to visit the bathroom or whatever euphemism she used for doing something she found embarrassing. So, I sat on the fire escape, patiently awaiting her return. Then I realised my mistake.

At boarding school, a vital part of our extracurricular education was a skill more generally taught by the British Army; namely how to execute a safe parachute landing. We only had trees, but the principle was the same: hang from a branch, drop, use relaxed knee joints as shock absorbers, and roll. The actual height could be measured using a piece of string; the velocity of a parachute landing being equivalent to a fall of twelve feet. (Information provided by a boy who had seen an old war film; modern parachutes might be different.) Most boys could manage a drop of nine feet (from bottom of shoes to grassy landing zone). Given that tree climbing was my best subject, I could win respect by dropping from branches eighteen feet in the air. Anyway, while sitting on the fire escape, I realised that Maggie might not have studied parachute jumping at *her* school, and so the thought of doing it now had frightened her and made her want to pee. I thought this very sad.

After quite a long time, my daydreaming came to an end and I walked down the escape to see where Maggie might be. The picture house was closed and the car park empty. As I began the walk back to the office where I had left my motorbike, I began to ponder Maggie's recent extraordinary behaviour. It could only be the result of a sexist education system in which girls were taught how to curtsy. For all I knew, Maggie had been sent to board at a school similar to the one across the lane from the boys' establishment I had once attended. What incredible acts of cruelty had gone on behind the high fence that kept them imprisoned? "When you smell flowers," her teachers might have said, "you must remember to say, 'Oh, how delightful.' Then we will have an exciting game of *Ring-a-ring o' roses, A pocket full of posies...*"
After three miles of walking, I was really upset – partly about Maggie's

assumed cruel upbringing, but also about an education system which meant that only boys studied 'parachute' jumping.

The following day I noticed Maggie walking past my office. Her lips looked as if they had been glued together. She seemed to be ignoring me, so that was the end of that.

Chapter Eleven

We now come to Helen, a goddess of the mountaineering world, to who this book is dedicated. How we met is too romantic to be included in this work, so her magical arrival in my life is only told in my general autobiography *Yeti Seeks Mate*. (The clue is in the title.) All you essentially need to know about Helen is that her obsessional desire to spend a night on the top of Ben Nevis is about to change my destiny beyond all recognition. So I parachute her into my world when we are sitting on the snowy slopes of Ben Nevis after spending the night on the summit. For obvious reasons, I was very much in love.

"That dawn this morning," said Helen. "I suppose it's always like that in the Alps?" (This was her first mention of the Alps.)

"Have you ever been to the Alps?" I asked.

"No."

"Neither have I. Would you like to do Mont Blanc next?" This is the highest mountain in Western Europe. I knew the answer was going to be no, but hoped my bold statement would make me appear to be a man of the world.

"Okay," she said casually. To her, this was clearly just a routine conversation which needed no further clarification. She seemed to assume that because Fred the motorcycle had brought her to Ben Nevis, he was also going to take us to Mont Blanc.

After returning to my houseboat two days later, the first thing I did was look at my world atlas to see where Mont Blanc actually was. The French/Italian border; its height 15,766 feet. Would that need bottled oxygen? Oh well, I would worry about that later. First I needed to modify Fred for his new mission of taking Helen and me across France. He classified these modifications as 'woman troubles'. His chassis was extended backwards by a couple of feet; a development he viewed in much the same way as a lady who, on realising that her bottom has suddenly doubled in size, refuses to go outside. To make matters worse, the extension was welded on, tending to suggest that it was a permanent fixture. It was on this steel foundation that I constructed a well-upholstered armchair in which Helen could relax to watch the world go by. Behind the backrest was a rack to carry camping gear for base camp, plus two sacks of climbing gear. Below, I bolted on old-fashioned car running boards to provide space for a spare can of petrol, a toolbox… and Helen's feet. I only did woodwork at school so, with the exception of the extended chassis, all other modifications were timber. By the time I finished, Fred gave the impression of being a brave, strong, manly machine, designed to cross the Sahara Desert, circa 1940. That was how I saw him, anyway. Others failed to see this image – but let them laugh; they did not have a young lady to take to the Alps, so I expect it was their way of dealing with all their jealousy.

I received a very practical letter from Helen three days before our departure date for the Alps. It simply said goodbye… and the rest of my life lay in ruins! Of course I knew that such a goddess of mountaineering would have hundreds of male admirers. I mean, she liked throwing herself into miles of nothingness by doing parachute jumps from real aeroplanes. All I had ever done was hang from tree branches and drop twelve feet onto the grass. How could I compete with all her other admirers, who worshipped the way she had rebelled against the sexist education system to become one of the very few ladies who lived for true adventure? "Tents," she had told me, "are silly." When she wanted to get to the mountains, she just put a bivvy bag in her rucksack and started walking. Apparently, her worst problem was old ladies, who woke her up when she was sleeping in bus shelters to ask if she was okay. To Helen, cars were boring, though she had once thought jumping onto the back of Fred rather fun. My intention had been to make her my lifelong partner. But to chase such a dream, I needed the sort of skills I simply did not possess.

Knowing myself to be a complete failure at everything, I walked the streets for hours, reflecting on a love no one wanted. The weather perfectly suited my mood: cold rain driven by strong winds, making me feel at one with nature. Eventually I wandered into the local picture house, where I could sit down to dry out. The film was just starting and, though I had not intended to give it any regard, soon I became mesmerised by the screen. It was the latest James Bond film, which began with him doing exciting things in the Alps. I had only ever seen them in illustrated books before, and their beauty in glorious Technicolor left me gazing up at the screen like a star-struck teenager. I had to do it; I just had to go! I tried to be sensible: a solo ascent of Ben Nevis was one thing, but travelling across Europe to climb alone in the Alps was another. Then I thought about how much I loved Helen. It had taken me years to get over Charlotte, and my current 'illness' seemed much worse. I wanted an instant cure. Mont Blanc ceased to be a mountain and became a gigantic lovesickness pill. At nearly three miles high, it was so much bigger than an aspirin that I felt certain it would work. I left the picture house inspired. Tomorrow, I would start heading south and keep on going until I came to the French/Italian border where, according to my world atlas, Mont Blanc might be found.

Chapter Twelve

It should be noted that I planned my expedition to Mont Blanc with military precision. For food, Fred's panniers were scrubbed clean, then filled with bulk porridge oats. The top box was packed with tins of sweetened condensed milk. I calculated this would feed two people for ten days; a length of time I could extend by opportunistic encounters with English-looking food. Navigation was even more precise. After checking my world atlas, I realised the compass bearing for Paris from Calais was pretty much due south. Helen had never been to Paris and had very much wanted to go. I was determined not to change my plans now because… well, why she had changed her mind was a mystery to me. It was a woman thing, I guess.

My dreams of Paris included walking along tree-lined boulevards, with birds singing and street vendors playing romantic tunes on accordions. In this idyllic setting, I would then go into a shop to buy a proper French road map, which would allow us to arrive at Mont Blanc in due course. In reality, after receiving Helen's goodbye letter I was clearly carrying an unnecessary amount of porridge. One of the saddest things I have ever done was using a tin mug to remove the oats from one pannier, knowing that from then on I would be eating alone.

From Fred's perspective, Helen's farewell letter was a beautiful piece of writing. It meant she would not be occupying his armchair;

thereby leaving it free to carry luggage. His chassis extension therefore only had to carry one rucksack and some ice-climbing equipment.

Anyway, so much for the trials and tribulations of Fred. I was quite devastated by Helen's letter and needed Mont Blanc to cure my lovesickness – or to die in the process, which amounted to the same thing.

Fred had very little understanding of geography. To him, Mont Blanc was somewhere down south; a place where it never rained and all roads were without potholes. There would be no annoying mopeds buzzing around like demented mosquitoes; just big, manly motorbikes similar to himself. He had no concept of the English Channel, or, more generally, that when you got to the seaside there was anything else beyond it. On arriving at Dover Docks, I followed the queue of other vehicles into the hold of a gigantic ship. To pacify Fred, I told him that it was a garage, then left him in blissful ignorance of the fact that, when the doors reopened, England would no longer be there.

After ascending to the top deck, I did my best to impersonate a great Hollywood actor running away to sea after an unhappy love affair. So there I was, leaning on the ship's rail, gazing romantically across the docks. It was a late-night sailing, so the floodlighting created a bleak world without colour. This suited my mood because, if I am honest, I was thinking about how fragile my solitary life now seemed. In particular, I wondered what risk of death was acceptable in an effort to cure lovesickness. When I'd first read Helen's letter, 10% would have warranted a shrug of the shoulders. Now, realising that this might be my last sight of England, 10% seemed a bit more worrying. I had never heard of anyone solo-climbing Mont Blanc as their first Alpine peak. So, sensibly, I had not bought a return ticket for the Channel crossing: to be found dead on a mountain indicates foolishness; to be found dead with a return ticket in your pocket signifies arrogance. Also, writing a cheque for a return sailing would have increased my overdraft, and my bank manager would be truly horrified if I died before he could give me a lecture on financial responsibility.

Presently, my thoughts were distracted by the ship's engines roaring into life. The deck began to vibrate, ropes were thrown to the quayside, and a moment later a great foaming mass appeared from the stern. The dock, the buildings – everything on land began sliding away to a chorus of angry gulls. Soon we passed the breakwater and ploughed into the main channel. A gale came from the west, bringing with it all the smells and sounds of the sea. A mountainous sea, black and angry, beneath the heavy clouds which raced above.

Everyone who leaves their homeland for the first time should do so by ship. It puts things into perspective and gives a sense of belonging. Leaning on the rail and watching the White Cliffs of Dover fading into the darkness, I became quite sad. Sad I was alone, and that my adventure was going ahead without Helen. Eventually I decided that this expedition was my destiny.

Then my thoughts were interrupted by a tap on the shoulder. I turned to see a great hairy man admiring my clothes. I was wearing the height of fashion, as illustrated in a book about Ben Nevis. I was very impressed by all the brave mountaineers breaking new frontiers of adventure, so took great care to buy all the same clothes. Hence, I often got some funny looks – because the book was first published in 1923. In 1923, baggy tweed breeches finished just below the knee, allowing two hairy white legs to make a brief appearance before taking root in a foliage of woolly socks and size eleven boots. I had gone for the more modern elastic braces; a belt being inappropriate because, prior to my relationship with Ben Nevis, my waist was approaching forty inches. Now, after all the exercise, it had reduced to thirty-two, so the breeches had lost any pretence of being in contact with my circumference. As I walked, they bounced up and down on their elastic cables, usually out of sequence with my body movements. Sometimes, after a really calorie-burning time in the mountains, they became positively indecent, so I had to crimp the tops with safety pins to stop people looking inside to see how my fashion sense had influenced my choice of underpants. My wool shirt was Scottish tartan; the sort a hardened crofter might wear. To keep my ears warm and leave my hands free, I always left the crash helmet on my head. From here it was less likely to be stolen, compared to leaving it with my bike.

"Going climbing?" asked the man.

"Yes – Mont Blanc."

"That's where we were going," he said, apparently fascinated by my clothes, "but it's in winter condition, so we are going to the Dolomites instead."

"Winter condition?" I enquired.

"Yes – you an ice climber?" he asked, apparently deciding my attire must have something to do with cold climates.

"Er… yes."

"That's okay, then; you will love it: ice everywhere. Come and join us; we are just going down for a coffee."

Visions of impossibly high ice pitches and crashing avalanches floated vividly to mind. I realised that what I had seen at the picture house was a bit of mountain James Bond could ski down; probably one of the lesser peaks in the Swiss Alps. I had no idea what Mont Blanc was like, other than that it was apparently covered with ice. I declined the man's offer and returned to my solitary gazing out to sea. England was now nothing more than a thin strip of land just visible against the dark night sky. Then it was gone.

On leaving the docks at Calais, I soon realised my survival depended on going wherever the crazy French drivers wanted me to go. However, because my journey needed me to leave the city, I considered finding myself on a quiet country lane a satisfactory outcome. Better still, a woodland to my right had dirt-track access. I rode onto this, parked by a convenient tree, and dismounted. Then I got into my bivvy bag and, using a rucksack packed with clothes as a pillow, lay upon a comfortable bed of leaves to drift pleasantly asleep.

Before continuing to describe my adventure, I need to explain about an aspect of my personality which a psychiatrist might find intriguing. "So, tell me about your childhood," he or she might say. "Was it unusual?"

"It is the only childhood I have ever known," I would respond, "so I consider it quite normal."

After establishing that I was the logical person in this conversation, I might eventually concede that my 'intriguing' personality probably began at a very early age, in an era when men who wore jewellery were considered excessively feminine. And for my generation, jewellery included wristwatches, which were essentially bracelets designed for fashion-conscious ladies. (I believe in posh society, ladies wore wristwatches, while men had pocket watches on gold chains. This defined both sexual characteristics and status.) But for normal men, like all those I met, the rule was that if you wanted to know the time, you asked a policeman. By the 1970s, unnoticed by me, attitudes had started to change. But I still had no interest in wearing jewellery. In truth I was unknowingly in the early stages of becoming an anti-watch anarchist. Eventually I would refuse to be governed by the artificial hours created by others. During my leisure time, I would get up when I wanted and sleep when I felt tired. Darkness was just something I dealt with as the need arose. And mostly this worked, or at least it added interest to my outdoor adventures.

But for my first night in France, it is only necessary to know that, after I awoke in my woodland home, like the surrounding animals I had no interest in knowing the man-made time. For a little while I watched the wildlife going about its daily business: some hopping, others slithering, while a spider hovering on its web did nothing in particular. I felt so sorry for those who, due to a misfortune in their childhood, preferred to wake up staring at a boring hotel ceiling.

Travelling on the wrong side of the road is far harder on a motorbike than in a car. With four wheels there is an internal left and right, so in France the driver only has to remember to remain near the kerb and let the passenger side take care of itself. On a motorbike there is no such memory aid. You are on your own, without clues. Nevertheless, I did tolerably well until I came to a roundabout. Well, these are always taken by going left – it says so in the Highway Code. The contrary view was forcefully put by a car heading straight towards me. I swerved, mounted the island (on my right), and bounced to a halt on the grassy middle. *Curious*, I thought. I waited on the island for some time, watching the occasional car whizz around me. In France, it seems, you not only ride on the wrong side of the road, but also have to go the wrong way around traffic islands. Those who choose to repeat my adventure would do well to remember this. After learning how French traffic islands worked, I took the compass from my shirt pocket, then set off along the road which best approximated to south, where Paris might be found.

After riding for an hour or so, my tummy told me that it was time to stop for breakfast. Not wishing to mess with my paraffin stove to make porridge, I stopped at the next village. This was the moment I had been dreading: my first close encounter of a French-speaking kind.

> *NOTE: In order to make the text more comprehensible for British readers, foreign words are always spelt as they are spoken. This also maintains the integrity of my original manuscript, written during the early 1980s, when international travel was less common.*

The only word I knew was '*wee*', which I feared might make the listener think I was asking the way to the toilet for a childish 'wee'. Thus, I stood on the pavement and looked through the cafe window. What I really wanted was fish and chips, but this seemed a little too complicated. In the end I entered the cafe, wandered up to the counter, and asked the man if he spoke English. He looked at me as if I had just escaped from a zoo, so I pointed to the coffee machine and said, "Coffee."

Instead of the coffee I had expected, he started telling me his life story in French. To this I nodded in what I hoped were all the right places. After he had finished he examined me enquiringly and seemed to be waiting for an answer. Because I had been pointing to the coffee machine, it seemed reasonable to assume that the man had just asked if I wanted a cup of coffee. I decided to try the only French word I knew, just to see what happened.

"*Wee*," I said.

The man started speaking French again. I responded by saying *wee* whenever he stopped talking; feeling that sooner or later it must lead to a definite conclusion. He seemed to be getting increasingly irate, and eventually pulled me a glass of beer. I consider alcohol to be the silliest thing ever invented but, out of politeness, took the unwanted drink to a table where I could meditate on the problem of obtaining food – or, more importantly, not getting frogs' legs or snails. I looked around the cafe to see what other people were eating. I suddenly realised that they weren't. Most were drinking beer, except for two who slurped coffee from soup bowls. I sneaked out, leaving the alcohol untouched. Cafes which did not sell food were too confusing for me to deal with. Compounding the problem by sacrificing my teetotal principles would have been reckless.

Wandering down the high street, I came to a cake shop. This was something I could understand. More importantly, it had things in the window I could identify. Peering further into the shop, I saw a pretty lady of about eighteen standing behind the counter. I went inside to ask if she spoke English. She replied in French. Now becoming accustomed to their ways, I shrugged my shoulders, like they do in France, and pointed to a cake. Now, you are not going to believe this – she stuck one finger in the air and said, "*Uh?*", just as if somebody had punched her in the stomach.

I tried not to laugh and said, "*Wee.*"

She put the cake into a bag, and I gave her some money.

"*Mercy,*" she said.

I looked at her strangely, but she did not seem at all alarmed. I decided '*mercy*' must have a different meaning in French, and it did not necessarily mean she thought I was going to attack her.

It was a very nice cake, so I decided to purchase a total of three. However, not wishing to confuse things by sticking two fingers into the air, I thought it best to obtain one item per visit. On the second visit

I could sense she was trying to suppress a smile, which I thought most delightful. When I entered a third time, she shrieked with laughter and handed me the cake, while trembling uncontrollably. Such behaviour alarmed me at the time, but I soon learnt that everybody did it, and eventually became accustomed to the practice.

My meal of three posh French cakes was clearly a great leap forward in both sophistication and not being hungry. However, they were not designed as an 'all-day breakfast', so around midday I stopped by a roadside caravan which served hot food. Here I asked the man behind the counter for some chips, and he responded by giving me a very long French loaf with a sausage in the middle. I returned to Fred, sat on his saddle, and began to munch the bread. I became quite excited as my teeth approached the sausage. But it did not last very long and, casting my eyes downwards, I saw nine inches of dry bread still waiting to be munched. I reasoned that the locals took the remaining bread home to make an elongated sandwich for their tea. On reflection, I could see the logic of this: if a French loaf is a metre long, why mess around cutting it up? Just push it into your mouth as the fancy takes you.

While doing battle with the loaf, I secretly monitored the toilet block on the far side of the road. It only had one entrance. I had been warned about these back in England – unisex, they called it. However, knowing about something and being faced with the reality of it are not necessarily the same thing.

It took about five minutes for my teeth to capture the last crumb of loaf. During this time, no females had gone into the toilet block. Taking a good look around, none seemed about to approach it. Because I only wanted to make a short, uncomplicated visit, I bravely crossed the road. After looking back to make sure that I was not being followed, I stepped through the single doorway; i.e. entered a place with no alternative escape route. It was then that I came across a mind-blowing concept. Next to the urinal bowls was a row of shower trays, each accessed by a semi-transparent curtain. I did not know which concept fascinated me the most: showers in a public toilet, or 'naughty' shower curtains in a unisex facility. Some vandal had stolen the shower heads, but to me that was unimportant – I did not want a shower and, even if I had, would not have taken one there. In fact, realising that I had been observing the surreal scene for some minutes, the fear of a lady entering while I was halfway through taking a pee meant I no longer had the courage to leave myself so dangerously exposed. I left the building and, I suspect behaving like most Englishmen, went to find my own private bush.

As I continued my wandering travel towards Paris, I noticed that the French frequently talked about *'olive oil'*. The lady in the cake shop had mentioned something about it as I'd walked away, but I'd thought I must have misheard. After the first day I realised a lot of people talked about it. Then I deduced that *'olive oil'* must be the French word for goodbye. I could never pronounce it the same way, but took to saying *olive oil* back anyway. So I now knew four French words.

When the fuel gauge on Fred's petrol tank dropped below half, I began looking at the signs outside any garage I happened to pass. All had a Barclaycard announcement and most had a second sign with a picture of a pink elephant on it. As my fuel reserves dwindled, I pulled onto every forecourt to show the petrol-pump attendant my particular species of card. In every case I got the same response: "*Nu.*" How could this be so? Back in England the credit card company had assured me the Access card was allied to Eurocard which, according to their literature, was, well, European. This is probably why the independently minded French refused to acknowledge its existence. The only cash I had with me had the equivalent value of thirty pounds. But if I ate nothing but porridge for ten days, I did not actually need money to buy food. Likewise, Helen's theory of sleeping in a bivvy bag covered all accommodation costs. The only expense of this expedition was therefore petrol. It was a perfect plan, or at least it would have been, were it not for the pink elephants. As Fred's reserve petrol tank dwindled to virtually nothing, I faced the inevitable and paid for the refill in cash, which left me with fifteen pounds. Paris was now well signposted, so I just went in whichever direction they pointed. Surely in a big city someone would recognise my credit card and issue funds against it. If not, I had just enough fuel to get back to Calais, from where I could return to England as a cheap foot passenger, draw some cash, and start all over again.

When quite near Paris, I came across a motorway. To stop people using it, the government had placed barriers across the access road and employed guards to defend it. My particular guard stood in his sentry box and demanded money.

"*Nu*," I said, speaking French for the very first time. "Motorbike."

The guard got quite excited by this and left his booth to point at a picture of a car on a nearby metal sign. Then he pointed to a ridiculous amount of French francs written by the side of it.

In response I dismounted and pointed to Fred. On such a narrow machine, this short journey was surely a fraction of what it would cost to travel to, I presumed, the South of France in a massive, wide car? Ah! Distance was obviously important. "Paris," I said.

The guard clearly thought I was speaking to him as if he were a bus conductor. (English translation: 'A tuppeny to the city centre, please.')

Realising my error, I expanded my phrase. "Paris, *mercy*," I said.

The guard responded by snorting, so I reluctantly rummaged about in a rucksack for my wallet. For security reasons this was well buried within my spare clothes. While searching through these, I noticed that the vehicles behind were starting to leave my queue, to create chaos by weaving into lanes controlled by more sympathetic guards. Like all sensible people, I kept my wallet in a special place where criminals were unlikely to look; that is to say, in a bag of underpants. Being a polite person, I avoided the extreme version of using pre-worn pants, but the toll collector did not know this. To him, I had a quasi-Hells Angel image and was extracting the cash from a biological weapon. He stepped back to examine the pants and general laundry scattered across the armchair. I removed a ten-franc coin from my underwear and handed it to the guard. In response he spoke so much French it was impossible to hear where he imagined the full stops to be. I panicked and gave him a fifty-franc note. He took it contemptuously from my hand using a finger and thumb. As he marched back to his hut, I followed for my change. Now it was my turn to get upset by a ten-franc coin. I stood there with my hand out for more, but he just lifted the barrier and indicated that I should pass immediately. It worried me that I had not yet reached Paris, but all I had left was ninety francs plus a card which lacked a pink elephant.

A little way down the road a lot of cars were crawling through another toll system which completely blocked the motorway. Security barriers to either side meant escape or retreat from this hungry money monster was impossible. I left the far side of that barrier with fifty francs to my name. On the positive side, I had only been in France for a day, yet had already acquired great wisdom, which I now impart to you: in France, beware cafes which do not sell food and showers that lurk in public toilets, but most of all, stay well away from motorways.

I had assumed that the toll barrier was guarding a major bridge, but beyond it lay just a few more miles of motorway which merged with the Parisian road system. Here, cars weaved about like colourful threads in a mechanical loom. Sometime in the afternoon, I blindly followed a yellow taxi onto a pavement. This would have been okay had I remained a few inches behind its back bumper. However, instinct told me that I should now do an emergency stop. My leader, having overtaken the vehicle that had annoyed him by driving at thirty miles per hour, then expertly accelerated back onto the road, while I was left stranded on the pavement. To me it seemed the French Highway Code considered a taxi had right of way over everything; equally, that a motorcycle with GB plates had no right to be anywhere in Paris. Of one accord, the pedestrians reclaimed their pavement and absorbed me into their midst. My return to the road was obviously going to be difficult, and I clumsily dismounted from Fred to push him back into 'the ring' for round two.

In addition to proclaiming, "So this is Paris", everyone who visits the city must go to see the Eiffel Tower. I therefore let the traffic push me in whichever direction pleased it the most. When occasional brief moments of calm allowed, I looked skywards, knowing that sooner or later I would come across the tower due to its size. Throughout the afternoon I followed many vehicles and saw most of Paris. The only thing I had missed was the Eiffel Tower. Then I came across a great pedestrianised hill and so abandoned Fred, my intention being to locate the tower from higher ground.

However, before I could set off, I heard a magical word: "*Fritz.*"

I looked around to see a bag of chips being handed from a mobile food wagon to a pedestrian. I fingered the coins in my pocket – parting with any of them would be foolish, yet somehow my search for proper English food had become a matter of pride. I went to the wagon and said, "*Fritz.*"

The guy behind the counter did not seem to think this unusual and gave me a bag of chips. That was five French words I knew: '*wee*', '*olive oil*', '*mercy*', '*fritz*' and '*nu*'. I had only been in the country for twenty hours. It is amazing how easy it is to learn a foreign language when you have to.

As part of our training schedule, me and Helen had planned to walk up and down the Eiffel Tower five times. I did not think we could get to the pointy bit at the very top, so had reasoned a total ascent of four thousand feet. If we gained that much height on consecutive days, we would reach the summit of Mont Blanc on the fifth; probably in time to watch the sun rising over Italy. Given all this, the fact I was now alone seemed a feeble excuse for not following the Eiffel Tower part of the plan.

Having resolved all tummy issues, I gave some consideration to a grand flight of stone steps which ascended the hill. On top of it someone had built a temple. I immediately realised that, in olden days, some French guy had been to look at the Acropolis and decided he could do better than the ancient, inferior Greek civilisation. After climbing the steps and walking around the temple, I was able to see most of the city. It was very big, with a mosaic of three-storey buildings reaching out to each flat horizon. And there, at the very edge of my vision, was the Eiffel Tower. It looked really odd: completely out of proportion, like a giant robot from outer space walking across a Hollywood film set on its four iron legs. After taking a compass bearing on the robot, I descended the steps to rescue Fred.

Anyone who has ridden around Paris on a motorcycle will understand the suicidal nature of attempting to do so while trying to follow a compass bearing. If a car swerves in front of you, there is no choice but to head in the same direction. Given that it is statistically likely that you will be heading in the wrong direction, it is generally necessary to stop at the earliest opportunity, do a U-turn, then attempt the same junction again, hoping that the next forced exit will be more to your liking. Then, without warning, I found myself following a car into a vast open space, at the centre of which was the Ark de Triumph (French spelling: Arc de Triomphe). Then, looking above the rooftops, I saw the point of the Eiffel Tower. A few seconds later I was pushed into a feeder road, heading towards a place unknown.

After finding somewhere to stop, I walked back to the Ark de Triumph, then located the exit road that went to the tower. Sometime later, sitting astride Fred, I reached the car park and came to a halt beneath a massive stone wall. This wall was actually one side of a great cube of rocks. Looking up, I saw it had one leg of the tower resting upon it. Only those who have seen this can appreciate the enormous scale of everything. I will merely say that the apparently little platform above the arches is actually a boulevard swarming with pedestrians who wish to visit one of the shops in the sky. But my intentions were more serious. Ignoring the lifts, I walked towards a flight of iron steps which ascended one of the legs.

At the bottom, a man in uniform was standing and eyeing me suspiciously. When I was about two yards away, he spread his arms and legs to touch each rail. "*Nu*," he said.

Ah, he wanted paying. "Where can I buy a ticket?" I asked, showing him the thirty-eight francs I had left.

"*Nu*," he repeated.

I got closer so I could explain more fully about my training walk to the top and back five times.

"*Nu*," he shouted again. Then he cautiously took a hand from the rail and pointed to the lift.

Then it all became clear. "*Nu*," I said, speaking in French. Then I walked up and down on the spot, while pointing to the top.

He did the same sort of walk, shook his head, then went back to defending his steps. I returned to Fred and sat on the saddle with my back resting against the rucksack strapped in the armchair where Helen should have been sitting. Then, gazing skywards, I fantasised about the best way to climb the tower without using the steps. Mostly it was Spider-Man territory, though some of the moves would have been within my climbing ability.

Then I was distracted by a voice in my left ear. "*Ubla nucti mem ungle whonton*," it said. The owner of the voice was clad in blue denim, from which hung a number of chains. He had a large Nazi cross around his neck and was wearing a crash helmet. To be approached by a Hells Angel at any time is rather disconcerting, and the fact that he was a Dutch one who thought I was *ubla nucti mem ungle whonton* did nothing to put me at ease.

"I'm sorry," I said, "I'm English."

The Angel appeared to go into a deep-thinking mode. I assumed he was searching his mind for some English words. Eventually he gave a satisfied nod. "Where going?" he asked in a strong Dutch accent.

"Mont Blanc," I said.

He responded with an evil grin. "Yes," he said. "Last year met boy and went seaside together." He then started doing something undeniably rude to Fred's handlebar.

Quite suddenly I remembered a film I had seen the previous year. It had included a scene in a nightclub in which two men were dressed like Hells Angels, but I wasn't. Clearly this one considered my 1923-fashion outfit represented some sect loosely associated with his own desires. "I like climbing overhanging ice and jumping crevasses best," I said, thereby communicating there was no possible chance that any companion of mine might return alive.

"Yes," he replied. "My last friend liked sea and swimming. We had fun." He then placed the back of his black leather glove on Fred's handlebar and slowly ran it to the end, which he tapped with a finger.

Given the intensity of the moment, he subsequently returned to saying things in Dutch.

As discreetly as possible I sat up straight, placed both feet on the ground, and bumped Fred off his stand. "Good engine," I said.

Hells Angels like noisy engines; particularly Harley-Davidson and Triumph ones. Fred, being a working man's Honda, was more of a quiet throb. Thus, when I demonstrated the engine by pushing the starter button, the Angel seemed not to notice. Showing no fear or alarm, he remained standing astride Fred's front wheel and gazed into my eyes.

"Have you seen my ice axes?" I asked. I pointed behind to the various pieces of ice-climbing equipment strapped to Fred's chassis extension.

The Angel let go of the handlebar and walked behind to examine what he probably considered to be my fetish equipment. Fred had never done a wheelspin in his life but, on this occasion, still managed a reasonable degree of acceleration – at least until a girl ran out from a crowd and stood in front of us. She was waving her arms and shouting something in German. I skidded to a halt. The girl was tall, slim, very pretty, and would have been completely useless on Mont Blanc.

"I'm sorry," I replied, "I'm English."

"Oh, err… *polly voo fonsa*?"

It was the sexiest voice I had ever heard, and my eyes became forcibly drawn to hers. She gave me a lovely smile.

"Er, *nict, nein*… no," I stammered.

She thought for a few seconds. "Er, have you got room for me?" she asked shyly.

"*Ubla nucti nem whonton*," called an approaching voice.

One of the few regrets of my life is that, on seeing the chain-clad guy bounding across the car park, I panicked. Twisting the throttle, I swerved around the girl. "*Olive oil*," I shouted as I headed towards the exit.

Chapter Thirteen

The vending machine was thirty feet long, seven feet high, and completely occupied a wall in a motorway service station twenty miles south of Paris. It hissed at anyone who dared go near it. Its main features were forty slots for eating money and fifty hatches for disposing of biological excretory products. It was labelled in French, liked totally French coins, and was almost certainly hissing in a totally French way. It was like playing Russian roulette with a hosepipe. I tried a few buttons and it squirted something into a plastic dish which might have been chicory with coffee flavouring. It contained no milk or sugar and, to all intents and purposes, was undrinkable. However, it did put me in the right frame of mind to reappraise the progress of my expedition.

I had now passed the point of no return: that is to say, if I spent all my remaining money buying petrol, Fred could manage around 180 miles before coming to a halt. His milometer told me that I had done 253 miles since leaving Calais. However, because I did not have the cash to buy a French road map, I only had a vague idea of where I might be, or how to make the return journey while avoiding both the motorways and Paris. In theory, I could head north until Fred could go no further, then hitch-hike back to Calais and… But this theory had no relevance to my situation. Fred was carrying sixty kilograms of equipment, some of which was quite expensive. For this expedition, me and Fred had to stay together as a team. Indeed, sitting in this bleak service station, I knew that Fred was my only friend in the world.

I had left England on a Thursday night, and so had arrived in Paris sometime during Friday evening. Hence, I had not been able to visit a city bank, where a cashier might see my Access card and immediately start *wee*-ing. Though, I had to accept that he or she was more likely to point at a picture of a pink elephant and say *nu*. I would not know the outcome of my visit until the banks opened on Monday. If it was the elephant option, then I could not think of a Plan B.

And so it was that I hatched a little plan. A few weeks before leaving England, I had read in a climbing magazine that a short way south of Paris was a famous climbing area. According to the rock gymnast who wrote the piece, during the last Ice Age the Alpine glaciers had extended all the way to England. These had contained the most beautiful boulders in the whole world; some thirty feet across. Then, when the glaciers melted, the boulders had simply dropped to the ground beneath. Now the area was a vast flatland, mostly covered by forest. But the boulders were still to be found in numerous clearings. Indeed, with a mattress underneath to soften any fall, even the most technical thirty-foot problems could be climbed without a rope. (This branch of climbing is called 'bouldering'.) I could not remember how far south of Paris this heavenly kingdom was, but its unusual name had stuck in my mind: Fontainebleau. So, sitting in my service station, sipping 'medicinal' coffee, the answer to my immediate problems became obvious. Establish a proper base camp in the forest of Fontainebleau, then set off in search of boulders. I would worry about whatever might happen after the weekend on Monday.

After leaving the vending machine area, I wandered off in search of someone who spoke English. The eventual victim was a petrol pump attendant. After I had explained my predicament, he agreed to answer a few questions. What does '*bonsure*' mean? How do you count to three in French? Have you ever seen this type of credit card before? (Answer: "*Nu*.") Will you take a cheque? (Answer: "*Nu*.")

How do I get to Fontainebleau? Etc. *'Bonsure'* and *'bonswar'* were duly added to my vocabulary. Both the words for 'two' and 'three' were unpronounceable, but for 'one' it seemed easier to stick a single finger in the air. For Fontainebleau he directed me thirty kilometres down the motorway.

"Are there any toll barriers?" I asked.

"The first one is just beyond this service station exit," he replied.

I thanked him for his help, then set off to walk around the boundary of the service station. There must be a staff entrance somewhere. Success. A short time later I was pushing Fred along a footpath that led to an ordinary road. With a compass hanging around my neck, I headed south, from where, if necessary, I could return to Paris after the weekend.

I found the forest of Fontainebleau most impressive from a tree point of view. However, the apparent lack of roadside boulders soon downgraded its general ambience to a picnic facility of no consequence. Anyway, given that my arrival coincided with approaching darkness, I soon gave up looking and pulled into a clearing just large enough to take my tent and Fred. (I reckoned criminals were less likely to tamper with a tent if they thought a great hairy biker was likely to appear without warning. So, whenever possible, I left them together, tying guide ropes to Fred's front and rear wheels.)

That night I cooked some proper *English* porridge (made with sweetened condensed milk, as opposed to Scottish porridge made with salt and water). Anyway, after dining alone I settled down to a good night's sleep. The following morning I breakfasted on more English-style porridge, which still left nineteen tins of condensed milk in Fred's top box. Then, with a full tummy, I set off in search of boulders.

Sadly, the man who wrote the article in the climbing magazine forgot to mention that a hundred or so boulders were not going to be that obvious in an area covered by twenty million trees. I walked along paths, through rough thicket, and squelched across ditches, all to no avail. Eventually I scrambled back to a road. Both sides were lined with trees as far as the eye could see. Then I did a quick calculation in my head, which simplified the problem down to one boulder for every twenty thousand trees – at which point, I abandoned my climbing quest.

Presently, I decided to spend the day doing a pre-Alpine training trek, which is a fancy way of saying a tourist walk, while thinking about climbing. Around midday I came across a town which I considered to be typically French, with all the house windows edged by wooden shutters. Every cyclist kept cars at a safe distance by strapping a French loaf sideways across their rear carrier. (The English later improved this idea by fixing a reflector to a strip of bendy plastic.) There was much *bonsure*-ing and *bonswar*-ing with everyone I met. Then a gang of children picked up on my English accent, and began walking alongside to ask me things in French. I realised they were playing a game of Confusing the Foreigner, which I accepted with good grace. Then I came to realise I had the advantage here, because an unruly mob has a tendency to become disorganised (as with the French Revolution). I, on the other hand, had complete control of my own mind.

"I am looking for the house where Joan of Arc lived," I told my first victim. Then I turned to another and explained I was living in the forest. Following the principle of divide and rule, I focused on the youngest. "I think the river that flows through Paris is very sensible," I said.

Their strategic game of confusion collapsed, and I was left to walk on alone, triumphant.

A little further along the pavement I came to a cafe, which I entered and successfully ordered a bowl of coffee. Then I noticed a newspaper stand in the corner and walked across to see what French looked like when written down. In one comic Mickey Mouse was speaking to Minnie in French. Even more amazingly, she could understand him. The image of mice speaking to each other in French made me giggle. I then picked up a Superman comic to find him hovering outside a New York skyscraper. A woman seemed to think it quite normal to open a window on the twentieth floor to discover a man flying about and wanting to speak French. But what really cracked me up was a Tom and Jerry cartoon. A mouse speaking French to a cat seemed absolutely hilarious, and I laughed out loud. Then I turned around to discover everyone in the cafe was staring at me, trying to figure out why I found children's comics so funny when I could not even speak their language. I shrugged, like they do in France, and returned to my coffee.

That evening (Saturday) I lay in my tent, listening to the rain dripping onto the canvas from the trees high above. It was too early to sleep, but too late to go out boulder hunting, so I pulled on my waterproofs and went for a short walk before nightfall. I had not intended to venture far from the road, and wandered aimlessly along what for me was a new path. Then it hit me – love at first sight. Waiting for me in a clearing was the most beautiful boulder I had ever seen. I climbed it via the easiest route, then stood on top, my conquest complete. Because the higher you get, the further you can see, I spied another boulder in the distance, even larger than the first. And so it went on, drawn deeper and deeper into the forest by bigger and better boulders. In fact I was enjoying my bouldering so much that I was quite surprised when it got dark. I tried to retrace my steps, but all the trees looked the same. It suddenly occurred to me that I had no idea where I had come from and, without a compass, no clue where I was going. Also, that the modern technology of an electric torch would have been useful, had I not left mine in the tent.

It was impossible to get lost in such an ancient forest without feeling that I was also moving back in time. I knew exactly how the peasants who had walked this way four hundred years earlier had felt as they prodded their way ahead with a stick to navigate between the trees. There was a daytime forest and a night-time forest. As one set of animals goes to sleep, another awakes. I was in the wrong phase; a human observed by a hundred unseen nocturnal eyes. I was not frightened, for I was the aggressor, but four hundred years before, when men, wolves and bears were equal, it would have been a different matter. I could understand how the book *Little Red Riding Hood* came to be written, and how much of its meaning had been lost to the twentieth century.

It is scientifically proven that, in the absence of light, the brain redirects its resources to the other senses. I became very aware of the wind playing in the treetops high above. I could feel the warmth of the living forest, and picked up its scents I would otherwise have missed. I became at one with nature and, after stumbling across a path, moved silently across a carpet of pine needles. The primeval instinct of survival was still inside me – you walked through a forest like this in silence. Hunter or victim, it did not do to attract attention.

When I finally came to a road, gentle rain pattered down and the cool wind, which had been playing with the treetops, made me shiver. On the positive side, the preceding absence of light had given me owl-like vision. I could clearly see the road for fifty feet in both directions but, having no idea where I was, the benefits of this were limited to not wandering off into a ditch. After giving the problem of returning to my tent some thought, I decided the best thing to do was to start walking, knowing that sooner or later I would come across a signpost for Paris. If I headed in that direction, it was inevitable that eventually I would join the approach road along which I had come. From there, I could easily find my way back to my tent.

My mood was indecisive and I made a couple of U-turns before I set off with any real determination. Eventually I came to a main road, on the other side of which was a signpost. I waited for a gap in the near-continuous flow of traffic. (French drivers believe it is unnatural to travel along a straight road at less than ninety miles per hour.) At the first opportunity I sprinted across – unaware of a low central hump. I crashed across the fast lane of the far carriageway and, for a moment, lay dazed, not quite certain how I had got there. Approaching headlights spun around my confused brain – no time to stand or think. As a reflex action, I made a mad scramble on hands and knees. Engines roared, kneecaps crashed into kerbstones and, head over heels, I rolled into a ditch. Tail lights, then total darkness.

After that my memory is a blank. I only assume I climbed out of the ditch and followed the signpost to Paris. The first thing I remember is reaching a junction I recognised. I then walked along my previous approach road, my kneecaps aching and my head sore. I forgot it was raining and that, having rolled into a ditch, I was dripping a trail of water from inside my waterproof trousers. It proved a good training walk; much better than climbing the Eiffel Tower. I returned to my tent as the early-morning light was just starting to creep into the sky. This is the advantage of establishing a base camp: just throw off your soggy clothes and crawl inside a sleeping bag to recover.

Chapter Fourteen

Monday morning saw me glaring at the closed door of a bank. Taking a compass bearing on the sun, I discovered it was now late morning, and still no one had come to open up. Paranoically I considered the possibility that someone was hiding inside, waiting for the Englishman to depart before letting in the public. I gave the door a gentle knock. Then, realising the resident might be a cleaner working with a noisy vacuum, I gave a louder knock. Getting no response, I sat on the pavement with my legs across the entrance. I closed my eyes, officially sunbathing, but in reality demonstrating my willingness to lay siege; the alternative now being to hitch-hike back to Calais.

"*Missure?*" said a voice.

"Yes?" I said.

"*Haah, Grand Briton, ah, Grand Briton, wee.*" (All spoken in French tones.)

"*Wee*, bank, money."

"*Nu*, building *societe, missure.*"

"Building society?"

"*Wee*, building *societe* closed Monday, *wee*." He pointed to a shop on the other side of the street and exclaimed, "*Le barnk.*"

"No, bank, money, *wee*," I responded.

"*Wee, le barnk,*" he shouted.

I stood up to assert my authority. "No, bank, money, *wee*," I said, raising my voice slightly, thereby giving the statement extra clarity.

"*Wee, le barnk*," he roared. Having proved that he could shout louder than me, he backed away to the other side of the street and pointed to a sign in the shop window. "*Le barnk*," he yelled, then promptly vanished into an alley. The French are so much better at shouting than the English. Chasing him to shout, 'No, bank, money, *wee*' would have been pointless.

Then I looked at the sign. It definitely stated, '*Le Banque Populaire*', but the building still looked like a shop. No bars, no bank architecture, just a '*Le Barnk Populaire*' sign stuck in a plate-glass window. Clever, eh? Camouflage even to the extent of misspelling the bank sign so it would not be recognised by those who gave it a casual glance. But it takes more than that to stop me.

On entering the building, I saw harmless-looking clerks sitting behind a counter similar to that of a travel agent. There were no safety grilles or anything to suggest the establishment was a bank. No longer timid about confrontation, I stood in the middle of the room and shouted, "Does anybody here speak English?"

All the staff replied in French, but at least I had an audience. I walked to the nearest clerk and showed her my credit card. Everyone left their desks to examine it with interest. After they had all managed to agree on *nu*, they handed it back. I counter-challenged with my chequebook and bank card. To my astonishment there was much *wee*-ing and nodding of heads. I wrote 'four hundred francs' in the little box, signed it, and let them fill in the rest. It caused a bit of confusion, but I was eventually handed the cash (about forty pounds). Of this, Fred needed twenty pounds to complete the adventure, leaving me sufficient to buy some cakes and a road map from a nearby shop.

NOTE: In order to confuse the English, the map uses metres – I convert these to proper feet or miles, which are easier to understand.

The French map revealed that the country was really big. However, running a finger down the pages, I located a route to Mont Blanc which avoided all motorways. This meant travelling through the western corner of Switzerland. Wow! There would be cowbells, cuckoo clocks, and the clip-clop of horses pulling hay carts…

I had hoped to make the Alps by Monday night, but then came the flies – hundreds of them. The first squadron attacked without warning at seventy miles per hour. Zit, zit, zit, splat – a direct hit on a tender cheek by an enormous hairy insect. For the most part I killed them outright, but those who had their impact softened by my beard crawled around the hairy forest, dazed and bewildered. Then I caught a sploshing insect right on my nose. As its entrails splattered outwards, I cried out in pain, eating a swarm of greenfly in the process. At that point I surrendered and turned up a narrow track where a sign indicated there was a campsite. I knew it would be expensive but was so covered in flies I had an obsessional desire for a shower.

After pitching my tent, I went for a quiet wander, which led me to many remarkable discoveries. The urinals were stuck to the outside of a building. Next to these were sinks for washing clothes. Bending over the sinks were two ladies, both elbow-deep in soapsuds. They seemed completely unconcerned that, just three feet away, men were letting it all hang out. The shower cubicles were also stuck to the outside of the building, but at least they were guarded by a saloon-type door to protect your rude bits in the middle. I entered one, undressed, then looked around for the taps. Some criminal had stolen them, so I dressed again and went to the next cubicle. But its taps were also missing. Then I remembered the shower trays I had seen in the unisex toilets earlier. Either stealing shower heads was a national pastime, or they had not been there in the first place. Then I noticed something peculiar. The drainage hole was large enough to lose a bar of soap – more like the size of a toilet. Confused, I returned to my tent to collect a water container. Bending down to fill this from a tap outside the cubicles allowed me to look under the saloon-type doors without being considered a pervert. I could see two pairs of legs, but no running water. More confused than ever, I went back to make myself a mug of coffee, since to do otherwise might have looked suspicious. Eventually I decided to risk going inside the previously mentioned building. There I was immediately surprised to see a lady emerging from a shower cubicle. I forgot that I was in France and backed away, apologising. She did not seem at all concerned, and replied in French. On reaching the door I looked for a sign which might tell me who had right of way.

The lady laughed, then beckoned me inside. Somehow she must have guessed that I was English. "It is okay," she said. Then she did up her bra and left.

I took a long shower. It was a beautiful feeling to have all the insects washed away. Once clean, I bravely stepped into the communal area, quickly pulled up my shorts, and made my escape outside.

After a nice meal of porridge, I explored the campsite in the hope of finding a proper toilet, but without success. By this process of elimination, I concluded that French toilets are modified shower units. I was not brave enough to use one but was told later that you had to squat in them. Apparently, they are called *pissoirs*; a word which, in part, has come into English usage. However, to this day I remain perplexed as to how you flush them without getting your feet wet.

The following morning, after leaving the campsite, Fred found himself travelling along a high plateau which thankfully lacked any potholes or hilly bits. Thus, he could focus on solving a problem which troubled him greatly. Since leaving England, the bulk porridge oats in one of his panniers had dropped by five inches, and the condensed milk in the top box reduced by three tins. So why had the weight on his rear suspension unit increased? Well, he had no understanding that any carried food had simply transferred to my digestive system, together with a few delicious cakes, and a one-metre French loaf, plus sausage. I had also purchased a road map, so yes, his load was heavier. He could only conclude that he had always been a downtrodden victim, and had no reason to think it would ever be otherwise. But neither did he have any understanding that his life was about to change in ways he could not imagine…

Chapter Fifteen

For me and the Alps it was love at first sight. That is to say, I fell for them and, because they made no effort to run away, assumed it was mutual.

This 'ka-pow' moment happened quite unexpectedly when the high plateau along which I had been riding came to a sudden end. Ahead, the road descended steeply into a wide, flat valley. This was covered with a shimmering blue haze which obscured any features it might have. Only on the distant horizon did the snowy summits of the Alps appear to float, glistening, between the haze beneath and a sapphire-blue sky. Fred could not understand why I had done an emergency stop to spend so long gazing at some pointy white things floating in the sky. They could have no possible effect on his own misfortunes.

Somewhere in the valley I approached a near-abandoned customs post. I did not want to stop, because I believed that on the far side of the crossing was the magical land of proper toilets (also known as Switzerland). Thankfully, the solitary guard gave me little regard because I had been in the country of shower toilets for five days and had no intention of stopping.

On arriving in the romantic city of Geneva, I screeched Fred to a halt, a little like James Bond arriving for a special mission. In my case, for obvious reasons, I leapt from Fred, grabbed the rucksack with all my valuable possessions – including ice axes and crampons – then ran to the nearest toilet. I ran down a marble staircase to enter an immaculately clean room set aside for males. Nothing was done with the hands. Taps were operated by foot pedals, as were soap dispensers and toilet flushes. Even the lights came on automatically as I entered, presumably to avoid any contamination via a light switch. I was not dressed for this emergency, wearing several outer layers of clothing, under which were hidden my braces. There was no time to undress, so I just undid the brace buttons and let gravity take the ultra-wide breeches to my ankles. Hence, in the cubicle, I was all tied up with a variety of cables and straps, with a heavy rucksack on my lap. But I felt safe in a world I understood – and eventually nature took its course.

After the panic was over, I began to wonder how the automatic light worked. Clearly, opening the door had activated the switch, but how did the door know if I was leaving or arriving? More to the point, what mechanism was able to distinguish between 'the visitor' being a very efficient Swiss gentleman, or an English male who liked to spend a quiet half-hour reading the newspaper? I mean, the Swiss invented cuckoo clocks so that everything might work in accordance with their efficiency regulations. However, before I could give the matter any serious thought, the lights went out. It was the sort of darkness you get in an underground bunker when the emergency lights are not working. So there I was, in a confined cubicle, lashed with straps and weighted down with a thirty-kilogram rucksack. There was no way I could get myself out of this situation in total darkness; only fight with the cubicle door, which opened inwards. After winning this battle, I staggered blindly around with breeches and underpants confining my ankles and everything else trailing behind. Eventually I felt my way to the door and opened it just a fraction. Immediately the room was thrown into glaring light, and I clanged back to the cubicle, hoping no one else would choose that exact moment to answer their call of nature.

After the toilet issue had been resolved, I went upstairs with the intention of telling Fred the good news about my weight loss. However, the stairs emerged in a shopping arcade, and here I noticed a shop which sold English biscuits. It crossed my mind that it would be nice to sit outside in the sunshine, eating chocolate digestives and drinking coffee from a Swiss vending machine. I went across to the bureau de change at the far end of the hall and tried to express my wishes. The dragon who lived behind the bars breathed heavily through her nostrils, thus using a universal language to state that she did not appreciate tourists who pushed a fifty-franc note into her cage. But I was hungry and needed Swiss francs, so stood my ground until she relented.

The motorway heading south from Geneva was a magnificent feat of civil engineering. Sometimes it was in the shade of a deep cutting; the next moment it appeared to 'take flight' above a 'bottomless' gorge. To either side, the foothills of the Alps towered up in a series of rocky walls. High above there were still a few streaks of snow, brilliant white beneath the afternoon sun. It was the sort of place where you might see James Bond speeding down the fast lane with a beautiful lady in the passenger seat of his sports car. I thought how wonderful it would have been doing this with Helen sitting in Fred's armchair and exclaiming, "Oh, what a lovely view." Occasionally, I took a glance to the far distance to check for toll barriers but, in this country, it seemed that such things did not exist. Here, quiet roads were probably more to do with a sparsely distributed population than anything the French had dreamed up to make motorways the preserve of the rich.

Presently, my mind adjusted to the magical surroundings. Then a long-forgotten memory floated by. I could imagine myself as a small child wandering the gaslit streets, before turning onto a bomb site to climb the crumbling walls of half-demolished houses. At the age of six I could not have believed that a world such as the Alps existed. Come to that, back then I had assumed that air always contained smoke; here it was possible to see distant summits with complete clarity. For the first time on this trip I felt a long way from England.

According to my road map, the nearest town to Mont Blanc was Chamonix. I had imagined this to be a small settlement where most of the locals made a living by herding goats or letting their spare room to the odd tourist. Indeed, I believe that forty years earlier this was the case, but the new motorway from Switzerland and the road tunnel beneath Mont Blanc had put Chamonix on a major transport route to Italy. Now the town was dominated by concrete hotels which had obviously been built in a hurry. I believe it only became a posh ski resort after the war, which probably accounted for the pavements being crowded with people parading as if on a fashion catwalk. On the positive side, the horde of fashion icons meant that there were many shops selling postcards, most of which had a photograph of Mont Blanc. I bought a few of these, then headed west to a place in the countryside which had no tall buildings to block my view.

It was very easy to identify Mont Blanc from the postcards. It consisted of a snow-covered summit, with a ridge descending towards the right. After a little dip, there was a great snowy dome, which a postcard told me was called the Dôme du Goûter. To the right of this, a snowfield fell away to a place where both the postcard and my vision came to an end. However, it was fairly obvious that the best way to approach the summit was from the right. The only weakness in my plan was that the postcards ignored the foothills, leaving the first eleven thousand feet of ascent to the imagination.

Looking at my map, I could see that if I continued west I would eventually come to a side lane which ended in the mountains, a mere eight kilometres before the Dôme du Goûter. This distance represented the foothills, which my map considered a blank space. French mapmakers have a strange interpretation when it comes to minor roads in the Alps. The one I had chosen clearly had its origins in a footpath which had been widened to a single track capable of taking farm vehicles. At one place it zigzagged up the hillside with the various tiers separated only by a vertical wall. The insides of the hairpin bends were sloped down at forty-five degrees, while the more gentle sweep around the outside was too badly potholed to be navigated by a heavy motorcycle. Despite what Fred might actually believe, he was a rubbish rock climber and kept running out of power, and so threatening to stall. I would have no chance of holding him on such a steep hill, and if I rolled back, my only method of survival would be to leap off and watch him tumble into a ravine. In light of this, I pulled in the clutch and screamed the engine to the top of the rev counter. Then I threw him back into gear and, rising up like a stallion, he bravely cleared the final part of the bend. That, in any event, was how Fred liked to see himself. To the casual observer, a better animal comparison might have been a terrified kangaroo. Anyway, by occasionally slipping the clutch, I lowered the gearing enough to get up the steepest bits. In this way I zigzagged up the mountain until the track eased gently to sloping meadows.

My arrival in the farmyard at the top of the track was the most spectacular I had ever achieved. Air-cooled motorbikes were never meant to do eight thousand revs while only travelling at two miles per hour. The baked-on oil of yesteryear was practically on fire and sent up clouds of black smoke. This gave body to the dust cloud which had followed me up from the main road. Around the farmyard stood a rustic selection of buildings, and from every window many faces were staring at the dust cloud from which I was slowly emerging. Then the faces disappeared and the doors flew open. This was not a village as I had been expecting, but an adventure centre for children. They came at me as a swarm and, though only about thirty in number, it was quite sufficient to surround me in three complete circles of excited jumping-up-and-down enthusiasm. Most were about twelve and all were female. Their only purpose in life was to ask me things in French. A few of the older ones took my imprisonment as an opportunity to practise their English. One girl even managed to say something I understood, and what a compliment, because it translated to 'the mad Englishman'. I was not just another climber; I was here to represent England and was determined to do my country proud. Well, in actual fact the words I managed to decipher were "English, solitaire, cowboy, cuckoo" – but I liked my translation better.

As the swarm began to disperse, a few adults wandered forwards. This worried me because it was obvious that they had never seen a mountaineer in this part of the world before. An older man, dressed in the manner of a farmer, examined my ice axes as if they were some newfangled gardening tool. Why? According to my logic, this was much the best place to start climbing Mont Blanc – surely people would be coming this way with climbing equipment all the time? However, because none of the adults spoke English, for now it would remain a mystery.

As my map had predicted, this mountain settlement was where the road came to an end. To the far side of the old farmyard was a gate, beyond which a cart track headed in the general direction of Mont Blanc. After pushing a badly traumatised Fred across the yard, I chained him to a tree. I could only hope there was not a local action group called the Society for the Prevention of Cruelty to Motorcycles.

Before leaving England, I had weighed my total luggage; the result being forty-five kilograms. If Helen had been with me to share the load, that would have been fine. But on my own, getting to base camp was clearly going to be a challenge. Not wishing to admit defeat, I began ascending the cart track with my back carrying a framed rucksack, to which I had strapped a tent, a sleeping bag, saucepans, and anything else that would not fit elsewhere. On my chest I had a rucksack in reverse. This contained a rope and sufficient gear to allow an abseil retreat from any faces which proved too difficult to complete. In each hand I had bulging shopping bags: one filled with porridge and condensed milk; the other overflowing with whatever else I might need if I had been about to climb Everest. To summarise, I was not so much a human being as a badly designed and overloaded yak. After a short distance my legs gave way and, lashed down by a pyramid of equipment, I collapsed in the middle of the track. After untangling myself from my Himalayan luggage I continued in stages, taking half the load a few hundred yards, then using the downhill walk to recover, before making a second ascent with the remainder.

Nevertheless I made reasonable time and by late evening had established a base camp on gently sloping grassland, with a good selection of equipment and five days' supply of food. That night I lay in my tent, listening to many cowbells clanging in the valley below. It seemed strange to think that I was lying in a solitary tent above an Alpine meadow. It crossed my mind that in a week I would either be dead or have a solo ascent of Mont Blanc under my belt.

I wished Helen was here now, wrapped in my arms, just lying still and listening to the sound of cowbells drifting upwards on the cold night air.

Chapter Sixteen

Those wishing to repeat my Mont Blanc ascent route should be aware that, from now on, many of the heights are based on information provided by my leg muscles. These lack objectivity and their unit of measurement is best summarised as 'Are we there yet?' However, during much of my early ascent I could see a really big mountain over to my right and, by looking at this, was able to monitor my progress. Sadly, this kept telling me that I seemed to be walking on the spot.

Anyway, when my legs (incorrectly) believed I had reached 4,413 feet (the height of Ben Nevis), I stopped to ponder my situation. Looking right, I gazed down into a U-shaped glaciated valley. Previously I had never been able to understand why geology teachers got so excited by these. But now I realised that my lack of amazement was due to British valleys no longer having a glacier at the bottom of them. The one I was now admiring contained a tumble of ice blocks, many the size of a house; the crevasses between them able to swallow a double-decker bus. The fact it was moving, albeit very slowly, explained how such natural wonders could move megaton boulders five hundred miles from the Alps to an area which eventually became the forest of Fontainebleau. On this particular glacier, I could only see the middle section, but logic dictated it began somewhere in the high mountains and ended in the far-distant lowlands. Quite suddenly I was overcome with sympathy for the long-suffering geology teachers of Britain who, while on wet and windy field courses, tried to get a gaggle of bored schoolchildren excited by the U-shaped valleys (as opposed to the V-shaped gorges created by water erosion). From my present observation point the far side of the glacier ended in a cavernous mouth where ice and rock gnashed together in an act of mutual destruction. Beyond this natural power struggle, the face of the previously mentioned really big mountain presented a wall of ice-covered rock which I believed matched any challenge the Eiger could offer.

As well as estimating how high you might be, it is useful to know the direction in which you need to be heading. For my current situation this was easy, because I knew roughly the position of my base camp and that I needed to pass the summit of the Aiguille du Goûter en route. This was marked on my map at 12,500 feet.

I am going to ignore describing the first part of my ascent because it was rather unpleasant, and higher up there was something far more gruesome awaiting me. However, the most basic facts are that when slowly trudging up the foothills, I was surround by a great swarm of carnivorous insects and the temperature was forty-two degrees centigrade.

So, leaving out the boring bit, I eventually came to an unremarkable section of hillside, about five thousand feet in altitude. Here my compass directed me towards a great tangle of brambles and tall, spiky bushes, the latter designed to tear the flesh from arms and face. Possibly it was such masochistic thoughts which made me rummage around in my rucksack for a thermometer. I had initially purchased this to record temperatures on Ben Nevis; getting slightly excited when the red line dropped a smidgen below minus twenty degrees centigrade. I had expected Mont Blanc to be even colder. Ironically the greenhouse effect within my rucksack had now taken the thermometer to the top of the scale at sixty degrees centigrade. To consider the air temperature in the shade was pointless, because I was above the treeline. All that remained was hard, cracked earth and the previously mentioned unfriendly vegetation. My survival therefore depended on excreting great quantities of sweat, but this broadcast my presence to the insects, who thought nothing of flying a mile to obtain a really tasty breakfast.

Leaving my masochistic thoughts, I looked left to study a slight path; the sort possibly maintained by hoofed animals. This confused me. Surely it should also provide a sensible walking route for those attempting Mont Blanc? Yet it was deserted. Then I realised I had seen no one since leaving the adventure centre the previous evening. My original assumption that at least ten climbers a day would be heading in the general direction of the summit was clearly wrong. The animal track had the disadvantage of heading directly away from Mont Blanc, but I could see no other way of avoiding the bramble zone without losing height. So, taking this as the least-worst option, I walked along the track until I came to a shallow gully of hard-baked clay and scree. This cut through the bloodthirsty vegetation above; the lower section descending into woodland perhaps three hundred feet below. Using my fingernails I clawed and scrambled up the gully for about five feet, but the clay crumbled, causing me to slide back down until I could leap sideways to the safety of the path.

Thinking practically about how I might overcome this obstacle, I remembered a recent article in a climbing magazine about those who ascended the White Cliffs of Dover using ice-climbing equipment. Those cliffs are vertical and made of chalk, and to me it had seemed a very efficient way to commit suicide. However, my clay gully was no steeper than sixty degrees so, as an experiment, I strapped crampons onto my boots, then removed two ice axes from my rucksack. One of these was a long-shafted walker's axe which extended my reach over particularly crumbly sections. The other was a short-shafted tool for more aggressive, deeper placements. Essentially, my hands and feet had become claws of steel. Swinging axes and kicking crampon front points into the clay, I began climbing the gully which, treating the clay as ice, proved easy. I improved this method further by spacing my feet about a yard apart to create a stable triangular shape. Unfortunately, when wearing tennis shorts this opens up a whole new 'menu' for insects who have no regard for respectable dining etiquette. Meanwhile, the more polite diners among them settled beneath my crash helmet to enjoy a meal of blood and trapped perspiration. When I could stand their frenzied feeding no longer, I pushed the shaft of the walker's axe into some particularly loose clay, which released a hand to have a good scratch below. I then moved my fingernails up my body until I reached my crash helmet. I removed this and balanced it on the axe. The effect on my head of removing the helmet was like taking the lid off a pressure cooker. Steam rose, and the insects who had not actually drowned took flight.

Meanwhile, my helmet rolled off the axe, bounced down the gully, smashed into some rocks, then disappeared over a precipice. Because I had joined the gully in the middle, I had no idea where the helmet ended up – possibly in a cowpat down in the valley, to be found by a farmhand who might wonder how it had got there? The loss of my helmet was not an immediate problem because in France it was legal to ride a motorcycle without one. But if I did ever return to England, I did wonder how I might explain to a policeman that it had fallen down Mont Blanc. Would he sympathise with my misfortune or simply arrest me for taking hallucinatory drugs? But thinking about England was not going to bring my helmet flying back up the gully, so I continued to climb without it.

After a routine ascent, my leading axe hooked itself onto a solid rock shelf. Looking up, I saw a really strange geological formation. All I could see from below was a stone lip and, behind that, a vertical wall of rock. This gave me the impression that I was beneath a giant elongated bookshelf. After planting the second axe onto the ledge, I pulled myself up to look across the shelf. To my astonishment, somebody had put a metal tram track along it. It was an outrage! When people first thought about climbing Mont Blanc, they did not take a train. They put on their boots and, very much like me, began marching towards the summit. If this track went all the way to the top where, like on the summit of Wyddfa, there was a cafe, I would be most cross!

But back to my next move. While ascending the gully there had been axe-holds above me on which I could hang and so maintain balance. Now, presented with a flat shelf, I faced a most awkward move. The normal procedure is to jump, straighten the arms, then gracefully bend forwards to swing up a leg. (This manoeuvre is called a mantelshelf. It is considered very bad form to put a knee on the shelf, because skin or trouser contact is less predictable than a solid rubber sole.) However, I thought the jump would not work very well when standing on crampons; their front points sticking into loose clay. Also, I had a rucksack pulling me backwards. In addition, back from the edge, the smooth rock shelf was covered with loose stone chippings. Though these are excellent for laying railway sleepers, they are completely useless as climbing holds.

The next bit was really embarrassing. I hooked my long-shafted ice axe over a tram rail, then pulled myself forwards to use it as a handhold. As my centre of gravity changed, my feet shot outwards, landing my belly on the edge. Without bothering to stand up I wriggled across both rails to sit with my rucksack resting against the rock wall on the other side. It seemed a good place to rest and inspect my poor, insect-eaten skin, which now consisted entirely of red blotches.

My self-pity came to an end when I heard the blast of a horn. I looked around to see a train laboriously struggling up the track towards me. It gave the impression of being very old, as if it had just escaped from a museum. Given this, I decided it was completely harmless, so merely bunched up my knees to remove my legs from the rails. I could not understand why the driver continued to blow his horn, and was now leaning out of his cab and waving his arms around, like they do in France. When the train was about fifty yards away, it entered my cutting, allowing me to see things from a different perspective. Or, more precisely, the train now looked like a charging rhinoceros which was at least two feet wider than the track. The driver seemed to think he had right of way, so I tried to push myself upright. But my crampons merely skidded across the loose chippings, sending my feet flying upwards. On my second attempt to retreat, I immediately sat back down, because I was still attached to my rucksack by a waist strap. Also, to prevent dropping my axes they were tied to my tennis shorts, which represented a severe form of bondage.

While being forced to sit would normally only be embarrassing, the fact my rucksack extended my back like a camel's hump meant I was pushed eighteen inches further into the danger zone than a 'thin' person. Realising death was fast approaching, I remembered that 'impossible' feats of strength often occur in dangerous situations. In films, this might be Superman stopping a train by standing in front of it. In my case, the waistband of my tennis shorts was not designed to withstand the sudden, determined upward thrust of me jumping up. Thus I stood, but my shorts fell to my ankles. Then, having no time to jettison my rucksack, I turned to face my nemesis; my body now reduced to the width of my shoulders. Then there was nothing else to do but wait for something to happen. Luckily, the widest part of the train was the stepping-up boards beneath the coach doors. (This placed them level with my knees, which are narrower than my waist.) This proved a satisfactory alignment, and eventually the train rattled by with a few inches to spare. Then it trundled onwards, and the gloomy, confined space between death and rock returned to sunlight. I concluded that all French drivers were the same: crazy.

There are two sorts of torture. I imagine the worst kind is when somebody else is inflicting the pain and looking for an excuse to kill you. The better sort is depicted by a monk inflicting self-flagellation, because he is presumably deriving pleasure from enjoying a previous sin. Also, he can stop whenever he wants. So where did my degree of torture rank as I trudged up a train track, squirting sweat, being eaten by insects, feeling severely dehydrated, and running a medically dangerous high temperature? Well, just possibly I obtained a little insight into what it was like for wartime prisoners being force-marched along a Burmese railway track.

The first relief came when I was directly above, rather than below, the bramble field where, earlier, I had diverted from my compass bearing to walk away from Mont Blanc. Maybe I had gained four hundred feet in altitude and, by these small stages, I would surely conquer the mountain… eventually.

A little later I was again plodding along the track when I saw the train returning from wherever it had been. However, here the ridge was broad, and I stepped aside to give the driver a friendly wave as he approached.

"*Bonsure*," I cried as he passed.

He, presuming that I could speak his language, shouted something back in French, but I have no idea what it was.

Things began to improve after a sharp right-hand turn. Here the track was cut into a steep rock face. I assumed that in winter the resulting shelf would have been completely banked with snow, but now this had melted to leave a vertical wall of glistening ice. From the top, a waterfall cascaded down, and, ignoring the medical dangers of rapid cooling, I proceeded to have a shower. The sticky sweat washed away along with all the insects. Then I threw back my head, opened my mouth, and sucked in the falling water. Finally, after filling my water bottle, I stepped into the sunshine, opened my arms, and stood awhile to watch the steam rising from my body. Feeling almost human again, I continued my journey by plodding up between the gently inclined rails.

Presently I came to a place where the cliff bulged out, which caused the track to disappear into a tunnel. When it became obvious there were no trains in the vicinity, I wandered into the darkness. After a short distance I noticed a man-sized tunnel cut into the right-hand wall. Out of curiosity, I diverted into this. On reaching the exit hole, I looked out to discover that I was halfway up a cliff face. Strangely, the summit of the really big mountain mentioned earlier was still higher than my observation point – by quite a long way. On the positive side, I could see the clearing where I had made base camp, but it was too far away to make out my tent. It is quite satisfying to observe where you started and realise how far you have come. Either that, or very worrying to discover that you have made less progress than you thought, and return to find that your tent has been stolen. I considered this side tunnel a good place to sleep – except that it was a bit draughty and, having lost my crash helmet, I no longer had anything to protect my ears from frostbite. I needed a proper snow hole with the entrance draughtproofed by a rucksack. Anyway, after my shower I was fully awake and excited about whatever might lie ahead.

I returned to the train tunnel, then continued to the higher exit, where I had the surreal experience of stepping onto a station platform. The rails were to my right; the buildings on my left. These appeared to have no roofs; their walls supporting a great snow cliff. As a result, I got the impression the doors merely led to the interior of the mountain. At the far end of the track a set of buffers told me this was the terminus. It was deserted, so I assumed the last train of the day had left. After a moment to ponder, I walked to a snowfield at the end of the track. Here, looking up, I discovered that it was the sort of snow a child might sledge down. Indeed, near the station there were many footprints, together with evidence of snowball fights. Essentially, it was a playground and, I assumed, picnic area for adults who wished to sunbathe. More importantly, it was the type of snow into which it was easy to dig a tunnel. Given that the snowfield extended onto the roofs of the station buildings, after gaining a hundred feet in height all traces of civilisation had vanished. Then, lost in a world of happy thoughts, I ascended, while occasionally looking around to admire the scenery.

At the top of the snowfield, a ridge curved upwards to my right. To my left, the wind had sculpted a half-crater in the snow, about the size of a tennis court. Its rim circled around the bowl to join a low rocky outcrop behind. Nestling beneath this was a little cabin. There was no glass in the window openings, but the remnants of a shutter still hung loosely from its rotten frame. Such architecture probably dated it to the 1800s, while its location suggested it had been built by an eccentric person who wanted to be left alone. After descending into the crater, I walked to the cabin and pushed the door. It squeaked open on rusty hinges to reveal that the building was unoccupied. I thought this most strange, given there were two long benches on which to sit and a great scattering of straw across the floor, making it an ideal place to sleep. This cabin was essentially a hotel for softies.

After porridge, I settled into my sleeping bag, sinking slightly into my luxurious bed of straw. As the night progressed I gave some consideration to why someone had built a hotel in such an isolated setting. Eventually, I reasoned that before the abomination of the train this was the furthest it was possible to get on the first day of the Mont Blanc ascent. Back then, only rich people could have indulged in such adventures, using local guides to carry their luggage. "We want a hotel there," an aristocrat might have snorted down his nostrils to a manservant, "and make it really posh, with benches and stuff." Then the train happened and this hotel became irrelevant, causing it to be abandoned.

Having resolved this dilemma, I turned my attention to the avalanches thundering down the still-distant peaks. The shock wave from one appeared to shake the cabin, but I did not consider it important. From now on, hopefully, I would be sticking to climbing ridges. Initially the avalanches were every fifteen minutes or so but, as the freezing night air took hold, things settled down and eventually all was silent. I had never stayed in a hotel before and confess I found the experience most pleasant. But I failed to sleep because, looking up to the window opening, I could see the stars twinkling through the frosty air. I could not get it out of my mind that I wanted Helen to share this moment with me, in the same way that two people who are very much in love want to sit together in a picture house. As the last stars faded into the first light of dawn, I got up, made porridge, then went outside to enjoy my breakfast beneath a clear blue sky.

Once breakfast had boosted my calorie levels, I turned my attention to the bowl of sculpted snow which curved around my dwelling place. The top was vertical or overhanging, so I got out my short-handled ice axes to test what was possible. Sometimes the snow took my weight; often it did not, causing me to roll harmlessly down into the bowl. I considered this a most enjoyable part of my Alpine learning curve.

After lunch, I turned my attention to the ridge, up which my climb would continue. Mostly it was a blade of snow, though occasionally rocky towers projected upwards in a most attractive way. It lacked any footprints, which I thought most strange because, give or take the odd zigzag, I had kept to a nice compass bearing, so knew this ridge was heading in the general direction of Mont Blanc's summit. The ridge turned out to be a dividing line between east and west, so my progress opened up increasingly spectacular views. Of particular interest was the grand sweep of an icy snowfield which descended towards Chamonix on my left. This confirmed my location, removing any lingering doubt about where I might be.

While ascending the crest of the ridge, I came upon a carefully built pile of rocks. These are quite common in the wilderness because they signpost the way across sections which have no obvious path. They are called cairns, and are particularly useful in snow-covered landscapes. However, on this obvious ridge the stones merely got in the way, forcing me from the crest to traverse the steeply angled snow beneath. Here I happened to look up and see a flat rock embedded in the cairn. It had been engraved with a man's name and the number twenty-seven which I presumed to be his age. To me it looked like a monument to record a death, though I was confused as to how it had happened on this gentle ridge. Only later did I learn that around seven thousand people have died on Mont Blanc (up until 1980), so 'death cairns' are a common sight. In this environment, something as simple as tripping over a shoelace can be fatal.

After passing the monument, a further ascent brought me to a place where the ridge widened to become a triangular plateau. To one side of this was a small hut of timber construction and pleasing appearance. Most of it was buried by snow, but the area around the door had been trampled underfoot. Walking closer, I noticed a snow cave to the side of the trench and, though now unoccupied, it had obviously once been a sleeping place for two people. This suggested it might be possible to buy a cup of coffee in the hut, so I advanced to the open doorway – and that was as far as I got.

Inside, wielding a large broom, was a lady of about nineteen. I believe men who judge females entirely by appearance are shallow, so will merely say this particular lady made my knees go all wobbly. Then she looked up from her sweeping, smiled, and said, "*Bonsure.*"

My own voice failed to respond. Rather, given her gentle tones, I felt a strong desire to acknowledge her superiority by giving a submissive bow. But, given the state of my knees, and the rucksack on my back, this would have sent me crashing to the floor, prostrate beneath her feet, which was the opposite to the manly effect I was hoping to achieve. So I just stood there gormlessly.

"*Dunka shern,*" she said.

"Er..."

She responded by raising her eyebrows to indicate a question. "Hello?" she enquired.

"Yes... I mean, *wee.*"

Her following speech informed me that she had learnt many ways to say hello but, for complicated things, she could only speak French. Eventually she looked me up and down. "Mont Blanc?" she said.

"*Wee,*" I replied.

"*Solitaire?*"

"*Wee.*"

Her face displayed a frown of concern. She cared about me!

The unexpected appearance of the lady had so discombobulated my brain that I forgot all about the coffee. I turned and retreated to a safe place on the plateau where I could think rationally. Only then did I realise that I had failed to notice anything about the interior of the hut apart from the lady. I wondered if my ability to lose peripheral vision represented either an evolved survival strategy or a weakness. Certainly, when I had earlier directed all my attention to the train rattling towards me, it had given me the strength to stand up, regardless of circumstances. Conversely, the more dramatic and unexpected appearance of the 'hut lady' had forced me to sit down. After getting the logical part of my brain back into gear, I realised that the lady could not sensibly walk to work every morning. Possibly she lived in the hut for the entire summer. So, she liked mountains. I decided that if I ever came to be lying injured beneath a cliff, I would like her to find me and nurse me back to health. Guess I had been reading too much romantic fiction again!

Meanwhile, back in the real world, I walked to the edge of the plateau and gazed up at the Aiguille du Goûter. The face was about two thousand feet high, its upper section mostly ice-covered rock; the lower section, where it was less steep, attractively decorated with windblown snow. Looking down, I noticed that the face ended in a sudden drop, beneath which was the head of the glacier I mentioned earlier. Strange to think that if I fell from the face I would disappear into the jaws created by the ice moving away from the headwall (known as a bergschrund), never to be found – until my ice-preserved body reached the foot of the glacier in the far-distant future. "Oh," some scientifically advanced human would say, "I can see from his clothes that this specimen is an early pioneer from 1923; we'd better give the museum a call."

Looking up from the glacier, I studied the cliff which dominated the higher face of the Goûter's left-hand side. It gave the appearance of a castle's buttress from which rocks could be dropped onto the troops of an invading army. However, because of its location I shall call it the Bastille Buttress (the French spelling of 'Basteal'). After giving my route options some consideration I concluded that, to avoid the buttress, I would need to traverse to the centre of the face, which seemed to offer a much easier line of ascent. To start this traverse it was necessary to cross a wide snow gully which, to simplify things, I will call the Bastille Gully. This began near the top of the Bastille Buttress and ended in a sheer drop to the bergschrund a few hundred feet below.

Using a long-shafted ice axe as a walking stick, I stepped carefully across the Bastille Gully until I came to an area which had clearly seen much stone fall. I looked up to make certain nothing was whizzing down. Then, without warning, I felt a little giddy. So I removed a second ice axe from my rucksack with the intention of traversing while facing the slope; this allowing me to kick proper foot placements with crampons. Suddenly the world started spinning. I could not understand what was happening. *It will pass*, I thought, and pressed on for another two sidesteps. And that was as far as I got. I tried to summon all of my remaining consciousness to get out of the stone-fall channel, but my legs seemed to be made of lead. I twisted the axe straps firmly around my wrists and plunged both shafts deep into the icy snow. Then I passed out.

Chapter Seventeen

I seemed to be floating through a starry black void from which I was trying to escape, but it kept calling me back. Then I became aware of something cold against my nose. My face began to tingle, as if a million tiny pins were lightly touching the skin. Slowly the tingling spread down my body. Eventually it reached my feet, and I seemed to be bathed in a strange radiation. Slowly the tingling began to fade as mysteriously as it had appeared. Then the darkness dissolved into snow, and I remembered that I was hanging from two straps wrapped around my wrists. I closed my hands around the axe shafts and re-kicked my feet into the snow. I was safe, but not yet ready to move. Using the time to think, I remembered reading an article about altitude sickness. It had said that if the patient cannot be brought down quickly, it generally results in death. I had ascended too quickly, giving my body insufficient time to make the physiological changes needed to function within a lower air density. (Blood cells change shape, haemoglobin levels increase to absorb more oxygen, and the diaphragm strengthens to increase the power of the lungs.) In addition to poor acclimatisation, I had recently dehydrated my body to dangerous levels. And though the hotel accommodation in the cabin had been superb, I had failed to get any sleep. I realised for my next attempt the only solution would be to descend, spend a couple of rest days at base camp, then start all over again – only this time, more slowly.

By the time I had retreated to the hut, I felt a little better. The lady looked at me – she had probably seen this a hundred times before. I was just another failure, inspired by dreams, but living beyond reality.

"Coffee?" she asked.

"*Wee.*" (Strange that she was speaking English, and I had replied in French.)

After I had sat on a bench by a long wooden table, the lady went through a side door which gave access to a small kitchen. I imagined this to be part of her living quarters. I wondered what grade she climbed after finishing her shift. "I am just nipping out to climb that new icicle which has appeared from the top of the Bastille Buttress," she might say. "Back in a mo."

My romantic musings were distracted by her placing a large bowl of coffee on the table before me. As could be expected, it was expensive but, given the context, worth it.

Without warning, I came over all funny again. Though my eyes were open, my brain was unable to register any light signals, and so believed itself to be in a place of total darkness. I felt sick and began to think that I was going to keel over and die. Then something extremely strange happened. In my recent fantasy I had thought how nice it would be to capture the lady's attention by requiring a rescue from beneath a cliff face. Now it became a real possibility that I might fall from my bench and crash-land at her feet, it became the worst thing imaginable. Though my vision had completely gone, I could remember where the door was. As if in a dream, I moved my body in a way which is difficult to define, and discovered that I had arrived in a different, colder environment. I was now standing on snow and promptly fell over: the outside world, I hoped, would think I was sunbathing.

After I had recovered, I noticed a well-trodden track in the snow which headed to the edge of the plateau, a little to the left of my ascent route. I followed the footprints to a descending snowfield which looked quite harmless, so sat down and used my bottom as a sledge; the footprints guiding my steering. Within a few minutes I had descended two thousand feet and was fast approaching the train terminus. Using my boots to brake, I gently stopped, then stood, feeling completely recovered in the denser air. Descending the track was an easy plod, so I reached the top of a clay gully without difficulty. Looking down, I decided against using it for retreat, so continued along the track until the landscape on my left looked more friendly. A little later I was wandering through a wooded glade when I noticed a most peculiar 'nest' in a treetop. I quickly realised this was an upside-down crash helmet. It had fallen and landed within twenty yards of my random descent line. My ability to successfully retrieve the helmet validates my previous belief that tree climbing is an essential skill which should be taught equally to boys and girls in all schools.

After recovering the helmet, I returned to my tent without further incident. Here I had a fine meal of porridge. This restored my brain to good order, allowing me to ruminate about what I had just experienced. I soon realised that everything could be reduced to three fundamental problems.

The first of these concerned the lady in the hut. Her initial angelic appearance while holding a sacred broom was obviously destined to remain deep within my brain for the rest of my life. To file her away under the access code of 'the lady in the hut' was too cumbersome. So, after much consideration, I decided she was called Felicity – because it sounded vaguely French, and because in English it translated to 'great happiness and pleasure'.

The second problem was food; specifically, porridge and condensed milk. For Scottish mountaineering, this is essential for good health during long winter nights. Because I had imagined that the Alps would be colder, on my first attempt I had carried a paraffin stove plus cooking utensils. In reality, summer Alpine conditions are more gentle (excluding the north face of the Eiger and the like). For my second attempt, I decided I would abandon all kitchen equipment and take four French loaves. Spread with margarine and filled with cheese, they would initially be bulky in my rucksack, but become less so as the ascent progressed. I also decided to carry a dozen packets of salty crisps. Having said all this, most humans have enough stored fat to go without food for a couple of days. But in extreme circumstances sweating can use up to two litres of water an hour, which needs to be replaced regularly. For my second attempt, I decided to carry four litres in plastic bottles. Throughout the day I could supplement this supply by munching the odd snowball. Also – and to my shame – I decided that during the ascent I would visit the Felicity hut for coffee. This would involve parting with large quantities of cash which I did not have...

Which brings me to the third and final problem: my bank manager. A nervous middle-aged man, he did not like talking about overdrafts with people who lived on houseboats, rode a motorbike, and spent large amounts of cash on mountaineering expeditions. However, he was back in England, while my chequebook was in the South of France. I reckoned that it would take many days for the two to meet. Of course, eventually I would have to kneel before him and beg forgiveness for my sins. But just at that moment, I needed coffee more than a happy bank manager, and so I would worry about him later.

Having resolved all my problems, it became obvious I would need to break camp and return to Fred. We would then both return to the valley and, after visiting the bank, I could buy some delicious French cakes for breakfast – or would it be tea? I had lost all track of time. But that did not matter, because I had decided to spend two full rest days before starting my second attempt on Mont Blanc... this time with a full tummy.

Chapter Eighteen

Two miles from Chamonix, in the aristocratic resort of Megève, there is a campsite so posh its utility block includes proper British toilets. In one of the cubicles some witty person had written, 'You sit on it.' On the wall above the washbasins a handwritten message states, 'This is not a toilet.' I guess you get a better class of graffiti in the South of France.

The well-manicured lawns of the campsite were densely populated with tents – the sort principally designed to display the affluence of their occupants by having many partitioned bedrooms. (I suppose their butler needed somewhere private to sleep.) There was only one proper mountain tent, outside of which stood a manly motorbike with wooden cladding and an armchair seat. He seemed to be contemplating the unfortunate circumstances which had brought him here. Inside this utility tent I sat cross-legged; my head lightly brushing the 'ceiling'. Though, in the context of backpacking, it would have been large enough for me and Helen to stretch out with plenty of elbow room, as it happened, the interior now contained a lot of needlessly empty space.

Having no one else to talk to, I half-listened to Fred expressing his dissatisfaction at my recent behaviour and future ascent plans.

But, I interrupted, *the English do things properly. It is most improper to cheat by using the train. It would be too embarrassing.*

Oh, I like that, said Fred. *So far on this trip I have had my handlebars fondled by a Dutch Hells Angel, done seventy miles per hour to take you to a lavatory in Switzerland, and been abandoned to a flock of hysterical teenage schoolgirls at an adventure centre. And as for that ridiculous rack which projects two feet behind my rear wheel, it makes my bottom waggle every time I go around a traffic island. So don't go telling me about being embarrassed. I will deliver you to the train station, but there is no way I am going back up that mountain again, for it will surely kill us both.*

I could always say you made me do it, I mused. *Take the train, I mean.*

Don't you go blaming me for anything, he retorted. *I can deliver you to the bottom of that steep hill if you want. Then you can stagger up the death zigzags, carrying everything but the kitchen sink on your back. Though I have absolutely no intention of taking part in such a foolish endeavour.*

But the train – it tried to kill me!

Just at the moment I find that a most delightful concept. But if you want my advice, you should leave your tent on this campsite for a few days with the stuff you don't actually need inside. Travel light, like me in my youth, before that Helen person sat on top of me and asked to be whisked away to Ben Nevis. Have you never thought about getting yourself an imaginary girlfriend? I believe they are much lighter to carry around. Anyway, do you want a lift to the station or not? It seems silly doing the bottom bit twice – unless, of course, you enjoyed it. Cuckoo, cuckoo.

If you ever tell anybody about this I will... I will...

You will what? Tell whichever lady you are trying to impress that I made you do it?

Yes, that's just what I will do.

I feel there is a weakness in your argument somewhere, replied Fred, *but I can't quite think what it is... probably because I am a motorbike!*

Two days after my acrimonious conversation with Fred, I awoke on a bed of straw and quickly remembered I was back in the 'hotel' above the first snowfield. Given my good night's sleep and skilful training programme, I was feeling particularly fit. (The training programme refers to the military-style march at Fontainebleau and my previous exercise on this mountain.) Also, on this occasion I vaguely knew where I had to go, and in particular that, once above the Aiguille du Goûter, I would be on the ridge covered by the postcard, which appeared to lack any difficult climbing. So now, perhaps prematurely, I offer the following advice to anyone wishing to follow in my footsteps.

My previous idea of taking all the equipment necessary to do an abseil retreat was unwise, if you balance the frequency of such events against the possibility of collapsing from exhaustion due to extra weight in a bulkier rucksack. In particular, it had required carrying a hammer axe to bang chunky nine-inch nails into the mountain; proper placements being expensive and generally impractical to recover. Conversely, nails cost a few pennies so can be left to rust away in their own good time. For my second attempt, I only had three axes and crampons, the principle being 'less weight equals greater speed'. Essentially, I had come to attack this mountain as a man with claws.

HEALTH AND SAFETY ALERT: I have only used nails in situations where I could gently and carefully bring my weight upon them. I doubt they would hold the snatch loading of a fall. This is not official advice, just my personal opinion.

For my second attempt, I reduced bulky items to a sleeping bag, spare clothes and a snow shovel, plus the claws. My first aid kit also included a whistle, torch and compass.

Anyway, back at the hotel, after getting up and having a good stretch, I stepped outside to be greeted by a fine sunny day. I needed to hang around at this altitude to acclimatise so, after having a cheese sandwich, I went up to sunbathe on the snow above my residence. I was aware that sometimes it became cooler, and subconsciously knew that a cloud had passed before the sun, but paid it no regard. Maybe an hour passed in this lazy fashion.

Then I heard a female voice. "*Yickle spraken ding donkton*," it said.

I opened my eyes to see a lady of about fifty-five standing above me. She was wearing a long, floaty floral dress which came down to her ankles. From my privileged lying-down position I could see that she was wearing boots. On her head was a straw bonnet, the rim of which was wider than her shoulders. This necessitated a yellow ribbon to keep it in place; the bow neatly tied beneath her chin. In one hand she was carrying a wicker basket.

I explained that I was English. She replied that she was from Bulgaria and complained of being a little out of breath.

"I have come up on the early-morning train," she added.

From her basket, she recovered a large plastic bag, lay it on the snow, and sat down beside me. She then offered me half of a fruit loaf. This hotel had room service! Given that I had only eaten a cheese sandwich for breakfast, I accepted her offer.

"I just wanted to see if I could still reach this cabin," she said. "Thirty years ago I stood on the very summit of Mont Blanc." The sadness in her eyes was terrible to witness. *Before I got old*, she might have said. *And now this is as far as I can get.*

During the small talk which followed, she mentioned something called the Tête Rousse Hut, which I found most confusing. Eventually I realised that she was referring to the Felicity hut. However, because she was from Bulgaria and had just given me half a fruit loaf, I let the matter pass. She then told me that the guard on the train had warned all passengers that a storm was due, probably before tonight. For the first time, I took a good look around. Storm clouds had gathered on the horizon. High above, a few wispy clouds raced across the sky, as if surveying an island they were waiting to attack. I thought back to the previous evening's sunset, when the entire sky had turned purple. Did that mean something? What would a shepherd say about it? Nothing, probably, because purple sunsets were a feature of the higher atmosphere; weather systems of which I had no experience. After thanking the lady for her warning, we went our separate ways: me to climb the ridge; she returning to the train. For the time being the storm clouds seemed happy to swirl above the foothills. Perhaps down there it was already raining, and my gentle summer's day only existed at altitude.

Later, when I entered the hut, Felicity seemed surprised to see me. Wow! On my previous visit I had only made a brief appearance in her doorway, yet she remembered who I was! Oh, and she had witnessed my retreat, when my face would have been as white as the snow – but I preferred to forget about that. After giving me a surprised blink, Felicity returned to racing around in order to provide her numerous guests with bread and soup. I merely asked for coffee, whenever she was ready. This casual approach was due to my new plan of spending two days between eleven and twelve thousand feet. Then, fully acclimatised, I was certain to complete the ascent without incident. This was at the cautious end of the acclimatisation spectrum, but I had no intention of passing out again.

Slowly the other guests got up and left, leaving just me and Felicity in the hut together. But she was too busy clearing tables for any friendship to develop between us. Then, not wishing to outstay my welcome, I stood up and unstrapped the snow shovel from my rucksack. I was quite happy to display this act to Felicity, because it demonstrated that I was intending to use my strong arms to build a man cave. And yes, she turned to look at me!

"*Nu*," she said.

I shrugged, indicating in French that I would be fine.

She shook her head, then held up her hands as if to play an imaginary piano. "Crackle-crackle," she said. Next she clapped her hands. "Boom-boom," she added. Finally she examined me carefully until her gaze settled on my boots, which had cost five pounds from an ex-army store. She pointed to the floor. "*Gratis*," she said. She then placed her gentle hands together on her cheek to indicate sleeping.

No Italian opera had ever created such a heroine as Felicity. Only a lunatic would deny her angelic wish that I sleep on her floor. I indicated my compliance by separating the shaft of the snow shovel into its short sections, and re-strapping them to my rucksack. She nodded her approval. I responded by ordering another coffee.

Eventually a new intake of guests arrived, presumably from the train station. Once more I was surrounded by a wall of confused noise, so, to avoid getting a headache, I went outside to see what the weather was doing. It now conveyed a note of anger. Heavy storm clouds blotted out the sun and it had become very dull. There was something in the air to warn of approaching danger. That, I reasoned, was my senses reacting to static electricity – my hair standing up, and my clothes (being dry) also taking up the charge.

While I was still waiting for things to happen, Felicity came to stand beside me. She was looking at the Aiguille du Goûter through binoculars, presumably to see if any climbers were still on the face. She looked concerned. By way of explanation, she offered me her binoculars. I wished she hadn't. Previously I had thought the face to be quite pretty; its ice-covered rocks brushed with swathes of snow. With binoculars I could see some climbers, so was able to judge its scale against the insignificance of human life. It made everything look much steeper. I guessed this was what the people on the Channel ferry had meant by saying the Alps were still in winter condition. Presently, I moved the binoculars to the top. I had already noticed a glint of aluminium perched on a ledge and assumed it to be some sort of hut. Now, magnified, it looked as if an alien spaceship had been put there to bring some ugliness into the world. However, on the positive side, I thought it might be possible to call in for a coffee on the way up.

I returned the binoculars to Felicity, who continued to watch the climbers progressing up the face. Finally she said, "*Seif*", smiled, and went inside.

I thought it strange that it had taken all day for the weather to prepare itself for the storm, yet, when it came, it seemed to happen instantaneously. One moment I was looking around, smiling; the next, a blanket of hail thudded from the sky, bouncing painfully off my head and covering the plateau in a carpet of large 'ball bearings'. A few seconds later, lightning flashed, while explosive thunder blasted my eardrums. I was besieged by the anger of the gods! Though some might consider the word 'besieged' to be overdramatic, it should be remembered that lightning does not generally strike the ground, but blasts its way unhindered between clouds of differing electrostatic charge. These electron surges follow the laws of physics and not those of men, who falsely consider their atoms sacred. Hence, with hair standing on end and tingly sensations in the fingers, a human truly becomes part of the natural world. The hail only dropped from the sky for a few seconds; then the atmosphere, having dumped its heavy 'blanket' of ice, became calm for a few moments. Next a hurricane-force wind brought a second blast of hail, only this time horizontally across the plateau. Two bedraggled climbers, buffeted by the storm, zigzagged their way from the lower snowfield to the hut. I followed them inside and shut the door behind me.

> *HEALTH AND SAFETY ALERT: The Alps often have electric storms. Generally the lightning is so fierce the rock it strikes turns to glass. (Metal just vaporises.) To be among the clouds during such a storm is an awe-inspiring experience, though possibly best avoided when sleeping in a snow cave with a metal-framed rucksack blocking the entrance. Or when attached to a rope, which acts as a lightning conductor.*

I discovered the hut catered for three types of visitor: the super-rich, who took a bunk in a side room; the less affluent, who got to sleep on the dining-room tables; and the waifs and strays, who required compassion, so were offered the floor.

Sleeping on a hard floor is best done by distributing your weight across the widest possible area; that is, bottom and back rather than the hip and shoulder joints. Hence, I spent the first part of the night gazing both at the ceiling and occasionally at the lightning which illuminated the room. The associated thunder caused the hut to shake; the shock making both the floor and my bottom vibrate in harmony.

Witnessing these powerful forces returned my mind to the 'death monument' I had seen on my approach to the hut. As it was a fine sunny day, its purpose had confused me. But had a storm like this caught me on that spot, I would have been lifted skywards, helplessly twisting and turning within a great swirl of hail. The best I could have hoped for was to be unconscious before a downwards vortex of wind sent me crashing into the mountain to be entombed in a snowy unmarked grave. A better option was to be lying on a hut floor and merely thinking about the storm raging outside.

The following morning, I went to look outside and discovered everything was covered with fresh snow in a fashion much loved by those who design Christmas cards.

HEALTH AND SAFETY ALERT: That's a new coat on a bed of ball-bearing hailstones. Take extra care in such conditions.

I now knew Felicity to be an expert in sign language. So, after coffee, I signalled that I was just going off for a spot of local exploring, and would be back before nightfall. I then pointed to a small pile of stuff in the corner of the room which I would not be needing today – basically, a carrier bag of cheese sandwiches, a snow shovel, and extra-woolly clothing. Felicity nodded consent, and so I left the hut with a lighter rucksack and good reserves of coffee sloshing around my tummy.

After generally admiring the scenery, my attention turned to a prominent ridge which rose directly up from the plateau. I decided it was too steep for any ball-bearing hailstones to accumulate, so any recent loose snow would have been blown away in the storm. It seemed the perfect place to play – a bit like the crumbling bomb-site walls I had ascended as an infant. This ridge provided many interesting rocky steps, topped with snow and coated with ice. I climbed up, down and around, picking out all the best bits. Lost within my own private world, I carried on searching for more problems, which kept changing their character as the midday sun caused melting to start.

HEALTH AND SAFETY ALERT: Due to my previous mountain experience being limited to northern latitudes, I understood about the dangers of frostbite, getting wet, and winter darkness lasting sixteen hours. I therefore failed to appreciate the main danger on this exposed ridge was the sun. Later, I was to see a lady walking away from the mountains with her face a mass of scabs and her lips blistered with pus. Sunburn at high altitude can be fatal.

That is not to say that I was totally unprepared for Mediterranean conditions, because I had ridden south, facing the sun. By this method, I had become moderately brown. However, that is not the same as climbing into a zone where there is less atmosphere above to absorb the sun's radiation. Though I did have one defence: a baggy, knee-length, long-sleeved, grandfatherly thermal vest of the sort frequently worn as nightshirts during the 1940s. Being made of white cotton, it also gave good protection from the sun… Ah! Now I come to think about it, I suppose the garment might actually have been a wartime nightshirt, which I co-opted into becoming a very warm vest. But whatever it was, it conformed to all the rules of sensibility: come rain or shine, or simply as something I could bunch up inside my breeches to cushion my bottom when sitting on a cold surface. Protection of my head and ears was a natural side effect of wearing my crash helmet. I only mention these details because, from what I witnessed, some Alpine climbers pay great attention to fashion. I wish to point out that, on this occasion, I was wearing tennis shorts beneath the vest, though any observer standing before me would not have known this.

However, before getting a reputation as a fashion icon, I return to my situation on the ridge where, having found good holds on a spire of rock, I was having a good think about my medical condition. It seemed that my lungs were working to a new level of super-efficiency, which meant my muscles had plenty of oxygen at their disposal. I could detect no signs of dizziness, nor any headache. Then I looked around and realised I was halfway up the ridge. Going down to the Felicity hut suddenly seemed extremely silly. Also, though sunburn was an increasing danger, the combination of the helmet and the thermal vest meant only my lower legs, hands, and face were truly exposed. On these I had smeared olive oil.

> NOTE: Terrible advice. Olive oil is okay for Birmingham people who want to sunbathe on the beach at Weston-super-Mare, but not at twelve thousand feet on the French/Italian border. Thankfully, I realised this before my skin took on the complexion of a fried egg.

So, having decided that I needed to find shade, I looked down to the gully which ran up by the side of my ridge. (The same gully on which I had lost consciousness during my first attempt.) A little higher up, this entered the shade of the Bastille Buttress. That was clearly the place I needed to be.

After descending to the gully, I discovered the snow took my axes and crampons well, allowing me to quickly reach the shade… where conditions immediately changed. What had looked so easy from below revealed itself to be a mere dusting of snow, under which was a skin of fragile ice and scree of small stones. They were so loose and at such an unnaturally steep angle that the whole area was a landslide waiting to happen. Good axe placements were impossible because anything more than a gentle tap caused the ice to shatter like a porcelain dinner plate. To make things harder, the ice was too steep to take a flat crampon, which meant I had to rely on the front spikes – not difficult, but exhausting on the leg muscles if done for any length of time.

Progress was very slow because kicking a foothold which did not shatter took many attempts. Then came the moment of suspense as I moved my weight to the new foothold and carefully straightened my leg. During this manoeuvre, my life was as fragile as the ice holding my crampon front points. I had to repeat this with my other leg before I could even think about advancing with my axes.

By these four movements – which frequently took a minute each – I gained eighteen inches… and I still had about four hundred feet to go. But humans are well adapted to such situations – all it requires is the ability to carefully plan the exact moves, while the adrenal glands prepare the mind for whatever lies ahead. However, as this climb was to take most of the afternoon, the prolonged exposure to adrenaline was less easy to deal with. I became impatient and wanted to move quickly. Then I remembered the almost-fatal mistake I had made when becoming stranded on Lliwedd three years earlier. There, impatience had left me swinging from a clump of vegetation. This Alpine climb offered no such luxury. A single mistake would send me accelerating towards the jaws of the bergschrund far below. So, for the time being, all that mattered was remaining totally focused on finding the next placement; never knowing if, purely on the grounds of random probability, it would take the additional force generated by my repetitive sequence of moves.

Eventually I reached the headwall, where I was able to slip my fingers into a rock crack. A slight twist of the wrist and my arm was locked into something solid. The prospect of death vanished instantly, to be replaced by a serene feeling of calm. Mont Blanc actually seemed to like me… or at least, had not yet rejected my unsolicited advances. The headwall itself seemed awkward but, to my left, a rock chimney held a deep bed of ice. Bridging up the chimney walls allowed me to make quick progress until, about ten feet from the top, the ice gave way to soft, slushy snow, up which I ascended aggressively to the plateau… *Oh, help!* There was nothing on the other side. Even two feet from the rim, the snow was no more than three inches thick. Had I kicked the snow any harder, I would have walked straight through it. My second response, after *Help!*, was to blink in confusion. Then, looking down, I had an aircraft's view of the Chamonix Valley nearly two miles below. I had reached the place where the picture on my postcard began. Success!

Two seconds later I was instinctively scrambling left to reach a pinnacle of rock. As far as pinnacles go, it was a fine example of geological engineering. Its mushroom-shaped crest was a bit wider than my bottom, letting me sit down. Also, it was quite late in the day and a cool breeze was drifting pleasantly across my skin. I removed my rucksack to recover a bottle of water and a cheese sandwich. (Or, more precisely, *the* cheese sandwich, because it was the only food I had with me.)

After my picnic, I tried to imagine Helen sitting by my side, also admiring the scenery – but failed. This was mostly due to the limited space on which I had settled like the Buddha, calm and composed, far above the world of men. If Helen were here, she would have needed to sit on my lap, facing me, with interlocking limbs. Could my humble mortal body have coped with a surge of romantic hormones and, if not, would our safety be compromised? Then the phrase 'dinner for one' popped into my mind. The romantic fiction I had often read dealt with the trauma suffered by ladies rejected in love and left to sit all alone in a restaurant. I had never understood that situation until now, when I had become a 'dinner for one' victim.

Presently, I looked down to the ice gully I had just ascended. I knew virtually nothing about roped climbing. Was it even practical to protect that particular route? Or would one person falling just take down anyone else on the same rope? I was glad Helen had not come with me. Dinner for one was a small price to pay for not killing the person you love. I manoeuvred around on my spire to gaze down on the hut where Felicity lived. In a eureka moment, I realised that there are actually three types of women. The first category was those who did not want to go out with me – like Helen, or Charlotte from my schooldays. The second category was those who had never given the matter any thought – like Felicity, who was much nicer because she had never actually rejected me. Finally, there were the ladies I had yet to meet. After these romantic thoughts faded, my attention returned to the rock on which I sat. It made me feel a little like a cartoon character who had been unexpectedly deposited on top of a telegraph pole. The only obvious way off was across the snow ridge I had just left at such speed.

The next bit of my climb was mentally challenging because I had no idea where I was going. It only needed one insurmountable obstacle to force me into a retreat down the gully – in the dark! Better to take my chances up a short, rocky cliff in daylight. This soon led to a slab of slightly overhanging snow. After climbing through this, I found myself gazing in wonder at the vast Mont Blanc plateau. To me it looked like a stormy sea, instantaneously frozen by a magical hand. A few seconds later I was standing on this, transfixed by its beauty.

As I wandered vaguely in the direction of the Goûter hut, I saw two men, their faces painted with white plaster – super-strength sunblock. One was posing for fashion photographs; the other prancing about to get his profile just right. On seeing me, they raised their sunglasses to look underneath – I assume to watch my motorcycle crash helmet bobbing towards them between the brilliant white snowdrifts. As I approached, they said something in French. I opened my mouth to speak, but the recent overdose of adrenaline left me unable to reply. After a few moments, my admirers looked down to my lower legs, then at my ex-army boots. Their boots were like the ones used for the moon landing, which I thought implied there was a better class of second-hand shops around here. After staring at me for a short while, they said something else in French.

"English," I squeaked through parched vocal cords.

"Where have you come from?" they asked.

My shoulders slumped with exhaustion. With great effort I lifted an axe and waved it behind me. They looked confused. I left them pondering the puzzle and made my way towards the higher hut.

Chapter Nineteen

From above, the Goûter hut could be viewed as an ugly aluminium building perched on a rocky outcrop just below the summit. Inside it looked like a motorway cafeteria and came complete with a chef, who wandered around waving a big saucepan, while speaking Chinese to anyone who would listen. However, a far greater concern was that I did not know if the hut had a two-way radio. If not, then as far as Felicity was concerned, I had simply wandered into the mountains and disappeared. This situation was made far worse by the fact that I had left my food, extra-woolly jumper, and snow shovel in her dining room. What would be the result of my assumed disappearance? A helicopter search, or simply a collective shrug from the rescue service? But whatever it was, I would have to go back down to announce my continued existence… then repeat the Goûter climb with a dwindling supply of cheese sandwiches.

After locating the hut guardian, I asked if he could radio the Felicity hut to say I was safe and would not be returning tonight.

"Uh," he said, as they do in France.

I pointed in the general direction of the Felicity hut.

"Tête Rousse?" he said.

I was not aware there were two huts, so grumpily said, "*Wee*."

This was sufficient to make him radio down, and eventually he returned to tell me it was okay to sleep here tonight. Given that it was a horrible hut, I thought this a bit presumptuous. But, on the practical side, my snow shovel and warm clothes were in the Felicity hut. Without a snow tunnel to hide from the wind, I was likely to get a bit cold as the night wore on.

"Okay," I told the guardian, hopefully in a tone that let him know that it was all his fault.

Having sealed my fate, partly out of curiosity and partly because of need, I followed a sign to the toilets. These turned out to be a garden shed with no floor, but two planks with a gap in the middle. Looking between these, I saw a great flow of sewage extending down the mountainside beneath. The updraught brought a terrible smell, together with a great swarm of flies. My respectable English bowels instinctively clamped tight, so resolving the immediate problem. (And because I had no food with me, it was unlikely to be an issue for the next two days.)

On the night of my residence, the hut had about two hundred guests. These could be divided into three distinct categories. Firstly, there were those who arrived with bulging wallets, expecting pampered hotel accommodation. The second group came under the category of eccentric worldwide citizens who, for one reason or another, had a sudden desire to climb Mont Blanc, but did not know how to go about it. These employed a guide who, for a price, would drag, push, or otherwise get their cargo to the top. The final group could be classified as sensible people who just wanted to enjoy life. On the night I stayed there, only three guests fell into this category – all British. Besides myself, there were two ladies in their early twenties who worked in a typing pool. In 1980 'girls' were paid less than men, but these ladies had saved diligently for six months to buy a package holiday in Spain. Fortunately, when in the travel agent's they had come to realise that such trips were likely to be extremely boring, so had changed their minds and booked a guided ascent of Mont Blanc instead. Neither had climbed anything before – so respect to them.

The category with bulging wallets were essentially looking for ways to escape their dull lives of dinner parties and the like. To emphasise this, I pass on something a guide told me about an incident he had witnessed on the Matterhorn the previous year. On the day in question, he had been relaxing in the headquarters of the local mountain rescue team when an American lady walked in.

"Hi," she had said, while pointing to the rescue helicopter outside. "How much to hire that?"

The rescue team looked perplexed. So the lady explained that her son had just employed two guides to take him up the mountain, and she wanted to sit in the hovering helicopter by the summit to take his photograph as he stood on the top. The team boss explained that the helicopter was only for emergencies.

"Oh, I don't mind what it costs," said the American lady. She then placed eight hundred dollars on the table, which she thought would make things clear. (In today's value [2024] that's about seven thousand pounds.)

But the Swiss like to do things by the book, so refused the offer. In response, the lady grabbed the money and rushed out, screaming hysterically that she was going to report their insolence to the local council.

Returning to my stay in the Goûter hut, I was approached by an American man who asked if I knew where he could buy some more film for his camera. I replied that I did not.

"Hell," he retorted, as if I had just announced that the world was about to end, "I've only got five rolls left."

For those who have no memory of the predigital age, a film was something you put in a camera and eventually took to the chemist to be chemically developed. It was quite expensive, so an average British person might use a roll of thirty-six negatives per year. On my visit to Mont Blanc, I took two photographs during the entire climb. But the Americans, especially the super-rich, did things differently.

After recovering from the shock of being unable to buy any more film, he took me outside and asked me to pose on a mound of snow. While I was doing this, he kept leaping about, saying things like "Great

– hold the axe a little higher. Fantastic! Oh, the folks back home will love this."

After thirty or so 'fashion shots', I pointed out that he now only had four rolls of film left. With a great deal of confidence, he told me that his guides would have to sort it. What I noticed most in this statement was that he used the word 'guides' in the plural; I assumed one to haul him up with a rope and another to push his feet from below… or a third to rush back down to buy an emergency supply of film.

Anyway, after all my international socialising, at around 10pm a member of staff asked if I was climbing Mont Blanc tomorrow. When I confirmed, he told me that he would wake me at 2am. I think this was something to do with starting before the sunrise melted the snow – or perhaps he just had a sense of humour. Whatever the reason, I had no intention of getting up at that unearthly hour. So, when the gas lamps were turned off, I settled myself on the floor and prepared to enjoy a good night's sleep.

At 2am the lights were relit, and a great magnitude of guests emerged from their sleeping bags to unstack chairs and place them around the tables, ready for their Cordon Bleu breakfast. This meant anyone still lying on the floor was either trampled by boots or poked with metal chair legs. I had no choice but to stumble upright and then, because I had no wish to endure financial ruin to eat a single meal, leave the hut as quickly as possible.

My escape to the outside was completely disorganised. One hand was dragging my unravelled sleeping bag; the other my rucksack. It is not a good idea to leave a high mountain hut wearing only the underpants and thermal vest in which you have slept. I quickly dressed in every item of clothing I had with me, thereby trapping a refrigerated layer of air next to my skin. Why I sat on the icy step I have no idea, though it was probably something to do with putting on my boots. In any event, it was the coldest thing my bottom had ever experienced. Within a few seconds I had pushed myself back up, which turned any dampness on my hands to ice. Because my breeches had briefly defrosted the step, I had a circle of ice around my bottom.

After strapping on crampons, I walked to the base of the Dôme du Goûter. Illuminated by starlight, it looked nothing like its picture-postcard image. Now, it sparkled and looked so magical it could have been an illustration from a fairy-tale storybook. Except its crest was two thousand feet above my present position. (Height measurement an educated guess.)

The first part of my ascent was more like a sleepwalk, taking turns to open one eye, then the other. Stars can be very bright at that altitude, especially when you have a headache. Then the thin air started to take effect, causing my breath to swirl into ice crystals. Out of necessity, I walked into these, which made my face tingle. This gave me the courage to open both eyes at once. Then a blackness mysteriously appeared before me. A reflex action caused me to stop. For a few moments I stared into an apparently bottomless crevasse. (The snow here can be half a mile thick, so however pretty it might look, it is best to remain fully awake while walking.) After taking a few steps backwards, I took a good look around. To my left, I was surprised to see the central crest of the dome, up which I had previously believed myself to be walking. To my right, a lot of precipices disappeared into darkness. All very dramatic, but not a place I particularly wanted to be at this unearthly hour in the morning. (With hindsight, I can say that I had wandered onto the Italian side of the mountain.)

After returning to France, I climbed the dome, then descended into an ice valley of ghostly shadows. After the first traces of dawn crept into the sky, I could make out some finer details of my surroundings. Strangely, these included a small building. Walking across to it, I opened the door to discover the floor was strewn with sweet-smelling straw. On this a lot of people were snuggled into sleeping bags, while emitting a cacophony of snores. Near the far wall, three hairy mountaineers were making coffee over a paraffin stove. They seemed rather cross that I was standing in an open doorway, so letting cold air into the luxury refuge. Realising I had intruded on a gathering of experienced Alpine mountaineers, I retreated. To me, anyone who had avoided paying an absolute fortune to sleep on a bit of dining-room floor required godly respect.

A short distance from the hut, a ridge of dazzling white snow rose into a bright blue sky. I recognised it from my postcard, so knew that its gently curving crest represented the highest place in Western Europe. I plodded gaily upwards with an ever-increasing sense of being above the world. The mountains James Bond had skied down were several thousand feet below and now looked like toy models. Eventually the sun caught the summit of Mont Blanc and quickly travelled down the ridge to meet me. As I stepped from the shadow, the sun warmed my ice-cool face and cast the mountain's huge triangular shape to the French side on my left. To my right, dawn was breaking over Italy. In the valleys twelve thousand feet below, sunrise was still an hour away.

'Follow the ridge forever upwards' was the motto of my legs. Hence, I was so busy admiring the eight-thousand-foot precipices to my right that I walked straight past the summit without noticing. I descended the ridge on the other side for thirty feet before realising something had changed. I stopped and looked around, slightly confused. I had been walking upwards for days and the fact I had now run out of mountain to climb seemed unreasonable. I retraced my steps and found the highest bit of snow on which to stand. Wherever I looked, things went downwards. I remembered the words of the schoolgirl at the adventure centre who, when I had arrived on my motorbike, observed, "English, solitaire, cowboy, cuckoo." Now, as I gazed across the lesser Italian Alps, I smiled quietly to myself. England had won.

The photograph of '*my Alpine wandering*' was actually taken on the summit of Mont Blanc, with Italy in the background. I did not state this with the photo, hoping some readers might enjoy speculating on whether or not I got to the top.

Chapter Twenty

My descent of Mont Blanc *mostly* passed without incident. However, while I plod 'endlessly' downwards, I will leave you to consider why, on bigger mountains, more people die going down than climbing up.

For the ascent, it is often possible to wait for good weather and safer snow conditions; for the descent, these are more unpredictable. In addition, tiredness and prolonged exposure to cold can affect good decision-making. Also, when going up you are normally facing the mountain, so might rectify a stumble by stretching out a hand to grab something. For a descent, unless you are walking backwards there is nothing in front of you, so a stumble becomes a dive. Equally important, during an ascent any slip simply means you stop moving, giving you a split second to think about how best to react. Going down, gravity immediately accelerates your direction of travel.

But on Mont Blanc, none of this applied to me. What *did* happen was that, on reaching the Aiguille du Goûter, I continued down using the regular tourist route. While this turned out to be an easy scramble, it was sufficiently steep to require using my hands to maintain balance; so I had to face the rock and take backwards steps. To the right of the scramble was a thick cable which I could use as a handrail. It was frequently pegged to the mountain, the idea being that, once clipped on, any fall would be halted after sliding down to the next peg. Anyway, I was descending near the side of the cable when I passed a guide standing on a good ledge. He was securely lashed to a peg to bring up a client on a safety rope. Not wishing to get in his way, I stepped around him while politely saying, "*Bonsure.*" He pretended I did not exist – though I strongly suspect he was thinking, *Scumbag, wandering all over my mountain by himself. He should be employing me, by law. Long live the French Republic.* Even after I said, "*Olive oil*" he still ignored me.

After descending a further twenty feet, I felt a violent downwards force on my leg. I lunged for the fixed wire and grabbed it. Then I felt my waist being hugged. Looking down, I saw a very heavy, sweaty, and presumably desperate man using me as a climbing frame. As much as I like helping people, I assumed he was wearing crampons and would soon want to use my shoulder as a foot ledge. So I decided to escape by wriggling free and stepping over the wire. Because I was not clipped on, I then stepped away to stand on a ledge. Now clear of the danger, I looked up to see the guide hauling the man up on a taut rope. Soon his 'cargo' was above me, allowing my descent to continue without further incident.

On reaching the hut, Felicity turned to look at me. Me, and nobody else! She pointed a finger in the general direction of Mont Blanc. "*Sommet?*" she said.

"*Wee,*" I replied.

"*Heros!*" she exclaimed. She then used her delightful body language to explain that, because of this, I could stay here tonight "*for gratis*".

The last thing I wanted was to sleep on a hard wooden floor. Felicity, understanding my doubtful expression, pointed to a side door, where I knew the rich people stayed.

"*Voo heros,*" she said. "*Chambre, gratis.*"

'*Voo*' – I had heard that word before, as in '*Polly voo fonsay?*' ('Do you speak French?'). Bravely, I pointed to her. "*Voo?*" I questioned.

She nodded. "*Voo,*" she repeated, pointing to me – as if I were somebody special! How could I resist her charms?

That evening I came to realise just how world-famous Mont Blanc actually was. The most notable international team using the hut were from Mongolia; six men, none significantly less than seven feet tall. Their biceps were so massive they could hardly bend their arms, which meant they had to crane their necks forwards to slurp coffee from their bowls. To balance this fearsome appearance they displayed continuous smiles, which revealed they all had broken, crooked or missing teeth. I guessed this was the result of forgetting to duck when they tried to walk through standard doorways. A team from China represented the other end of the spectrum. None of the men were over five feet; the ladies somewhat shorter. Both sexes were dressed in identical Communist Party uniforms and appeared to take great pride in representing their country as a single, disciplined unit of efficiency. (China was then undergoing Chairman Mao's Cultural Revolution.)

When bedtime arrived, I walked into the small dormitory to discover that it had bunks crammed wall to wall around a tiny central space. Each guest only had a sleeping bag's width of mattress. To reach this it was necessary to crawl from the bottom of the bunk or, if in a corner, climb over others to reach the pillow resting against the wall. I imagine this claustrophobic configuration would work quite well if every human was incredibly small. The Mongolians, being longer than the beds, had to lift up their knees to prevent their feet overhanging the mattress. Possibly the Chinese could have filled in the gaps, but both groups insisted on staying together. Anyway, the idea that each individual would have an equal amount of bunk space had no meaning in reality. I found myself squashed against a great, hairy Spanish guy, who rolled over and laid his arm over my face. Behind me, a German lady with a fat bottom seemed to believe that I liked playing sardines.

Such a cramped room, with forty-eight sleeping people, is very noisy. A great snoring chorus was frequently interrupted by grunts as elbows tried to secure a bit more mattress from their neighbour. My previous belief that ladies only ever broke wind quietly and in private was completely shattered by the German lady pressed against me. I was almost asleep when I was startled by what I at first imagined to be a ship's foghorn. It proved to be a thirty-second warning that a great mushroom cloud of gas was going to erupt from the top of her sleeping bag, forcing me to hold my breath for as long as possible.

The next morning I staggered into the dining room like a survivor of a wartime coffin ship. Then I saw Felicity and everything became wonderful again. A little later, when it was time for me to go, she followed me to the doorway to wave goodbye.

"*Olive oil,*" I said.

She tried to imitate my British accent. "*Olive oil,*" she replied, smiling.

Then I walked into the snowy landscape, knowing I had finally met a lady who had not actually rejected me… but also that I would never see her again because we lived in different countries.

After returning to my tent in the valley, I asked myself the question, *Now what?* Then I thought about the massive glacier which began high on Mont Blanc and ended in a great ice wall, perhaps half a mile from the main road to Chamonix. It was well within walking distance from my campsite. So that afternoon, I went to take a closer look and discovered that beneath the final ice cliff there was a family picnic area. A few visitors were using the ice wall to practise their climbing, and having great fun in the process. That was okay, I supposed, but I quickly ventured onto the glacier above. One moment I was surrounded by a crowd of holidaymakers; yet ten minutes later I seemed totally alone in a magical world of sculpted ice.

I returned the following morning; this time fully equipped to explore whatever secrets the higher section of the glacier held. I descended into its crevasses and became lost within a fairy-tale world of translucent blue ice – sometimes tunnels and caves; other times opposing cliffs topped with arched snow bridges. I particularly remember standing in an ice tunnel which had clearly been carved by water. A little stream ran down its centre, its source presumably being meltwater from the surface. Near my feet was a man-sized hole down which the stream disappeared in a whirlpool. This setting triggered four of my five senses. The blue ice, illuminated by the light coming from the tunnel entrance, was beautiful to behold. The sound of gurgling water was very relaxing. My face was tingling in response to the sub-zero air temperature. And smell? Well, I was in an ice cave with completely pure air, so my nose was confused by the complete absence of any scent.

Anyway, standing there in my own sensual world, I thought about Helen. She had told me how she "simply adored potholing". Doing that through this ice tunnel would have overwhelmed her happy hormones. I hoped that whoever had won her affections would treat her properly, and bring her to nice places like this. Then I continued deeper into the tunnel, my torch lighting the way – a solo adventurer following a path Helen had decided not to take.

However much fun 'ice-potholing' might seem, it is worth remembering that while you can choose where to access a glacier, leaving it somewhere else might be far harder. Before descending into any crevasse, I hammered two nine-inch round-head nails into solid ice. The pressure on the nail head melted the ice, which then refroze to lock the nail in place. I left about three inches of nail poking out to hold my weight for a gentle abseil.

> *HEALTH AND SAFETY ALERT: Climbing or abseiling on a nine-millimetre sheathed rope is a lot harder than doing the same on the thick multi-stranded ropes hanging in school gymnasiums. Before leaving England I had hung a climbing rope from a road bridge and learnt how to ascend it using 'prusik loops' (knots which can be slid upwards but lock under load). Do not go into crevasses without leaving a rope in place, confident that you can also use it to climb back up. Nine-inch nails are not designed for mountaineering.*

Being an insignificant speck of life within a magical kingdom of ice greatly helps the moral development of an anti-wristwatch anarchist. For what did time matter when the slowly moving ice would have begun its existence as a snowfield in the high mountains thousands of years before? The only problem in judging my life against geological time was that I needed to be back at work on Monday morning, and today was… I had no idea.

On returning to the valley, I asked a few people what day it was. Most replied in French, but eventually one gentleman told me it was Friday. I looked at the position of the sun and modified this to Friday afternoon. This meant I had two days to reach England; not a problem for rich people, who can use the French motorway system, but I dared not extend my unauthorised overdraft any further. Like any other true mountaineer, I was now officially skint, so limited to travelling home using only back roads. I resolved the problem by riding to Switzerland, from where I picked up the free autobahn system. Briefly, I pulled into a service area where I slept beneath a rather nice hedge. In the morning I picked up the Belgian motorway system – again, free. I saw Luxembourg somewhere, but it did not last very long. Then, in the Netherlands, I slept under another hedge where it rained all night.

I returned to my houseboat at six o'clock on Monday morning. There, I heated some water for a tin bath and sat in it to wash away the sweat accumulated on the glaciers of Mont Blanc and the journey home. Then I dressed in office clothes and by nine o'clock was sitting at my desk, gazing vaguely at a handwritten accountancy journal. But all I could see were images of beautiful blue ice.

As the morning progressed I came to realise that the journal, still untouched, was now completely irrelevant to the meaning of my life. By midday I had accepted the truth: that accountancy was boring, and I needed to become a professional mountaineer. But how? I was too old to become a world-famous climber, and possibly a bit unorthodox to find employment as an outdoor instructor. This left only one option: to become a writer on the subject. My plan, worked out in my dinner break, involved going to climb somewhere interesting – perhaps the really big mountains on the edge of the Amazon jungle – and then returning to deal with all the publishers who would want to buy my epic adventure story. This business plan would have worked perfectly, had I possessed the financial resources to take two months off work and the knowledge of how to travel anywhere other than by sitting astride a motorbike. But I had my Mont Blanc odyssey – and we all have to begin somewhere.

That night, I returned to my boat, sat at the kitchen table, and put a blank sheet of paper into my clunky 1948 typewriter. The rest of my life had begun. So, thank you, Helen, for pointing me in the right direction – with a little help from James Bond. And thank you, Felicity, for just being a really nice person.

In addition to resolving my romantic illness concerning Helen, Mont Blanc's pure air also cured my asthma.

Chapter Twenty-One

With hindsight, I can say that my decision to become a published writer within three years was extremely optimistic. (It actually took forty years, so did nothing to finance my mountaineering.) On the positive side, this delay means that I can write my adventuring story as an ordinary person doing things normal people can achieve on a fairly basic income. (You are unlikely to have a dazzling career if mountaineering becomes your passion in life.)

In addition to learning how to write creatively, I thought it wise to study the technical aspects of climbing. For this, I joined a local mountaineering club and targeted the best climber available. This happened to be a fifteen-year-old boy called Simon. He was so fanatical about the sport that he used all his school dinner money to buy climbing gear, so was often hungry. His pocket money was used for training sessions at the indoor climbing wall. He had no transport, which was where I came in. I had a motorbike, and enough cash to feed us both during our weekend adventures.

With regard to the sleeping arrangements, the club had access to an otherwise abandoned, semi-derelict mountain farmhouse in North Wales. The ground floor had no doors or windows, which did not seem to worry the occupants; possibly because they were a flock of sheep. The upstairs had one bunk bed built wall to wall across a secluded end room. It was twenty feet wide and so, unlike the Felicity hut, even on a busy weekend there was plenty of elbow room. The hut had a proper kitchen but, in practice, everyone tended to go down to the cafe in the nearby village of Capel Curig for breakfast.

So, for an ordinary mortal like me, Simon was an ideal teacher. All I had to do was feed him in the morning, and he would spend the rest of the day teaching me how to climb properly. The arrangement was based on the idea that he would lead me up routes on the Saturday, but on Sunday I was expected to belay him on much harder problems.

WORD DEFINITIONS

To belay (verb): The act of feeding a rope up to a lead climber, or taking the rope in from a climber lower down.

Belay or stance (noun): A place where a climber stops, secures themselves to the rock, and manages the rope for the person who is actively climbing.

Pitch (noun): The route a climb takes between two stances.

Runner (noun): A piece of equipment, plus attachments, secured to the rock by an active climber. The rope is fed through this, thereby reducing the fall the leader takes to that runner, plus the same distance again, until the equipment hopefully starts to slow the fall. (Climbing rope is slightly elastic.)

There are many more rock-climbing terms to learn, but do not worry about those for now. When *you* put *your* nervous face around the entrance door of *your* local climbing club for the first time, *you* should be welcomed, and the language explained before *you* begin *your* first climb.

Naturally, on Simon's Sunday practice sessions I had no intention of following, but he often spent half an hour trying to overcome a single hard move, so I only had to belay him at the bottom of the climb. Occasionally he fell, which was also part of my training; gaining valuable rope-handling experience.

After I had been going to the club for a couple of months, Simon took on a second novice, Rob. He had discovered the joy of climbing relatively late in life but now, aged thirty-five, it was his religion. More importantly, he had a car, and together we made certain that Simon built up his food reserves for the following week so he could continue diverting his dinner money to useful climbing equipment without unduly worrying his mother.

Before I continue, it is necessary to explain the confusing system for grading the difficulty of any particular climb. This is because the sport began in the late Victorian period when the footwear would have been hobnail boots. Mostly it was an upper-class 'game'; the working class having no transport and being required to work sixty-hour weeks with no paid holiday. Hence, the first three grades became known as 'easy', 'moderate' and 'difficult'. Nowadays, 'moderate' rarely gets a mention in rock-climbing circles, but may be found in books on scrambling. 'Difficult' is considered an easy climb for a first-time novice wearing ordinary boots. The grade 'very difficult' was added during the early days but, with modern equipment and a safe leader, the novice might now be presented with one of these as a first route. The next grade up, 'severe', is best typified by a climb called the Tennis Shoe, a 460-foot route up the Idwal Slabs in North Wales. It was first done in 1919. The name gives a clue to the improving footwear. The next grades up are 'very severe' (VS) and 'hard very severe' (HVS). These represented the hardest climbs throughout the 1940s, due to most fit men being taken away to fight in the war.

In the early 1950s, the climber Joe Brown changed everything. He had lots of advanced equipment, like nuts (as in nuts and bolts). He would thread a length of cord through the nut, which could be wedged into a crack to provide a runner or belay anchor. Though, in that era, pitons were the norm, as was clumsy hemp rope often stolen from shipyards. I expect the 1950s generation would have considered a nine-inch nail a luxury. Anyway, in 1952 Brown climbed the savage corner crack known as Cenotaph Corner in the Llanberis Pass, Snowdonia. His admirers looked at that and realised that a challenge previously believed impossible had been conquered. Did HVS need yet another adjective? No, they went with a single word: 'extreme'.

Needless to say, with sticky rubber climbing boots and a rack of climbing gear costing (possibly) over one thousand pounds, climbers tackled ever-greater problems. Today, Cenotaph Corner has been reclassified as E1, with harder climbs being graded E2, E3, etc. Those who suicidally ascend E6 can think about turning professional. With the advent of purpose-built indoor climbing walls and extensive 'gym-like' training sessions, there is no significant difference between the top male and female climbers as both can, heroically, manage E8 routes.

Climbing with Simon meant that after my first year of roped climbing I could safely lead on VS routes and a little harder if I went second, where falling was (theoretically) only a matter of being embarrassed and shouting, "Sorry" to the leader.

My first serious embarrassing incident happened on a route called Grey Arête (HVS) on Glyder Fawr, a mountain near the A5 in North Wales. Rob was absent that weekend, which meant I was solely responsible for keeping Simon amused for his normal Saturday ten-hour climbing fix. The difficulty of climbing Grey Arête was increased by our approach, first ascending the Idwal Slabs via Tennis Shoe Direct (VS.) This led to a near-vertical headwall, which we ascended using the Original Route (VS) and the Grove Above (S). In total, 675 feet of continuous climbing. So I arrived at the bottom of Grey Arête with aching legs, tired arms, and low blood sugar. Simon gave the impression he was having a nice walk in a park; effortlessly pulling himself up a vertical sequence of opening moves and climbing out of sight. The continuous speed of the rope attached to Simon's harness told me that he was not bothering to put in any runners, but his definition of 'easy' was different to mine. After 120 feet of rope had snaked up behind him, he called, "Safe", which meant he had reached the first stance and was hopefully tied onto something solid.

Two minutes later he shouted, "Taking in", referring to pulling up any slack rope until it went tight against my harness.

"That's me," I called up.

Simon would then have put the rope through a device which locked it in place in the event of a sudden loading (i.e., a fall). Then, after presumably making himself comfortable, he shouted, "Climb when ready."

Nothing about all this shouting made any sense to me. It looked neither safe nor something I could climb, given my aching arms. But Simon never came back down to apologise for being horrible to me, so somehow I struggled and grunted my way up to his stance. When both climbers are of equal ability it is normal for the second person to 'lead through', thereby avoiding the need to change who is secured to the belay.

"Sorry," I said, "I am in no state to lead the next pitch."

Thankfully, because we had arrived on my motorbike, it was not in Simon's interest to have me taking a leader fall, which might break a few bones. After I had been lashed onto the rock, he led the second pitch. Then, when the time came, I could do nothing but follow.

The first serious concern happened on the third pitch, when Simon stopped to look at a savage crack which curved away to become a minuscule ledge. Before undertaking this challenge, he placed a nut in the crack. "Runner on," he called down. This meant he was not entirely confident of doing the crack without taking a fall. Though, as it happened, he completed it without too much effort. "Nice," he shouted down. (If he thought something was 'nice', it meant it wasn't.)

It worried me that this rarely visited crag was at an altitude of nearly three thousand feet, meaning retreat would be impractical. And in truth, when looking away from the face, the rest of the world seemed a long way down. After climbing the difficult moves, Simon put in a second runner before moving significantly to the right. *Without* this additional protection, if I fell, I would have taken an enormous pendulum swing. He was expecting me to fall – good assessment! By wedging my hands into the crack, I managed the first bit by leaning out, thereby pushing my feet onto the cliff and walking up the rock. Then the crack veered to the right, forcing me to make a long reach, which allowed me to get two fingertips onto a tiny hold. I needed to stand on tiptoe to give myself just a little more reach. My feet slipped, and my fingers, having no chance of holding all my weight, lost their grip. I slithered down the rock a few inches, then the rope went tight on my harness.

"You've climbed things like this before," shouted Simon. "Stop hanging around; I'm hungry."

This was the first fall I had experienced while roped climbing. I was therefore confused as to why I was just hanging there, harmlessly, like a rag doll pegged to a washing line. After I had tried to climb, but fallen from the same move six times, Simon was getting quite cross.

"It's too hard," I whined.

"Stop being such a crybaby – just do it."

"I am not crying!"

Simon did not think my comment worthy of a specific response. "There's only one pitch above this," he shouted, "then it's just scrambling to reach a nice footpath – you'll like that."

Being tempted by the prospect of descending via a footpath made me think about many things. Firstly, over the previous five minutes I had gained a lot of experience in falling. I now realised that for the second person it was generally nothing to worry about. Secondly, I was also hungry. Thirdly, I had to make that move, because there was no way Simon was coming back down. So, rather than clinging pathetically to the crack, I let go completely and hung there with all the grace of a sack of potatoes. Then I lowered my arms and waggled my fingers to relax the muscles, so increasing blood circulation. At the same time I was building up my psychological strength. *I can do this move – have to do this move. Felicity is watching me through binoculars. If I become Spider-Man, she will exclaim, "Heros!" and want to be my girlfriend. If I can believe this, anything is possible.*

I still fell off, at least twice more I think. The third time I truly managed to believe that Felicity was watching me. This meant my brain focused totally on hanging from two fingers while my free arm made a long reach to a wider section of the crack. Curling my hand around this allowed me to hang comfortably from the much better hold while working out my next move. I arrived at the stance a little later.

"Fun?" asked Simon.

Did that require an answer? I decided it was best to remain silent until we had climbed the wall above, and so reached the promised footpath.

After losing all fear of falling (as a second), my climbing improved greatly. A month later we did the same sequence of routes again; this time taking alternate leads. This made everything much quicker, though before we started Grey Arête I worked out that I needed to lead the second pitch, so that Simon was leading when we came to the hardest move.

We now come to the delicate issue of three men frequently going away together at weekends, when none had girlfriends – nor, apparently, any interest in rectifying the situation. It must be remembered that in the early 1980s it was still illegal to be a homosexual until you were twenty-one. My own opinion was that if 95% of men were homosexual, it might improve my chances of getting a girlfriend. That suited me just fine.

Only once did Simon, Rob and myself have a man talk about our lack of female companionship. My coping mechanism was to blame the sexist education system. Rob said he had had a girlfriend once, but she did not like rock climbing, so they had to part. But Simon was the most sensible. "Girls get in the way of climbing," he proclaimed – which I thought showed great insight for a teenage boy who had the body of a super-athlete. Anyway, I agreed with Simon. From then on, it was my choice not to have a girlfriend, and nothing to do with the fact I was so ugly that no one wanted me. So, at least our brief conversation established that we were all heterosexual.

Chapter Twenty-Two

Joining the mountaineering club introduced me to a concept of which I had no previous experience: a social life. Simon, Rob and myself often went out in the evenings. Sometimes we climbed buildings; other times bridges. Once, when we were climbing trees in a secluded suburban avenue, the police arrived.

Before proceeding, we need to consider the vexed problem of how to climb a tree when all branches lower than a high-sided vehicle have been sawn off by the council. Tree surgeons attend college to study the subject, and then wear special clawed boots. In Canada, where they have giant redwood trees, proper competitions are held. But this book is about ordinary people doing normal things, so I just use FootFangs and ice axes. (I never climb the same tree twice, and those who criticise my single visits should think about the council with their horrible buzzy chainsaws before passing judgement.) So anyone walking by knew that we were from a proper mountaineering club, I always wore the clothes I bought for my Mont Blanc adventure.

Anyway, when the police car arrived, the officers got out and looked at Rob, who was belaying from the pavement. Slowly the policemen looked up to investigate where the rope was going – to me, though the officers would not have known this because it was late at night and we were climbing using head torches.

"Safe," I called down.

"Off belay," shouted Rob.

I pulled up the rope, doubled it over a branch, and abseiled down to land near the officers. We had been in similar situations before, so had some experience of how to handle things. I explained to the officers that, living in the city, the nearest proper rock climbing was at Cleeve Common, some forty miles away.

"No," said Rob, "Kinver Edge is less than thirty miles."

"But it's rubbish," I retorted.

The officers were clearly confused, so after I had removed my FootFangs and thrown them into Rob's car, the officers considered the situation (whatever it may have been) to be resolved.

Having implied that our nights out were rather exciting, honesty dictates I now confess that most evenings we used an indoor climbing wall. But besides these venues, we never went anywhere else. Anyway, one evening I was at the indoor climbing centre, practising various low-level moves on my own. (There was a red line above which you could not go unless roped.) My lowly status in life was because Simon and Rob refused to have anything to do with me when I was wearing my 1920s fashion outfit. Rob and Simon were at the far end of the gym, taking it in turns to belay each other, occasionally loudly proclaiming, "He's nothing to do with us." But paradoxically it was my outfit which attracted all the attention, not their fancy designer sportswear. So there I was, a mere six feet from the woodblock floor, when Rob came running towards me. His face was white with shock.

"I thought you did not want anything to do with me," I said curtly.

"It's Simon," gasped Rob. "He's got himself a real, actual girlfriend!"

Both me and Rob ran across the hall in a state of panic. We reminded Simon that many great climbers had fallen in love and given up their true religion shortly afterwards. But Simon seemed unconcerned. In fact, his only response was that we could meet her this weekend, because he had invited her to the club hut. He then said that her name was Christine. Apparently, she attended his school as an O level student. He also mentioned that, in order to acquire a "full set of gear" before the summer holidays, she had a Saturday job in a climbing shop. He then told us that because of her work, she could not join us until Sunday. If two days of climbing was deemed necessary, he added, she would bunk off school on Monday. Essentially, Simon was describing a female version of himself. (Or at least, that was his fantasy. No sixteen-year-old girl could be that perfect.)

As planned, Simon, Rob and myself arrived at the club hut on Friday night. The following day we left the hut early to visit Wyddfa. It was January and, as was often the case in the 1980s, the north face was in wonderful condition: vertical sections fully covered with climbable ice, and any chasms filled with consolidated snow. Simon, as always, went for the hardest routes – those vastly more technical than the Alpine climb I had done beneath the Bastille Buttress. But we were roped, and three men together often do things which are not entirely sensible.

After the day's climbing, we returned to the hut; myself ecstatic with the recent adventure, but muscles completely exhausted. I guess it was much the same for Rob, but men do not talk about their physical weakness. As could be expected given the weather, Simon's girlfriend had not arrived. We tried to console him, but he merely shrugged.

"She probably got a bad hitch," he said. "I expect she'll turn up in the morning."

"Hitch?!" I exclaimed in a bewildered voice. "From Birmingham?"

"Not like she's got a car," said Simon.

"Well, yes, but…"

"She finishes work at 5.30 and walks a few miles before sticking out her thumb. Hitching from the city centre is not safe."

She is not coming, I thought. *He's just trying to put a brave face on his rejection. Never mind; it means tomorrow morning we can sit around the gas fire, waiting for her not to show. Then, about midday, we can go home.*

The following morning I looked out of a tiny attic window to watch the wind bring alternate swirls of snow or rain. Simon suggested we went climbing in Tremadog. A well-known cliff, stretching about two miles, marks the edge of the national park. Due to it being close to the seaside, it is noted for generally having good weather. But none of this was important today, because we had to wait for Simon's girlfriend to not arrive – after which we could all go home.

Footsteps began tapping up the stairs at ten o'clock. Then an angelic face peeped into the room. Its expression displayed curiosity; a bit like Alice in Wonderland after she had fallen down the rabbit hole, I expect. A few seconds later I noticed that Christine was carrying a massive rucksack, on top of which a great deal of snow sloped up to her woolly hat.

"Sorry I am late," she said casually. "Two bad hitches, and got dropped off in the middle of nowhere at about midnight."

"What?!" I exclaimed.

"It's not safe for a girl to hitch after the pubs chuck out," she said, "so I slept under a bridge. The hitch this morning dropped me in Betws-y-Coed." She then mentioned she had walked the rest of the way. Though only four miles along the A5, it included a steep uphill; a road up which my old Honda 90 had a top speed of ten miles per hour. Added to this, Christine had never been to the club hut before, and she only had a few scribbled directions about where to turn off the main road to begin her walk into the mountains. After finding the correct dirt track, she would have seen our apparently abandoned building occupied by sheep.

Being selfish, me and Rob ignored Christine's various misfortunes and gave a collective sigh of relief. She would not want to go climbing today. Perhaps me and Rob could drive home, and leave Simon and Christine to go climbing tomorrow. Presumably they would then hitch back together.

"Can I have a cup of tea before we start?" asked Christine. "I had no food with me, so haven't eaten since yesterday lunchtime."

"Surely you went to the chip shop?" said Rob.

"No money," replied Christine.

I had never set out on my adventures without at least a pound in my pocket. But literally, Christine had left work on Saturday night with no money. Then I realised this did not make sense because Saturday staff got their wages on the day they worked and, as a schoolgirl, she would be on twenty pence an hour. I went to the kitchen and, while warming my hands over the heating-up kettle, pondered the money contradiction. When I returned to the lounge, Christine was excitedly showing Simon a camming device. These have cogs and expand when pushed into cracks, so can be placed in overhanging rock. James Bond had them, but they were (then) very rare in the world of normal climbers. Christine's device had cost her four weeks' pay, hence her having no money for food – though Simon seemed very impressed because it meant they could now tackle harder routes together. I hesitate to include the word 'safely'.

After Christine had finished her tea, she refused another, because it would be dark in six hours. So we all collected our gear and loaded up the car – the sensible course of action being to drive directly back to Birmingham. But instead we headed to Tremadog; the best plan now being to visit Eric's Cafe at the foot of the crags – that's Eric Jones, the pioneering climber and explorer. A less sensible thing to do would be to go climbing. Anyway, after getting out of the car we all looked at the crags towering up a few hundred yards from the road.

Rob then did something very brave. "Sod it," he said. "I'm going to the cafe."

Following normal etiquette, we all looked at him with expressions of disbelief and horror.

"Girl!" exclaimed Simon. (A corruption of the word; its new definition being 'a person of either gender who plays with dolls and wears pink underpants'.) It was the worst insult that could be said to a man.

But Rob just walked away… to the warmth of the cafe and probably a fry-up breakfast. On the positive side, this left three climbers; so one leader trailing two ropes to bring up the others. (Had we remained as four climbers, it would have meant two parties with two leaders. Now, I could just follow Simon.)

"One Step in the Clouds," said Simon.

The route name says it all. Three pitches, the 'one step' being a lunging traverse near the top of the second pitch. Those who make

Summit of Ben Nevis, Christmas Day, 1979.

Alpine Wanderings, 1980.

Opposite page: All three show me climbing at Cleeve Common near Cheltenham in 1981-82.

This page: Re-living my childhood play-times on Brean Down in Somerset. Actually forty years old, I still had a mental age of twelve.

Above: Just having some fun.

Left: Overcoming a typical problem on this route.

Typical Grade III snow and ice climb. This example on Wyddfa's north face.

Cresting the ridge to reach the summit of the north face route (opposite).

Opposite page: My father's house in Birmingham was ideal for practising moves when stuck in the city!

This page: I enjoyed many social evenings out with Rob from the mountaineering club.

Right: Rob leading on a road-bridge over a canal.

Bottom: Rob traversing across a bridge wall, while I stand below belaying him as leader.

A typical night's 'accommodation'. This particular sleeping arrangement in Arctic Sweden, en-route to Kebnekaise.

After travelling and living in my lorry, I made it my static home in Porthmadog, North Wales, in 2009.

the pointless gesture of looking down will note the considerable drop to the trees and boulders at the base of the cliff, with the road two hundred feet below that. On a fine, sunny day with a slight breeze, it's a fun route because, though the 'one step' move has no significant foot ledges, the rough rock helps to maintain balance. How snow and ice would affect this move I had no idea; nor was I particularly excited about finding out.

You are completely mad, I thought, but how could I make such a statement with a lady standing next to me? "Okay," I said.

Christine led the first pitch and brought me up second. I was then tied safely to a wall above a good ledge. Simon came up last, which meant he could 'lead through' without changing the rope arrangement with Christine. As he passed he clipped the rope leading to my harness onto his and, a few seconds later, had walked to the far end of the ledge. From here he began ascending a thin finger crack, using toe-sized knobbles for his feet. A howling gale meant we could not hear him, nor indeed see him, as the climb went diagonally up a slab above our stance. As I shivered, occasionally brushing snow from my face, Christine happily chatted away about this and that, completely ignoring the strange British obsession with talking about the weather. I was becoming increasingly hypothermic, so looked at the rope to see how quickly Simon was climbing. Not very, presumably because the wind was trying to blow him from the cliff. Or perhaps it was due to him wearing specialist rock boots; these were a little like ballet shoes with smooth, sticky rubber soles. They were excellent at 'feeling' dry rock, but pretty hopeless on ice.

Then the rope stopped moving for at least five minutes. I guessed that Simon had reached the 'one step' and so had needed to leave some slack rope for his sudden move, thereby making any fall quite serious. I was now really, really cold. Simon eventually and successfully made the move, then quickly advanced to the second stance. Having no other means of communication, two short tugs came to Christine's rope. A few seconds later her rope went tight, which meant it was her turn to follow. She removed her gear from the rock and loaded it onto her harness.

"See you later," she said, as she moved along the ledge, then climbed out of sight.

Now it was just me on the isolated ledge, waiting for the two tugs on the rope to tell me that my turn had come...

After the climb, we all returned to the road, where Simon mentioned he wanted to do Shadrach next. I had done it in summer and found it quite hard. In these conditions I considered it a suicidal adventure. Then I thought about Eric, the cafe owner. He had solo-climbed the north face of the Matterhorn because he'd thought it looked interesting. Simon and Christine seemed to have the same mentality. What twist of fate had caused all three individuals to be in the same area at the same time? More to the point, what had caused *me* to be here?

"But Christine hasn't eaten for twenty-four hours," I said. "She needs food. I'll pay."

"Oh, it's fine," said Christine. "My mum will have supper waiting for me at home."

Your mum, I thought, *would be too busy having a nervous breakdown to cook anything if she knew half the things you get up to on your weekends away with Simon.* "But it will be dark in two hours," I protested. "A rope of three will never complete Shadrach in that time. I'm going to the cafe."

I never climbed with Simon again. To him I had transitioned into a hideous creature whose sissiness was beyond his comprehension. And anyway, he now had a partner with who he could romantically share a double bivvy bag, snuggling down within the beautiful, remote mountains. And here I pause for a romantic sigh, inviting you to do the same.

This chapter concludes my study of ladies: from Maggie, who failed to climb a simple picture-house wall; to superheroines like Christine, who ruthlessly destroyed the preconceptions upon which the sexist education system is based. As for me – well, on that day in Tremadog I realised I was just an ordinary guy who wanted an ordinary girlfriend who liked climbing ordinary things.

Chapter Twenty-Three

I am such a hypocrite!

While agreeing with Simon that girls "got in the way of climbing", I was frequently placing personal advertisements in national mountaineering magazines, in the hope of finding a lady who might grow to like me. Clearly this was a delusional aspiration, but my brain could not accept a fate which included spending nights in an igloo with a great hairy man. I needed a lady I could hold in my arms without feeling awkward. Also, someone who would not snore very loudly, then eat all my porridge in the morning.

Sadly, those who responded to my advertisements had, presumably, visualised me as a mega-hunk with a manly personality and a motorbike well suited to whisking them to exciting places. Instead, any meeting began when they opened their front door to see me standing on the pavement with Fred parked nearby. So, to cut a long story short, with three exceptions, my search for a girlfriend had no influence over my future life.

The first of these exceptions was a lady aged around twenty-five, who obviously disliked men of weak character. As I sat on her sofa, she asked what climbing routes I had done and was planning to do in the near future. When it became apparent I could not lead E3, she cut the interview short by saying that tomorrow she would take me potholing instead. At the time, I found her extreme views regarding how a man should lose his potholing virginity quite terrifying, so naturally she never wanted to see me again. But it did inspire me to seek less demanding underground adventures, and I soon became dedicated to mid-range potholing; a sport enjoyed equally by men and women.

The second lady to influence my life lived in the far north of England. After riding up from the Midlands, I arrived on her doorstep on a Saturday afternoon. I thought it a long way to travel but, if things went well, knew it would be possible to pick her up the next time I rode to Scotland. But she obviously wanted to take things more slowly and suggested we went for a walk along a disused railway line nearby. When we came to a rough stone bridge, I naturally began to climb it. She seemed happy just to watch. I tried to get her involved, but she failed to even get off the ground. The rest of the afternoon progressed in much the same way. Maybe I worked out twenty short routes up different bridges, but her success rate remained zero. After waking up on her uncomfortable sofa the following morning, I asked if she might want to go potholing in the nearby Yorkshire Dales. She replied that she had to work. Thankfully, I was now accustomed to face-to-face rejections, so returned home and thought no more about her. Then she sent me a letter to say how much she had enjoyed our weekend together. And another letter after that. But I had already decided that a five-hundred-mile round trip was too far to travel in pursuit of romantic dreams. I concluded that my future girlfriend needed to live no further from my houseboat than Derbyshire or the Mendip Hills. All of North Wales was fine, because it was where I hoped to take her anyway.

The final lady I wish to mention had a far more traumatic effect on my mental well-being. This yet-to-meet person only lived sixty miles away, which I considered local. Initially, my letters entertained her and she responded in a positive way. One of her letters informed me she was climbing 'severe', but was nervous about leading and wanted someone else to take any serious falls which might occur. I was a man – I could protect her! But more than the general climbing matters, her writing style allowed me to deduce that she had a nice personality. Also, as a farmer's daughter she would be well accustomed to wearing wellingtons, should our relationship progress to potholing.

And so eventually I set out to visit her and whisk her away for a fairy-tale ending. This fantasy was helped by Fred having an armchair seat in which she could relax. Also, I still had my proper 1920s fashion clothes, and my bright yellow crash helmet highlighted my attention to health and safety issues. On arriving at her farm, I parked Fred in the cobbled yard and tapped the door of the house. An amazing lady in her mid twenties answered. Her clear complexion was devoid of make-up and a quick glance down revealed that she was wearing sensible pumps. Her nails were short, so there would be no hysterical tantrums if one got broken while doing a delicate climbing finger hold. This was it; the one I had been searching for. Wow!

The lady, however, had more to take in, because she had to consider both me and my motorbike parked twenty feet away. This took her about three seconds. "I've got to wash my hair today," she said.

Then the door closed, leaving me staring at the cruel wooden barrier which had unexpectedly come between us. I wanted to shout through the letter box that I could wait and, if it got dark, we could go potholing instead. But that rather contradicted her statement about hair-washing.

The lady from the farmhouse stands out because of her hair. From that day, I resolved never to show any interest in a lady who had the sort of style which took all afternoon to wash.

While placing my personal advertisements in the climbing press, I became aware of a lady named Alison Hargreaves. You might remember that I mentioned her earlier as the eight-year-old who got a bit lost on her first attempt to climb Wyddfa, and accidentally traversed the Crib Goch ridge in the process. With such an excellent start in life, she was obviously destined to achieve great things. So, while still a schoolgirl, she was invited to attend an international women's mountaineering fest; a three-month extravaganza of climbing offered to only the most able lady climbers in the world. Anyway, one day I opened my monthly climbing magazine to see her standing for a group photograph of female mega-rock stars. Truthfully, my eyes immediately focused on Alison, who was so angelic the others failed to even register in my peripheral vision. I wish to clarify that Alison was in the sixth form, and what captivated me most was her delightful smile, which portrayed a friendly personality. I was also completely realistic about the fact that the only contribution I could make to her life would be to stand on the ground and write poetry about the graceful way she climbed beneath overhangs, with her long hair trailing gently in the breeze. But of course, she had no need to respond to my personal advertisements. But I hope she saw them, and they made her laugh, before she moved on to read the sections of the magazines she thought important.

Returning briefly to my late teenage years, my desire to be successful in my studies and so get to the same university as Charlotte meant that I spent all the time either working or occupied with one of my course books. So I reached my early twenties with no experience of 'going out' – by which time Charlotte would be completing her university degree and have lost any memory of my existence.

But life moves on. From the age of twenty-two, once a week I began going to the pictures. Then, slowly, I became braver about expanding my horizons into completely new areas of social activity.

I had read about eating-out situations, but it was not part of my upbringing. However, I knew it was a lot more complicated than going down the chip shop to have 'dinner for one' while sitting on a park bench. But I was becoming increasingly curious about the Indian restaurants I passed on my way home from the picture house. They seemed very exotic, and I often found myself gazing through the windows of a very posh restaurant called The Houseboat. I could see flickering candlelight, and many people sitting at tables, waiting to be served. Finally, around the age of twenty-six, I bravely walked in and scurried to the darkest corner to sit down before the waiters even realised I had entered.

Presently, a very respectful gentleman approached and gave a slight bow. He was immaculately dressed in white robes and a turban. After we had exchanged 'good evenings', he gave me a menu. He left before I could order, but magically reappeared as soon as I placed the menu on the table. I ordered a coffee, plus what turned out to be a new experience in food. I found the exotic meal most enjoyable, and became a frequent late-night visitor during my late twenties.

The thing about Indian restaurants, I discovered, is that the environment seems to encourage ladies to do strange things. In particular, if they see a man sitting alone in a dark corner, they think, *Why is he there? Will he buy me alcohol? Would he like to give me money for no longer being alone?* My response was to look at their painted faces and think, *I don't understand why you are trying to make yourself look like a goldfish.* And like most people, I am nervous of things I do not understand. I was never approached by a lady with an unpainted face who was not also suffering from alcoholic poisoning, so any 'girlfriend outcome' was clearly out of the question.

Anyway, when I was twenty-eight, as usual I was in The Houseboat, enjoying a meal and a non-alcoholic drink. I was sitting in a quiet corner minding my own business and causing no harm to anyone. Presently the peace and quiet was broken by a gaggle of girls who came crashing through the doorway. The waiters retreated into corners until the squabbling over chairs had been resolved. I decided this was the tribal ritual called a 'hen party'. The waiters seemed to understand it was extremely dangerous. They nervously approached the women's table, all the time giving the impression they were ready to run and lock themselves in the kitchen if the need arose.

After half an hour or so, one of the ladies, who seemed a little more drunk than the rest, began making a buzzing noise between her teeth. Pretending not to look, I lowered my head while lifting my eyes to observe the situation through my fuzzy, protective eyebrows. The lady was holding out a finger and staring at it as a hypnotised person becomes fixated by a swinging watch. Very slowly, the finger began to rotate while leaving the wrist static. From her mouth came the most remarkable impersonation of a helicopter I have ever heard. Increasing in both frequency and loudness, the helicopter began to take off. It then dragged her arm and body upwards, until she was standing alone in the middle of the room. After she had captured everyone's attention, the helicopter began to drift sideways. The waiters nervously wrung their hands at this strange English custom. Diners watched in astonishment as this crazy, buzzing woman hovered between them. When the helicopter was above my head, I stopped pretending not to look and gazed upwards. Quite suddenly, all movement and sound ceased. The audience held its collective breath. What was going to happen to the helicopter now the rotor had stopped moving? Total silence – the lady standing there like the Statue of Liberty, finger pointing to the sky. She smiled as if she knew that something really good was about to happen. Then, without warning, she let forth the frenzied howl of a diving aircraft. The hand fell from the sky and landed in the middle of my trousers. I leapt up with a scream to match hers. The waiters advanced, thought better of it, and retreated. A few seconds later the lady let go and rolled to the floor, laughing hysterically. I sat down, hands across my lap for fear of another attack.

The lady climbed up to sit on the chair opposite mine. "Hello," she said. "You looked lonely – thought you might like some company."

I understood this was all part of the 'dinner for one' drama, as played out in romantic magazines. The lady had simply sent out an emergency rescue helicopter; much the same as if it had been a mountain incident.

After this unusual introduction, things settled down until even the waiters felt it safe to leave their hiding places. They approached and, standing well back, leant over to sort out the table which I had almost kicked over on my upwards flight. Because the candle had been sent to the floor, they removed it, presumably believing it to be a fire hazard. Other than this, and their occasional knowing looks, they appeared to have completely forgotten the incident.

The lady had been chatting away for some time before she asked if I had a girlfriend. I knew from past experience that responding to this question with a simple 'no' was not a viable option. The more polite females would observe that I had gone as red as a traffic light; the less polite, probably sensing my awkward body language, would ask about my assumed lack of romantic experience. On this occasion, I decided to expand my answer.

"No," I mumbled, "but there is somebody I love."

The lady eyed me cautiously. The next part of the conversation was made awkward by the fact I could only respond by either nodding or shaking my head.

"So," said the lady, after the interrogation was over, "there is somebody you like, but don't see any more, and that's why you are sitting here on your own?"

I shook my head.

The lady ordered some more alcohol, on my account, then rested her chin between her hands and stared directly at me. "I'm confused," she said. "You will have to explain."

So I did, using the L-word all over the place. I told her all about the complications concerning Charlotte, her middle-class upbringing, university, and my unfulfilled dreams. The lady responded by hiding my coffee cup and ordering a bottle of wine with a second glass for me. I did not drink the alcohol, which meant the lady soon began sloshing it into her own glass. Finally, I got to explaining that I was sitting alone in the restaurant because I had just been to the pictures, and didn't see Charlotte any more.

Then, quite unexpectedly, the lady asked me something horrendous. She was obviously training to be a therapist; the sort who require insurance in case it messes up the rest of their client's life. "Did you ever have sex with her?" she asked.

Shock gave way to indignation. Charlotte's honour had been brought into disrepute. "No," I said defensively.

The therapist clearly took the Freudian approach to life. "And what about the ones you had sex with?" she asked. "Don't they mean anything to you?"

I decided to avoid talking about my non-existent love life. "I'm waiting for Charlotte," I said.

"Bloody hell. What, never... since school?!" She thankfully took full possession of the wine, filling and drinking her glass twice before continuing. "I think..." she continued. She paused to give me a haunting look. "I mean, don't you ever wonder what it is like?"

I shrugged my shoulders. "Wouldn't mean anything without love," I responded.

"In my experience..." The lady took a gulp of wine, then corrected herself. "In my *limited* experience," she said, "I think that is a load of bollocks."

"But when you love somebody—"

"When you first told me about this Charlotte thing, I thought you hadn't seen her for six months, not eight bloody years."

"Twelve," I corrected.

"Once you get past six months it feels like forever – eight or twelve years are, I guess, pretty much the same. Oh, don't tell me you're a monk who doesn't believe in sex before marriage?"

"A marriage certificate is just a piece of paper—"

"Thank God for that!"

"But I don't believe in sex before Ben Nevis."

"What?"

"Ben Nevis requires commitment," I explained. "You get to know your partner and, if you are compatible, stay together for the rest of your lives."

After learning of my moral philosophy, the helicopter lady alternated between gulping wine and saying rude words. I responded by telling her how amazing Ben Nevis was. Finally she looked directly into my eyes.

"Do you want to come back to my place or not?" she asked.

Because we had already talked about 'no sex before Ben Nevis', this was obviously an innocent offer to sleep on her settee. Why I would want to do that when I had a perfectly good bed at home, I had no idea. But perhaps, when she was not drunk and the paint had been scraped from her face to reveal what lay beneath, she was actually quite nice. Did she deserve a chance? At least she had not ignored me. Okay, her helicopter landing technique left a lot to be desired, but part of me said it was better than having a lady telling me to go away. "Okay," I said after much thought. "I will take you rock climbing this Saturday."

"What?"

"Oh, just for the day, in Derbyshire, nothing complicated." I decided not to confuse things by talking about the motorbike. She seemed confused enough already.

After a few minutes of incoherent rambling, she wrote her address on the back of a beer mat and passed it across the table. It was only then that I remembered her nails. She had forgotten to cut them for ages and, to hide all the dirt and germs beneath, had painted them bright orange. So unhygienic, but now I was committed.

"I'll pick you up at ten o'clock," I said.

She nodded, then staggered back to her friends where, a little later, I heard her say the word 'virgin'. The whole ritualistic group looked at me, making me believe I had been unwise to ask the helicopter lady out on a date. But, being an optimist, I hoped that once in Derbyshire, she might show me a more gentle side to her personality.

I was now well organised when it came to climbing, so at nine o'clock on Saturday morning I loaded a rucksack of gear onto Fred, plus a spare crash helmet for the helicopter lady. Also, a pair of nail clippers so that I might attend to her claws. Without this, even a one-inch-wide finger hold would be impossible. I decided to introduce her to Fred first, and the nail clippers once we were in Derbyshire.

After arriving at her road, I walked along, looking at the house numbers. *Oh, it's only one day,* I was thinking, *but thank heavens I have not committed myself to a whole weekend.* The lady lived at number 129, so I was rather bewildered to discover the last house in the street was number 86. I knew she was drunk, but had not realised she was so incapacitated that she had forgotten where she lived. I dithered and dallied for a little while; all of this compounded by the fact that *if* she had told me her name, I did not remember it. Presently I went to sit on Fred and ponder a well-established problem of philosophy: the difference between belief and knowledge. I clearly knew the lady had given me an address that did not exist, but my brain was incapable of believing she would let the chance to go climbing pass her by. Then slowly I began to smile at the irony of it all. My 'no sex before Ben Nevis' rule introduced a perfectly sensible delay between impulsive manly desires and logical thinking. If applied nationally, there would be fewer shotgun weddings and less subsequent unhappiness as both parties came to terms with their incompatibilities.

"How far did you get?" a friend might ask.

"The Kendal service station on the M6," I might respond. "Then I realised this particular lady was not for me."

As I meditated on these complex questions, I decided taking the helicopter lady anywhere seemed all wrong. Fred's armchair had been designed for Helen. I have no wish to talk about ladies' bottoms, beyond saying that occupancy of this armchair belonged to one very special person. I pressed the starter motor and hurried away, ultimately going to Derbyshire on my own.

That afternoon, I happened to be clinging to a ledge with my feet squeezed into a thin vertical crack. I had already hung a rope from the top of the face, and so was clipped safely into a loop. (There is a better way of doing this self-protection, which I shall explain later.) The important thing for now was that, if I fell while attempting the next difficult move, I would not hit the ground. Then, as my fingers caressed the ledge above, my mind drifted back to the geology field course and Charlotte. My conclusion on that day was that I understood rock a lot better than I understood girls. As true then as it was now!

Chapter Twenty-Four

It's early February 1981, and I am plodding up the Yeti Path on Ben Nevis, thinking happy thoughts about the forthcoming adventure. Because it is winter, I have brought the alarm clock from home: when darkness lasts sixteen hours, it is necessary to know how many hours have passed, otherwise the night seems to go on forever. Also in my rucksack I have a folding aluminium snow shovel. In addition to knowing the time, it helps to have a nice place to sleep.

So, travelling light, I had a most relaxing walk up to the col, then continued around the base of the mountain to stand beneath the north face – a spectacular display of rock clad with snow and ice. After admiring the scenery I continued below the cliffs until I came to the steep snow near the base of Tower Gully. Here I got to work with the shovel, digging out a cosy cave some six feet deep; an activity which kept me amused until supper time at six o'clock. I then pushed my rucksack into the entrance: a house is not a home until it has a 'front door' which you can close to keep out the cold night air. After consuming my porridge, I snuggled into my sleeping bag and adopted a sitting position with my back resting against the far wall. What the outside world might be doing had no relevance to me. Inside my home it was all very peaceful, the only sound being the ticking of the clock I had placed on a little alcove near my 'bedside'.

As the night passed gently by, I sometimes slept, or occasionally lay awake 'daydreaming' about nothing in particular. Could life be any more perfect that this? Well, only if I had a girlfriend with who I could share a double sleeping bag. Or maybe we could play a game of chess, or just talk. Sadly, the sexist education system which indoctrinated girls to dream only of doing housework and ironing men's shirts meant I seemed destined to remain a solo adventurer. It almost brought a little 'grrr' to the back of my throat when I remembered the curtsying lessons the girls had done at infant school. There had been no mention of doing interesting things like living in snow holes, where housework is non-existent. Maybe I should just focus on having an imaginary girlfriend who understood what it was like to be me.

At 7am I scooped some snow from the wall of my cave to prepare a leisurely breakfast of porridge, followed by coffee. At 8.30 I pulled my rucksack forwards to see a wall of snow. Strange – it had not been there last night. Digging a tunnel upwards at forty-five degrees, I broke the surface after about ten feet. I expect that's what happens when sleeping beneath a two-thousand-foot gully where the snow can accumulate. Or it may have been a simple avalanche which had gone over my head unnoticed.

My snow cave was pleasantly situated beneath the awe-inspiring cliffs of the Orion Face; a 1,500-foot wall of near-vertical, ice-covered rock. According to many, it offered the hardest winter routes in Scotland. I thought it very nice to look at but, as far as my feeble body was concerned, a complete no-go area. However, the gully I intended to climb ascended steeply up against the right-hand side of the face, until both came together at Ben's summit. As I gained height, the snow got steeper until, near the very top, it became vertical. I cut upwards through this at about eighty degrees, which allowed me to stand upright with all weight pushed down on my feet; the axe placements merely maintaining balance. When the cutting was two feet back from the apparent edge, my head came level with the summit plateau. So one moment all I could see was snow, which often touched my face; the next, I could see the summit, which looked vast. Because I was still ten feet out from the actual rock edge, I slithered from the cutting like a lizard, so distributing my weight over the largest possible area. When it was safe, I stood up and wondered what to do next.

Fortuitously, the summit has an elevated emergency shelter: a semicircle of corrugated iron, blocked off at both ends by steel sheets. The floor area is a little larger than the size of a double bed; the headroom in the middle just sufficient to allow a 'guest' to squat in comfort. When the shelter is being used as a hotel, if it is needed to deal with an emergency situation you must vacate immediately. Though during my stays to date I have never been disturbed and have mostly slept soundly until the first light of dawn filtered around the ill-fitting metal-hatch doorways. So, after my climb of Tower Gully, I decided that was where I would sleep tonight, which gave me about five hours of daylight to wander at will.

I began by descending Number 4 Gully – the only truly easy way down the north face – then circled around to climb Castle Buttress. This was nicely exposed to the wind, so a pleasant contrast to my gully climb of that morning. I got back to my summit shelter about an hour after dark. Here I prepared porridge and two mugs of coffee. Then I settled down for many hours of monklike contemplation.

Presently my mind floated back to my twelve-year-old self running away from boarding school in a blizzard. Crossing the hills back then had also been amazingly good fun, and this adventure was merely a grown-up version of the same sort of thing. Essentially, it was playing with snow (though the mountain rescue service might not agree with this observation). However, so far I had avoided all of the challenging situations which had occurred during my first Christmas visit to the Ben fourteen months earlier.

For my third Christmas on Ben Nevis I was living the dream: a whole two weeks of doing interesting things in a world of snow and ice. The lowland temperature was minus eighteen degrees centigrade, so both the unpleasant rain and the bloodsucking insects of summer were absent. Accommodation was plentiful, there being plenty of places to dig a snow hole above six hundred feet.

Given the length of my holiday, the first thing I did was establish a base camp near the start of the Yeti Path, using a brand-new mountain tent I had bought on hire purchase from Nevisport. Or perhaps a mortgage would be a better description, because it had cost me five weeks' wages. Anyway, the tent had bendy poles which allowed the canvas to flatten during more severe gusts; temporarily reducing the humans inside to a sandwich filling, but otherwise providing luxurious accommodation. Attentive readers will have noted the phrase '*more* severe gusts', which is not the same as *all* conditions – when shelter is needed the most. Also, the tent's space-age design meant I was unable to view it with any great affection, like my brave little ninety-nine-pence Woolworths tent with its broomsticks. That would also stay up in *more* severe gusts, which put it in the same category as the tent on which I had a mortgage… and which was ultimately reduced to a tangle of torn fabric in a violent storm, while I still had six monthly repayments to make.

During this third Christmas I naturally spent the main festive period sleeping on the summit, returning to the shelter shortly after dark. I found it most confusing that I failed to see another person for the whole two days. So where was everyone? What happened on Boxing Day that I did not know about? Surely there are only so many mince pies you can eat? As the holiday progressed I started to think about the infamous all-night Hogmanay parties which took place on Ben's summit every year. Apparently all the best Scottish climbers attended, which relegated me to an annoying, amateur and weedy Englishman. So, when New Year's Eve arrived, after it had been dark for a little while, I looked out of my tent in the glen to study Ben's southern flank. As expected, the tourist path was busy with torchlight. I decided the time had come to attend my first ever grown-up party. To me, it was akin to a Hollywood moment of mingling with the famous celebrities of the age.

After ascending the Yeti Path to join the tourist route, I discovered the partygoers had moved up, so enjoyed a pleasant solitary walk to the col and a little way up the flank. Then I noticed a light in the distance. After a short while there was a long line of torch beams bouncing towards me. I was totally bemused by this; after putting so much effort into reaching the party, why would anyone immediately turn around to leave? As the first person in the descending column approached, I questioned him. He responded that he could not see a thing. What had he been expecting to see – a lady cabaret artist parading in a state of undress? Essentially, the summit is snow and more snow. In the middle of Hogmanay, you did not go to see it, but to feel the ambience and perhaps sing 'Auld Lang Syne'. As the column of people passed me, they all said pretty much the same thing about the visibility. Most had English accents, so I decided that they had seen all the snow they wanted. But those with Scottish voices worried me more. What was there not to see?

At about 3,500 feet I walked into a blanket of still air with floating frost crystals. The beam of my head torch became a dull glow of reflected light. I could just see my hand in front of my face, but certainly not my boots. Climbing upwards was easy, because I knew how far I had raised my feet before dropping them back down onto the snow. But it was much harder to work out the angle of the snow from left to right. This had not been a problem when I had first entered the 'zero'-visibility zone, because the north face was a long way to my left. Hence, I had a large margin of error to play with. A far greater problem was an isolated gully which dropped down somewhere to my right. The normal way up the flank easily misses this but, in conditions like these, complacency can kill. Thankfully, my torch was lighting my compass, allowing me to slowly and carefully plod on.

At around four thousand feet it became more difficult because the width of the plateau narrowed, so it was necessary to get closer to the face – wherever it might be? But the air was perfectly still so, with the exception of my crunching feet, there was complete silence. This allowed me to use an echolocation system: throwing snowballs about. If they landed with a slight splosh, they had hit the mountain. If no sound came back, they had probably disappeared into an abyss.

Presently, I began walking downwards. Good! I had passed the summit, which had obviously been somewhere over to my left. I turned around and walked back, hopefully a little higher, then repeated the manoeuvre around thirty times, getting ever closer to the top. The summit can be identified by the crumbling walls of a ruined observatory – a Victorian eccentricity which once doubled as a hotel for fashionable tourists. They had mostly arrived up the zigzag path on mules. But on my echolocated ascent I had to keep kneeling down to feel for my footprints, which were hopefully a little lower down the slope. I would then lob a snowball towards the face, hoping to hear that comforting splosh. The danger was that I would become disorientated, miss the ruined observatory, and so step into two thousand feet of empty space.

Eventually, the various slopes indicated that the summit was close – but where exactly? My margin for error was now down to twenty feet. I turned around to retrace my steps, hopefully two feet to the right – bump! Having crashed into something solid, I groped around in front of me. It was definitely an ice-covered wall projecting two feet above the snow. Feeling my way along this, I got a precise location. I knew my way around the summit quite well, so walked directly to the shelter. I reached up and opened the door. My torch beam fell upon an unbelievable mass of bodies. All great big, hairy men – no ladies. I was horrified by the sexist nature of this gathering. Judging by the comments from those I had awoken, they were obviously all drunk; the party having ended some hours before. Wishing to be polite and honour their customs, I asked if it had gone midnight. An awful lot of rude words came back. I had believed that finding the summit had only taken me about four hours, but it must have been longer. It was now 1982. Not wishing to lie on top of a load of bodies – even if they were the elite of the Scottish climbing world – I retreated.

After walking a few paces from the shelter, I fell into something bendy, beneath which something wriggled. A human shape, which also said a lot of rude words. Feeling about, I realised that I had crashed onto a tent. "Sorry," I whispered. Retreating again, I fell over a guide rope belonging to another tent. For safety's sake, I began crawling in the general direction of the observatory wall. On reaching this I felt along it until I came to a narrow gap which had once been a doorway. I decided there was only one accommodation option left. I took the snow shovel from my rucksack and began building the domed wall of an igloo, using the doorway as a central support.

As I started work on the other side of the doorway to build the second half, with a proper rucksack entrance, a lot of people began shouting at me to "Be quiet." But I needed somewhere to sleep. Then someone gave me a time check like they do on radio programmes. Apparently it was "four in the morning", so I only needed a sleeping place for a short while. Half an igloo would suffice. I crawled inside, snuggled into my sleeping bag, and fell asleep.

A few hours later, I was sitting inside my sleeping bag with my back resting against the igloo wall. Importantly, my earlobes were nice and warm inside my motorcycle crash helmet. Before me, an army-style tin contained blazing fuel pellets (high-energy firelighters); the frame above supporting a metal pot filled with tasty porridge. Then a man knelt on the snow outside. After looking inside my half-igloo, he frowned, told me I was mad, and left. *What extraordinary behaviour*, I thought. After my meal, I put more snow in the pot to boil water for coffee. Inexplicably, while I was drinking this, more visitors arrived. I smiled at them all. In response, they too made silly comments about my sanity. Presently, I edged forwards to see what was happening outside. There were an awful lot of tents, but what really caught my attention was a group of three men sitting outside theirs. One of them held a Gaz stove at knee height, while another directed the flame from a petrol lighter onto the base of the cylinder. I thought it surprising that they did not know Campingaz was a trade name for butane, which remained liquid at minus two degrees centigrade. The third man was holding a frozen boot over the stove's meagre flame, which I thought looked rather funny, though possibly a little unsafe. And surely they knew it was possible to walk down a snow slope in their socks? On reaching a lower altitude it would have been warmer than the minus fifteen degrees centigrade on the summit, so the stove would have worked better, albeit still with the aid of the petrol lighter. But once thick leather boots have frozen into a squashed shape, getting them flexible enough to readmit your feet is still a challenge. After thinking logically about how those beginning their day on the summit of the Ben should behave, I suddenly became overwhelmed by sadness. There was not a lady to be seen. I felt certain their presence would have lightened the mood and introduced some sensibility to the proceedings.

I left the summit down the steep east snowfield and so reached the start of the arête which leads to the mountains running parallel to Ben's north face. This arête is the most interesting section of the Ben Nevis Horseshoe; it being very narrow with precipitous drops on both sides. A particular delight are the projecting rock spires which stick up from the crest like rotting teeth. Hooking gloved hands or axes over the tops of these allows you to lean out, thereby pushing crampon points nicely into their ice-coated 'gums'. So, not technically difficult, but the void beneath your boots means each move must be carefully planned and executed. Remaining totally focused on what needs to be done is the key to survival. The delicate nature of the crossing means that muscular activity is relatively low, so produces little in the way of internal heat. This caused the surface of my face to freeze and my fingers to lose all feeling. But the arête is not unduly long and, on reaching the broad ridge on the far side, I was able to snuggle my hands into my armpits. It is worth a mention that my beard had a thick coating of ice, while my bushy eyebrows developed two fine cornices which I could see at the top of my vision. Without these insulating features my facial tissue might have suffered deeper frostbite damage. So, do not trim your eyebrows, and ladies, wear the sort of balaclavas bank robbers use to cover everything but their eyes.

While I was having fun on the Ben, I confess to leaving Fred to fend for himself during what was considered the coldest winter since accurate records began. Thus he endured two freezing weeks on his own. This did something bad to his already worn-out engine. Anyway, his return journey to the Midlands was made on the back of an AA truck, with me riding in the warm cab. The cost of making Fred better was prohibitive, but he was taken away by a mechanic who wanted a challenge regardless of cost.

For reasons too complicated to explain here, I was given a three-wheeler van called Ethel which I could legally drive on a motorcycle licence. So, I now had a passenger seat and floor space in the rear – and who knew where that might lead? What did happen was that Ethel became the vital transport for a climbing and potholing club I started for my colleagues at work. However, our weekend expeditions involved some romantic situations of an explicit nature, so this aspect of my life is covered in *Yeti Seeks Mate*. I wish to clarify that Ethel was a very stable form of transport, because with two adults sitting in the front and sundry others squatting on the floor in the back, her weight often increased by 50%. This reduced her top speed to thirty-five miles per hour and, on the final steep hill to our North Wales climbing hut, the passengers had to get out and push.

Chapter Twenty-Five

In addition to my hectic climbing life, I was busy transforming my houseboat into a thing of great beauty. By the time I was twenty-nine, the inside had become virtually indistinguishable from an eighteenth-century cottage. (I had ripped out all the electric wiring and fittings, preferring the gentle glow of oil lamps.) In my living room, a brick-built fireplace provided all the heat I needed. However, less artistically inclined people – who only saw my boat from the outside – realised that its basic structure was a Portakabin, the bottom of which had been plastered with fibreglass to make it float. For reasons I do not understand, the British Waterways board had an insane desire to demolish it, simply because it was floating on their canal. I thought their attitude very strange, because it had been tied against the same bit of towpath for three years before 'the men in suits' even noticed it was there – or at least they had previously turned a blind eye to its existence. Sadly, the board were a government agency dedicated to making law-abiding citizens homeless. (My personal point of view.) My response was to get a boatyard to build me a forty-foot-long, open-topped steel box. I then hired a crane to drop my boat inside it. Demolish that, you bullies!

Strangely, it made them want to demolish it even more. And so what I now considered to be an iron battleship was craned onto the back of a lorry and moved to the River Avon. My ambition to 'arrive' in the stockbroker belt was thus completed before I reached the age of thirty. Before the lorry and crane took my battleship to an idyllic tree-lined riverbank, the location looked like a Constable painting. Nearby, an ancient and picturesque lock allowed navigable boats to visit Stratford-upon-Avon, a little way upstream. I believe my dwelling, ten yards from the lock, brought a postmodernist charm to the area. However, my nearest neighbour, who lived in a great mansion on the far bank, held a contrary view. (Our 'relationship' is too complex to explain in this adventure book.)

Anyway, it so happened that in order to deter common tourists from wandering to our really posh area from Shakespeare's birthplace, the authorities had left the road between virtually unchanged from its horse-and-cart origins. I therefore purchased a boat tender which I could row directly upriver to do my shopping in Stratford. Sadly, because of the legal fees arising from my disagreements with the waterways board, plus the cost of relocating my 'battleship' from canal to river, my finances were somewhat limited. So what I had actually acquired could also be described as a children's play dinghy. In size and appearance the 'vessel' was similar to an inflatable inner tube as used for large tractor wheels. However, rather than dull black rubber, my new 'boat' portrayed a happier image: banana yellow with splashes of green. The 'floor' was made of waterproof canvas, and the 'hull' (inflatable tube) had two separate compartments, which made it unsinkable – a bit like the *Titanic* before it hit the iceberg. My vessel came with a set of plastic oars, so was technically classed as a rowing boat. The fact it had cost fourteen pounds and ninety-nine pence from a toy store did not alter its ability to provide me with a cheap method of transport.

Given that I was residing in such a posh area, I decided to give my tender a classical name. After much thought I settled on *Romulus*, because it was mostly round. And, when I looked up the name *Romulus* in my encyclopaedia, I discovered it was a name the lady of the mansion would appreciate. *Ah*, she would think, *Romulus was the guy who killed a lot of people to become the founder of Rome. Such*

Latin-based knowledge clearly identifies the man on the houseboat as one of us. Perhaps I should invite him around for afternoon tea on my extensive lawn which leads down to the riverbank. That never happened, but I bet if a true Latin scholar had enquired about the name of my tender, he or she would have nodded wisely. "Romulus," they might say. "I know all about him. While at sea he was swept away in a violent storm, never to be seen again. Sounds about right!"

Anyway, one day I was drifting idly down the river after a shopping trip when I began to wonder if I could row *Romulus* around Brean Down headland, where I had done my first rock climbing at the age of twelve. I reasoned that, if I launched from the beach at Brean, my destination would be the River Axe; a narrow waterway which separates Brean from Weston-super-Mare (known locally as Weston). During the summer, a rowing-boat ferry operated across the Axe, taking up to six passengers at a time. Both sides of this crossing had boardwalks over the muddy approaches to the landing stages.

Back on the Avon, as I drifted home from my shopping trip I realised that if I returned to Somerset I could launch from the beach at Brean, return inland up the Rive Axe, and so arrive at the ferry landing stage. While to some this might seem an ambitious use of a children's toy, I should explain that I had researched the subject when I was a boy. In fact, back then grown-ups had thought it odd that a child should spend so many hours sitting on a rocky headland doing nothing much but gazing out to sea. To them, admiring scenery was an 'old person's thing'. But in addition to admiring the view, I was also watching the swirling currents which appeared at various states of the tide. I had thought then that, if I launched a boat from the beach at Brean half an hour before high water, I would end up near Weston on the other side of the headland – and quite quickly. Well, the Bristol Channel has the second highest tidal range in the world, so the currents are really fast, especially if a mile-and-a-half headland channels the water into a narrower gap. Sadly, at the age of twelve I did not have a dinghy – just a good imagination as to how it might work. Nearing my houseboat on the Avon, I stopped rowing and let the current take me home. Well, this method of transport seemed to be working okay. Then, while I relaxed, looking at the swans and stuff, I realised that something else – as important as buying *Romulus* – had happened recently. A few months earlier I had acquired Ethel. How fortuitous to have both a dinghy and the necessary transport to visit the seaside!

The following day I arrived at Brean and used a hand pump to inflate *Romulus*. After carrying the dinghy to the beach, I tied myself to it so that, if thrown overboard by a big wave, I was still lashed to something which floated. I did this via a climber's chest harness, so ensuring my legs would not become entangled with the rope. Getting seaborne was less straightforward than I had anticipated. Stepping into *Romulus* from shallow water merely resulted in cascading waves pushing me back to even shallower water. (Here, children paddled, ignored by their guardians, who took a greater interest in watching my repeated arrivals.) Conversely, pulling *Romulus* to deeper water made it impossible to board, because flopping my chest onto the inflated ring caused the vessel to flip over and land on my head.

After experimenting with boarding procedures for some time, I found what scientists call the 'Goldilocks zone' – that is to say, water that was neither too deep nor too shallow. This proved to be just before the swell broke into waves. Between the crests, the water only reached my tennis shorts, which allowed me to jump up from the sand and, with only minimal support from the dinghy, land inside. After this, the swell pushed me towards the shore, but after the crest had passed, I got sucked back out again. Frantic rowing therefore took me to deeper water, where I stopped because the current near the sea cliffs was already carrying me outwards at about eight miles per hour.

Within five minutes I was projected into the open sea. Here, as expected, I got picked up by a tide heading towards the Severn Estuary. This was really good, because the deeper-flowing current was surging in the opposite direction. It is called a tidal rip, and it makes the surface go all bouncy and bubbly. *Romulus*, with its near-round shape and no keel, spun across the surface, meaning that my view rapidly changed from the coast of Wales to the Severn Estuary, Brean Down, or Devon. This was a confusing experience, because the sea cliffs were quite close, so appeared to be flying by; whereas the coast of Wales, some miles distant, seemed to be stationary. Then, after possibly ten blinks, I saw Weston, which appeared to be relatively static, given the two miles of water which lay between us.

When completely clear of the headland, a circular current took me in the expected direction. I was still travelling quite quickly and believe I could have easily transferred to the River Axe current, had I not accidentally let go of an oar during all of the previous excitement. Now, with the single remaining oar used as a canoe paddle, *Romulus* sort of waggled rather than headed efficiently in any particular direction.

It is worth a mention that, had I attempted this adventure aged twelve, my inexperience in difficult situations might have caused me to panic. To survive you need to stay totally focused and committed to obtaining the end result. If I now failed to escape the circular current, when the tide turned I would be heading back out towards the Atlantic Ocean. Fortunately, at the age of twenty-nine I had the determination to paddle furiously towards *any* bit of sea cliff which nature decided I should reach. And so, when I bounced against a rocky wall I reached up to grab a good hold and quickly managed three complicated moves before the next wave arrived. After this initial ascent, I reached easier rock; *Romulus* now being hauled up behind me. It should be noted that if I had foolishly tied the rope to my tennis shorts the result would have been quite embarrassing. Waistbands on shorts are only designed to support their own weight, not an attached dinghy.

After about 150 feet of ascent, I reached a grassy hillside, where I deflated *Romulus* and carried it back to Ethel. So as you see, proficiency in deep-water soloing can be very useful in everyday situations. Hence, I repeat my much earlier statement: climbing should be taught in all schools; equally to boys and girls. Deep-water soloing can be combined with swimming lessons, because children naturally enjoy falling into water.

Whether Ethel's adventurous life in the mountains, and now at the seaside, was responsible for her front wheel falling off, I have no idea. Anyway, when it happened, it came as a shock to us both. Thinking logically, I subsequently borrowed a car with four wheels for an afternoon, together with a passenger who had a full licence. I used this vehicle to drive to a test centre, practising emergency stops on the way. Given that I had a year's driving experience, I passed first time. Until 1997 (when things became much stricter), a car test covered a small lorry. So theoretically, I could get into a lorry cab and take the vehicle onto a public road. I wondered where that might lead.

Chapter Twenty-Six

The most dangerous thing a man can do is take a lady potholing. Men who are romantically inclined should not even consider it unless they are willing to marry the female involved.

While these statements might seem a little extreme, you must remember that potholing includes gymnastic rock climbing, getting seductively wet, and wriggling through passageways just wide enough to take the shoulders. All this is performed by the dancing light of head torches. But this book avoids erotic situations, so I will merely say that the marriage proposal I made to my lady potholing friend was declined. Grief-stricken, I began doing all sorts of illogical things. My work suffered, life got complicated, and then, at the age of thirty-three, my houseboat sank. The combined result of these circumstances led to my homeless phase.

At the age of thirty-six I decided to stop being homeless, so found a job which no one else wanted. This involved unloading sacks of charcoal from shipping containers and stacking them onto pallets for UK distribution. While this monotonous activity caused my muscles to ache and my skin to become blackened with charcoal dust, it appealed to my romantic notions. Essentially, I was following in the footsteps of the great mountaineer Hamish MacInnes. Hamish was a very hard Scottish climber who had learnt his skill on Ben Nevis in the era of hobnail boots and hemp ropes. There being no money in his clan to speak of, he took the most physically demanding job he could find and, in this way, trained for his Mount Everest expedition. His plan involved hitching to Nepal and, when in the high mountains, feeding himself using the abandoned food dumps of a previous expedition. He had no documents allowing him entry into the Asian continent, no map, and ultimately nearly died of starvation. Well, I had now reached stage one of his career plan – that of carrying sacks of charcoal. In due course, the rest would follow.

One day, after spending eight hours engrossed in hard manual labour, I explained to a waiting forklift truck driver, Jason, that I was not really unloading charcoal, but on a training programme to prepare myself for climbing big mountains. He replied that he had just left the army, where he had liked the outdoor side of things. I quickly responded by saying that the temperature had remained at least five degrees below freezing for the past seven days, so Snowdon (Wyddfa) would be in excellent condition for ice climbing. More importantly, I had a wage packet burning a hole in my back pocket. Most of this would be used to pay back debts, but that still left five pounds for luxury items. So, within three minutes of my conversation with Jason beginning, it appeared I was returning to my beloved Welsh mountains. My partner was a sad comedown from my dreams of finding a lady to be my friend – but my co-worker had a car and was available that weekend…

I awoke on a narrow, badly angled car seat, whose springs had rearranged themselves to inflict maximum discomfort on the human bottom. After cautiously opening one eye, I realised the car interior was gloomy due to a coating of snow on the windows. The vehicle was rocking violently from side to side, which suggested we were in a gale. Then I remembered that, on my request, Jason had parked in the Pen-y-Pass car park. Here, mountains on either side greatly amplified high winds. The advantage of the location was that, being 1,180 feet above sea level, it minimised the walk to the north face of Wyddfa. We did not have a stove, but each had a can of Coke in his sleeping bag to stop the liquid freezing. These and a packet of biscuits represented our breakfast.

Once outside, a sudden blast of air blew us against the car, which at least pinned us upright. After using our icy fingers to struggle into windproof clothing, we distributed the climbing equipment between us. All of this gear dated back to my more prosperous times, when I had bought four axes, each with its own specific use. In addition to these handheld claws, I gave Jason my crampons, while I would be wearing the more aggressive and technical FootFangs. So we were well equipped but, in other respects, this was to be a typical teenage adventure. We had just enough money to buy two bags of chips after the climb, and there was probably sufficient petrol in the car to get us home. The only food in the mountains would be the fat reserves we carried in our bodies. Climbing at its best; certainly for Jason, who was twenty-two and used to military discipline.

After leaving the car park, a forced march up a snow-covered track took us deeper into the mountains. Every waterfall in the area had frozen and, because Jason had no previous ice-climbing experience, it was on these that we began. In a controlled environment of short-lived, escapable problems, we climbed using a rope, and Jason quickly picked up the technique required to ascend with axes and crampons. Jason then introduced a new concept into my adventures. He had a watch and, clearly believing himself to be back in the army, told me it was 1200 hours. Like I said, we were well equipped.

Given the high winds, I suggested we did a climb called Left-Hand Trinity, a Grade II mostly confined to a sheltered gully. It held great appeal for a novice, having no particular difficulty, yet finishing on the summit ridge after nearly one thousand feet of climbing. Our ascent began up a straightforward snow slope before deviating left to reach the bottom of a much steeper gully. Here we encountered a queue of people waiting to continue up our chosen route. This often happened in Wales because the winter climbing season only normally lasts a couple of months and is generally confined to the Wyddfa area. Our adventure was taking place on a Saturday in January, so absolutely in peak season. What I had not anticipated was a crowd of twenty people. It was clear to me that most of those waiting would not even begin the main part of the climb before nightfall, so would eventually give in and go home unfulfilled. However, the gully was wide enough to allow overtaking on the left, without interfering with the roped parties anchored to the right-hand wall. Going solo, which is quite normal on straightforward routes, is much faster. Our problem was therefore one of etiquette. To overtake and be gone is common sense. But Jason did not do etiquette. He was already wearing crampons and holding two axes, so up he went. I sneaked up behind, saying please, thank you, and sorry to those we were overtaking.

When we were about five hundred feet above the lower snowfield, it became apparent why all movement for the pre-existing parties had ceased. The snow had petered out and, in one place, diminished to a width of six inches squashed into a crack at the base of the right-hand wall. This necessitated leaning over, very much off balance, then hanging awkwardly from the axes as the snow groove twisted sideways. Elaborate efforts were being made to place protection, which accounted for those lower down now becoming stuck. This was now a serious etiquette situation, because the crack was only wide enough to take one boot. The best phrase to describe what happened next is 'pushing in'. This is most rude but, on the other hand, not doing so meant us going back down, and it was too late to select another route.

"Sorry," I shouted up to a gentleman who had roped himself to the wall at the bottom of the crack and was now giving Jason evil looks. (Justifiably so.)

The man's partner was about ten feet higher and trying unsuccessfully to protect his lead with assorted gear. In this situation Jason should have asked for permission to pass. It was then for the other party to either give consent or expect us to wait for hours while they sorted themselves out. In this case, Jason just began climbing directly up an ice-covered slab to the left. This was significantly off route and more suited to a Grade III climb.

"Do you want a rope?" I called.

"No, it's fine," he replied.

In my experience, people do not want to die, so, when unroped, they avoid making moves from which they might fall. However, I had never climbed with anyone from the army before. In that organisation they train you to go over the top, screaming; to kill or be killed. To them, death is an occupational hazard.

Jason was quite reasonably climbing ice at about sixty degrees. Less reasonably, he continued when the ice became very thin. In due course, it failed to take his weight and gave way. At the sound of crampons scraping over newly exposed rock, I looked up to see a thirteen-stone man overcome by the laws of gravity. There was no way he could stop, and instinctively I knew his fall line would take him hurtling at around fifty miles per hour into the climbers lower down. In the split second which followed, I decided to try to catch him. His initial trajectory looked set to send him flying off a tiny overhang two feet to my left. I stepped across, thrust the shaft of my walker's ice axe deep into the snow, and held up my left arm, ready to make a grab as he passed.

To my astonishment, he came off the slab in a crouched posture, fell two feet, and landed on my shoulder in a sitting position. This turned me into a piledriver, embedding my boots deep into the snow. My axe cut down through the slope, but my arm only had to prevent my body from crumpling under the increased weight. So my single axe, plus foot placements, held us both. Given that Jason's perch was only wide enough to take half of his bottom, my spare arm grabbed his waist to stop him falling sideways. It took a moment for our brains to catch up with events. He expressed no fear about this; only mild surprise that he was sitting on my shoulder, apparently quite comfortable. Then we both looked below to see many white faces staring up in horror at what had been set to crash into them. After that, they all seemed happy to give us permission to use the snow crack and, in so doing, be gone.

ETIQUETTE: *Popular routes often accommodate many climbing teams at the same time. These frequently intermingle at stances to have a good gossip, so making it something of a social event. Those joining the queue at the bottom accept the risk to themselves of the higher party falling, or dislodging loose rock. However, 'pushing in' without consent being freely given is unacceptable behaviour, for which I apologise.*

By the time we left the confined gully, the wind was trying to blow us off the mountain. This, together with the lower temperature near the top, made our faces painful with cold. When the gusts came, we had to keep four points of contact with the ice or rock to prevent being whisked skywards. At other times we moved very slowly. On reaching the summit I pointed to the cafe, abandoned for the winter. However, the walls offered shelter from the wind, and we squatted inside a bowl of snow which had formed on the leeward side.

Situations like this boosted my confidence. I felt that Wyddfa understood me. But more than this, I had just proved that it was technically possible to catch a falling climber. Also, I knew that even athletic ladies occasionally made mistakes. All it needed was for the two circumstances to align…

"My word," I would say, on finding a lady sitting on my shoulder, "you only weigh twelve stone."

"That's actually quite heavy for a lady," my new companion might respond, in a sweet and gentle voice.

Then, in the manner of James Bond, I might coolly raise an eyebrow and say, "But I'm taking you down the chip shop tonight, and was allowing for your healthy appetite. I'm Mike, by the way…"

I have heard it said that many men have fantasies about ladies, so do not find having an argument with my imaginary girlfriend embarrassing. In fact, I was more worried that she was going to dump me when she discovered I could only afford one bag of chips, which we would have to share.

Anyway, returning to the real world, I noticed that Jason's muscle coordination was erratic – and accompanied by repetitive twitching. Also, he had a lot of snow attached to his face for a person who was merely a bit cold. I suspected his core body temperature was starting to drop. I supposed that if, when in the gully, it had been a lady who had landed on my shoulder, I could now have given her a cuddle to keep her safe and warm. But there was no way I was hugging a great hairy bloke. So I said, "Forced march, at the double." This simple instruction reawakened his army training and, robotically, he obeyed.

After reaching the gentle snow slopes below the north face, the temperature became more agreeable. This allowed my mind to ignore the outside world and return to the lady perched safely on my shoulder.

"From where I'm sitting," she was saying, "the bald patch on the top of your head looks like a useful place to put a coffee mug."

"Look," I responded, "I'm sorry I thought you were twelve stone. But I've always believed it rude to ask a lady's weight, so don't know about these things."

"I'm the same perfect weight as Helen, who I believe you took to Ben Nevis."

"Fred thought she was two tonnes."

"Lucky for you that I don't actually have a cup of coffee, because if I did, I would place it on your bald patch, upside down."

Then, to my astonishment, her voice dropped an octave to say, "That was amazing." After a moment's confusion, I realised the voice had come from the real world, somewhere over to my left. I had forgotten all about Jason. Turning, I noticed the ice had melted from his ears, though not his hair, which acted as an insulating layer over his scalp. I felt my own head and discovered the ice had gone to reveal the bald patch I had first noticed some months earlier. I immediately decided to shave off my beard – couldn't have ladies laughing at me because I had more hair at the bottom of my face than the top.

And so when, two days later, that deed was done, I looked in the mirror at my naked chin and thought, *My homeless phase is at an end. I now have the money to buy a packet of disposable razors.*

By working every available hour, I recovered from my homeless phase very quickly. Within the year I had become a qualified riverboat captain in Worcester. By this time my salvaged houseboat had been mostly renovated.

A year after ceremoniously shaving off my beard, I came to be standing in a yard which sold lorries. My attention was particularly drawn to an ex-British Telecom wagon of five and a half tons. The box behind the cab was eight feet wide with three windows in the front section. Looking through these, I saw the area was set aside for a staff canteen. After the dealer had unlocked the outer door, I walked into the kitchen, then went through an internal doorway to enter a workshop in the rear. However, I saw it more as a mobile climbing club hut, which could bring wonderful things back into my life. I purchased the vehicle the same day, and before the end of the week had a camp bed screwed to the floor in the old workshop. Because of this, in future I will refer to this area as my bedroom. The outer door, though set into the side of the box, I will call my front door. So I now had two homes, as befitting my age, and the inclination to do adventurous things whenever work allowed.

Chapter Twenty-Seven

Like for most men, the arrival of my fortieth birthday came as a great shock. The associated midlife crisis was, like, huge! But even reverting to teenage language did nothing to reduce the traumatic experience of becoming old. Of course, if I had had a lady friend, she would have made things better by saying I only looked thirty-five, then gone out to buy me a new pair of comfortable slippers. But mutual love had passed me by, so the trauma had to be faced alone, occasionally sitting before my fire, wearing an old pair of thick woolly socks.

I join my midlife crisis on the 15th January 1993, which I remember as being forty years and twenty days old. On the morning of this crisis event I looked into my clean clothes cupboard to discover that it was lacking any underpants. This forced me to face the reality of owning a laundry basket overflowing with smelly socks and T-shirts. I had not done any washing since Christmas and now the time had come to spend two hours in the launderette, like an old person who lacked the excitement of having a 'real' life. I collected the overflow of clothes from the floor and pushed them into my largest rucksack. I then put my arms around the still-full laundry basket and left my houseboat overloaded with my domestic woes on display for all to see. After walking the quarter-mile along the riverbank to my wagon, I was feeling even more grumpy – especially as I had forgotten the washing powder. *Is this it?* I thought. *What my life has become?* Of course I could buy some more washing powder, because it would all get used in the end. But as I drove towards my 'date' with a washing machine, a Dylan Thomas poem floated into my mind. This stated one should rage against old age. Yet the best I could do was rage my way to the launderette at thirty miles per hour, obsessing about washing powder – because that is the sort of thing old people did. Then, quite suddenly I rebelled against everything. Recklessly I took a right turn and headed to the M5.

Two hours later, I was driving along the (then-) quiet lane which led to Brean Down. (I wish to point out that I had stopped in Weston en route to buy some new underpants, a pair of which I was now wearing.) It was on Brean Down that as a twelve-year-old boy I had first learnt to climb rock and, as a thirty-something man, had navigated around it on *Romulus*. Now, as an old man I parked near the headland and wandered onto the beach. I then walked towards Burnham-on-Sea where I had once gone to school. Back then I had sometimes returned home along the same beach, occasionally dropping my satchel onto the sand and going for a swim in the sea. (I still wore short trousers so, according to my logic, it saved Funkle Trumpet from doing the washing. She, being obsessive about domestic arrangements, had viewed the clean-clothes regime differently… and now she had been dead for fourteen years.)

And so, aged forty (plus twenty days), I came to be walking along the beach, with gentle waves rippling up the sand a few yards distant. My progress was lit entirely by the stars, which made me feel totally alone in the universe. Then, slowly, I began to see the world differently. In particular, I remembered how, during my fantasies of becoming a professional mountaineer, I had thought of doing an expedition to the High Atlas range in North Africa. This would include ascending Toubkal, the highest peak. This fantasy had never really gone away; merely hibernated as real life kept getting in the way. But my homeless phase was now behind me, allowing me to drift quietly into a different sort of existence where everything was comfortable and predictable. Was I really ready to settle down and only occasionally go climbing, while middle age crept around my tummy? Arguably, my life required something dramatic to happen. It needed chaos and unpredictability, so as to give it a new meaning. So why not go to Africa now? My wagon was only parked the other side of the sand dunes. It had a canteen and a camp bed screwed to the floor in the old workshop. So why not drive it to Africa and… who could say what would happen if I tried such a thing? And because my life needed chaos to rearrange it, the adventure seemed a wonderful idea. Added to this, my work on the boats would not start again until March, so theoretically I could go tomorrow and visit Casablanca on the way. That seemed a lot better than buying *myself* a new pair of slippers.

So, there it was: the 'signpost' – one arrow pointing towards a boring middle age; another to Africa. It took about an hour of wandering back and forth along the beach for the truth to dawn on me. The 'boredom' signpost pointed towards my wagon where, after a mug of drinking chocolate, I could go to sleep on a nice camp bed. The 'excitement' signpost pointed towards the sea, directing me to take off my clothes and go for a swim. Slowly, I came to focus on this fact. If I could do naked swimming in the Bristol Channel in January, then I had the sort of psychology which might reasonably include driving to Africa. If I could not do the swimming, then boring middle age had already arrived, and I had no business still dreaming of becoming a proper mountaineer.

Taking off my clothes was the easy bit, and walking into the sea only a challenge when the near-freezing waves began splashing towards my slightly overhanging tummy. Realising that I could not go through with it, I ran back to the beach. There I stood shivering and feeling most annoyed with myself. If I could not even go for a swim because the water was a bit cold, then clearly the notion of driving to Africa was just silly. Soon my mind was racing between a comfortable bed and Africa. Everything now boiled down to this one thing. Did I have the psychological strength to overcome the pain of swimming in water only a few degrees above freezing? I focused my mind on Africa, but to do that I must first prove to myself that I could overcome adversity. I returned to the sea. This time, when the waves splashed up my tummy I carried on. A few hundred yards further out, the water was up to my chest. Then I bent my knees and began to swim. It seemed I was going to Africa.

The following morning, I awoke to find myself sleeping in the middle of a workshop. Reaching out from beneath my duvet, I recovered the thermometer placed on my bedside locker – that is to say, an upturned cardboard box. The mercury was just touching minus two degrees centigrade, which told me that getting dressed needed to obey the same rules as a sprinter leaving a starting block: the time taken between leaving the 'safe' duvet zone and being fully dressed should be the shortest possible. A highly trained athlete should be wearing a base layer of clothes within ten seconds. This traps the skin's 'duvet warmth' until the more complex tasks of adding socks, footwear and a jumper can be completed. If, like me, on a dark winter's morning you find it is necessary to light a candle, a time of thirty seconds from duvet to fully dressed is acceptable. However, if you are not too fussy about going to work in odd socks, a back-to-front T-shirt and an inside-out jumper, lighting the candle is unnecessary, so a trained athlete should still be ready to start their day within twenty seconds.

So there I was, in the back of my wagon, fully dressed, yet without any need to go to work. *So now what? Drive to Africa, I suppose.*

We now come to the logistics of the adventure. Almost everything I owned was on my houseboat. This was moored on the River Severn, 120 miles to the north of my 'second' home, now parked near the Bristol Channel. This north/south divide, as politicians might call it, meant my world atlas, which included Africa, was on my bookshelf in Worcester. In the glove compartment of my wagon was my road atlas, but this seemed to believe the world ended at the bottom of Spain. But I knew Africa was on the far side of the Mediterranean, and could roughly remember the locations of Casablanca and Toubkal, so did not really need to see my world atlas again. And, further south, the Sahara (which I also wanted to visit) was, like, everywhere, so you could not really miss it. I had no climbing equipment with me but, as I had proved on Mont Blanc, this was of limited use for a solo climber. Anyway, Toubkal was in Africa, so I would not be needing my ice-climbing tools. I did not know how far my chosen mountain might be from the nearest road, but assumed it would be a multi-day walk or climb. In consequence, I would need my sleeping bag, which currently lay on my bed up north. (A duvet is impractical to carry in a rucksack.) But going back to get it, when I was halfway to a sailing from Portsmouth, was just too silly for words.

Things only started to go wrong that evening, when I got to Portsmouth. It was here that I had intended to visit the launderette and buy a cheap sleeping bag from Woolworths. But as things worked out, on nearing the city the motorway took me straight into the shipping terminal, where I found myself looking down a one-way boarding lane. An hour later, I was in the middle of the English Channel on a ferry, with no clean clothes or anything in which to sleep when away from my wagon. Oh well, it was Africa, so I would probably end up sleeping in the shade of a cactus plant anyway. Also, customs never checked my wagon, so I got away with importing the biological weapon of my laundry basket into France, where I expected to find a launderette.

My forward planning meant that, while still in Somerset, I had visited a branch of my bank. Here, in a world where cashiers spoke English, I bought both traveller's cheques and French francs. Having my passport in the wagon was more fortuitous than calculated. This was due to the time when my houseboat had sunk, causing me to lose all identity documents. Starting from zero, these had proved quite difficult to replace. Now I had more confidence in a residence established on wheels. This – my wagon – had a high-security padlock on the front door and various anti-theft devices in the cab. To me this seemed safer than keeping paper items on something that floated… or did not float, as the case may be.

Chapter Twenty-Eight

The French motorways, to which I had been so catastrophically exposed on my Mont Blanc trip, had, quite understandably, left me suffering from an extreme form of tollophobia. I cannot find this word in the dictionary, probably because it's rarely an issue in Britain unless a really long bridge or tunnel is involved. In such circumstances, the existence of a toll barrier is both predictable and sometimes reasonable. It's only when 'French highwaymen' disguised as toll collectors lurk in unexpected locations that I start to panic.

If you remember, I had got around the problem on my return journey from the Alps by riding through Switzerland, Germany, Luxembourg and the Netherlands; all countries which had dealt efficiently with the 'stand and deliver' problem of the eighteenth century. However, a quick glance at my road atlas, which had a small European section at the rear, immediately informed me that going through Germany was not a practical way of getting to Africa. But continuing my journey from Brean to Portsmouth would let me cross the English Channel directly to Le Havre on the western side of France. From here I could head due south, as dictated by my compass, safe in the knowledge that I was certain to miss Paris with all of its horrible toll roads. By this method I would arrive in Spain by the shortest possible route.

This plan mostly worked, at least until I found myself on a road that became increasingly bendy and occasionally had obstructions which gave my wagon only an inch of clearance. This bit of my journey came to an end at a low bridge which, sensibly, should not be there. Just before this obstruction was a patch of gravel on which a car might sneak a five-point turn. But any high-sided vehicle which might actually need to do this had no chance. Anyway, when the police arrived to investigate the traffic chaos, they used all sorts of gestures and pointing techniques to aid my short reversing manoeuvre. It was almost as if they thought it was all my fault, when truthfully the blame lay entirely on the French nation, which kept their motorways free of traffic by making them too expensive for ordinary people to use. After the police had helped me reverse onto a teeny-weeny verge without leaving any room for my driver's door to open, the traffic began to flow freely. Then a (presumed) senior policeman opened my passenger door. By pointing to his watch and waving his hands about, like they do in France, he 'told' me to stay put until midnight, at which time I could begin my reversing move.

"For two miles," I responded.

He shrugged his shoulders, then left me to figure the rest out for myself.

Besides this epic three-hour reverse, nothing of any interest happened on my journey to the South of France. Only as I approached the border with Spain did I trouble myself to take a short, relaxing walk to where the French and Spanish coasts met. Here, the Bay of Biscay forms an almost-perfect right angle, giving the ocean a square corner more common to swimming pools. But do not be fooled by this. I only managed a childlike paddle before near-freezing legs, and common sense, forced a speedy retreat to dry land.

Heading south from western France involves crossing the Pyrenees; a rugged mountain range often considered to be a mini version of the Alps. The road I needed clearly had its origins in the days when hardy folk led pack mules between the two countries. While it had seen some ad hoc improvements since, it was still steep, twisting and narrow. The authorities did not bother to erect any safety signs. To warn of danger, they simply left any lorries which had tumbled into the roadside ravines as twisted lumps of metal, reminding others to be careful. My wagon had a very low crawler gear which allowed it to get up desperately steep hills at three miles per hour. But it was never designed to do this for miles on end. Likewise, big, powerful juggernauts have crawler gears which let them ascend hills at, say, six miles per hour. However, this does not give them the power to overtake a wide vehicle travelling at half that speed. And so I became the figurehead of my very own convoy. Romantically, I was following the route Napoleon had once taken with his horses; these animals plodding up at much the same speed as my procession. As could have been predicted, after the highest point the road descended, allowing vehicles to travel at great speed. But I kept to thirty miles per hour, because my brakes were not designed for hurtling down precipitous roads. Also, my wagon was high-sided so, as well as avoiding low bridges, I had to take bends with extreme caution to stop it flipping over.

My arrival on a modern highway, which began in the foothills of the Pyrenees, finally allowed for overtaking. My British Telecom wagon therefore unleashed a brigade of roaring juggernauts. It was easy to imagine myself as a modern-day Napoleon invading Spain. After all the fuss had died down, I returned to being a humble wagon of no great importance. The highway was mostly clear of traffic, which allowed me to admire the scenery of a semi-arid landscape with a backdrop of hazy, distant, snowy mountains. More importantly, the Spanish road system is free to use, so I knew there would be no toll barriers forcing me to do emergency stops.

Eventually I reached the suburbs of Madrid, where I settled my 'second home' in a most pleasant area. The following morning, I was able to throw aside the duvet and dress at leisure. Later, wearing only T-shirt and shorts, I left my front door to wander along an avenue lined with palm trees. (I shivered occasionally, but was trying to prove the principle that I had travelled quite a long way south.) Whoever designed Madrid obviously had a 'thing' about grand fountains and palaces. I spent two days wandering about its clean, impressive centre. To me it spoke of an age when Spain had had an empire. Others might think more specifically about the year 1588, when Philip II sent his great Armada north. So, a city of history was now invaded by myself, all the way from England. I bet Philip never visualised my wagon coming as he inspected his mighty ships.

The highway south of Madrid is mostly boring. Also, according to my road map, the thick red line I was following only led to Granada in the south. From there, another thick red line went to Gibraltar in the west. Importantly, this meant my sailing to Africa would depart from a port where everyone spoke English. Unfortunately, keeping to these major highways meant I would be following a 'square' shape. While this might be sensible for a car whizzing along at seventy miles per hour, given my more moderate pace I realised it would be more sensible to take an east/west diagonal route, as dictated by my compass. So when I noticed a major road leaving the Granada highway in the required direction, I turned off to follow it.

Sadly, the road's grand status soon petered out as it entered a mountainous area unmarked on my map. As I ventured over rolling hills I was able to admire the green valleys, which were divided into small enclosures, giving it all a pleasant nineteenth-century feel. Next I found myself bouncing along a twisting, potholed lane at thirty miles per hour. Here, my greatest hazards were pack mules which, I concluded, seemed the most sensible method of transport in this area, given that I was now on a glorified cart track.

Eventually I descended to a charming little village, where I came to a halt in its single narrow street. Both sides had houses with balconies projecting above the road. Householders who sat on these, presumably having a siesta, were level with my roof. Once awakened, they greeted me as a wandering minstrel who had come to provide them with an afternoon's entertainment. But it was all very good-natured because, even though I had not the faintest idea what they were talking about, they were all giving me friendly smiles. I got out of the cab. "Malaga?"

I said to a man sitting on his balcony. He stood up and, a few seconds later, appeared at his front door. He then beckoned me to follow him to a sharp bend in the road. I thought that I could probably sneak under some of the balconies on the way, but others I could not. I informed my guide of this by shaking my head. The locals, all friendly and jolly, confirmed my view by welcoming me into their midst.

From my account of this little diversion, it should be obvious that using a compass to navigate leads to far more interesting situations than the academic study of maps. And I still got to Malaga only seven days after leaving England.

Chapter Twenty-Nine

I had no idea how to cross the Mediterranean, but reasoned a good plan was to do so at its narrowest part. I therefore arrived at Gibraltar to be told I was in the wrong place and needed to head a few miles west to the port of Algeciras. A little later, as I approached the port's entrance, two men ran out from behind the security building to block my progress. My determination to reach Africa, without knowing how it might be achieved, possibly lowered my defences to events which might otherwise have looked suspicious. So when one of the men walked to the driver's door and tapped the window, I opened it. In any event, I was blocked by his companion leaning on my wagon's radiator grille.

"Where going?" asked the man, now looking through my window. Because I had GB number plates, this was a sensible choice of language.

"Tangier," I said.

"I get tickets," said the man. "Bring here, eighty pounds. Very cheap."

I had been worried that crossing the Mediterranean might cost... well, I had no idea, but suspected a lot more than eighty pounds. The fact the men had run from behind the security office had surprised me, but the uniformed staff inside seemed to think it quite routine. Indeed, they were waving me on without even bothering to say hello. In consequence, I let the men who wanted to sell me tickets direct me to a patch of waste ground to the side of the main roadway. The obstruction I had created having been removed, the queue of traffic waiting to enter the port began to roll forwards. I noticed the security staff were making a lot more checks on the new arrivals than I had suffered.

Within five minutes the man who had previously spoken to me through my window returned with an official ticket. "Ship leave five minutes," he said. "One hundred pounds, go quickly."

The other man then jumped into my wagon via the unlocked passenger door. "Quick, quick," he said. "Special rate; next sailing 160 pounds."

Given my nervousness about not reaching Africa at all, I thought that pointing out the ticket price had jumped from eighty to one hundred pounds was inadvisable. Also, I had picked up on various clues that this method of travel was slightly unorthodox. As the men had said, they had organised a special deal, possibly reserved for nervous-looking travellers who arrived in a British vehicle.

Everything worked like clockwork. I was allowed to proceed onto a ship without either my ticket or my passport being checked… because I was a special customer! With my wagon parked in the hold, I went up on deck to romantically lean on the ship's rail to gaze across the sparkling blue waters of the exotic Mediterranean. I could not believe how easy it was to get to Africa.

Then, after we had sailed a short distance, I realised the sun was in the wrong place. I supposed an ancient religious cult might have considered this astronomical event to be a sign that the end of the world was nigh; though on reflection thought it more likely the ship's captain was drunk, so had forgotten he should be steering the ship towards Tangier near the Atlantic coast to the west, as opposed to south or east. Like most British people, I assumed every sailor on the high seas could speak English; this being the universal language used for international shipping communication. Not on the African ferries, it seemed. All the crew I told about the sun being in the wrong place replied either in Arabic or in Spanish, before shaking their head in English. Finally I found a lady working in the canteen who replied that she could speak English.

"Tangier?" I asked, pointing in what I hoped was a westward direction.

The lady looked confused.

"I am going to Tangier," I repeated, on the principle that speaking more slowly makes things clearer.

"Not on this ferry, you aren't," she said. "We are going to…" (a word I did not recognise). She then wandered off to serve customers who wanted to spend money rather than have a casual chat about geography.

It was dark when the ship docked somewhere on the North African coast. Did this vague location represent success? Given that ten hours earlier I had had no idea if it was even possible to cross the Mediterranean, I supposed it did. I then concluded the best thing to do was get out of the port, find somewhere quiet to park up, and so have a good night's sleep. And that was where things started to get complicated.

It was the sort of residential street which would have been a common sight in the north of England at the start of the Industrial Revolution. On either side, low-roofed houses rose directly up from the road; their front doors opening directly onto the street. Also common to northern England, the street was heading up a steep hill, possibly at a gradient which might force a small boy to push his bicycle as he set about delivering bread. And in keeping with the towns of Britain a century earlier, there were no street lights.

I was not concerned about the hill, because I had a crawler gear. Nor was I concerned about the space between the opposing houses for, taken slowly, a gap of one foot either side of the vehicle was quite adequate even for getting around the bends. There was no other traffic, but had I met something coming in the opposite direction, the higgledy-piggledy nature of the houses meant the natural occurrence of passing places. Given all this, the strange whizz-bang noises coming from above my wagon did not worry me greatly. Clearly it was a weather-related phenomenon.

Only when I realised it seemed to be following me up the street did I stop the wagon. The noise also stopped. I got out and looked back down the street. Now many front doors were open, illuminating what had previously been darkness. It appeared that some sort of street party was taking place. The central focus of the gathering seemed to be telephone lines. Previously invisible to me, they now lay across the road like lengths of de-flagged bunting. Looking ahead, I could just make out more telephone lines; these stretched between the houses, perhaps nine feet above the road. My vehicle was a few inches higher. Thankfully, the men seemed to be laughing, while discreetly dressed ladies peered nervously around their doorways to giggle. Then a man walked around to the front of the wagon.

Please don't hit me, I thought. "Sorry," I said.

The man looked down at my number plate. "No harm," he replied.

In England, I thought, *taking out a telephone system would be considered a major incident. Here, it seems to be just an excuse to have a street party.* "Do I need to wait for the police?" I asked.

"No harm," repeated the man.

After I had said sorry many times, I returned to my cab and began to reverse… until the engine lost power. I brought the vehicle to a halt. Meanwhile, ahead of me I could see a man with a stepladder was in the process of reconnecting the telephone lines. All of this friendly, laid-back behaviour certainly made me realise that I had truly arrived on a different continent – though I still did not know precisely where. Sadly, my wagon would not restart. Given that I was completely blocking the road, I foolishly decided to reverse using the gravity of the hill. Whatever was wrong with the wagon could then be sorted out in the morning, on a piece of waste ground yet to be identified.

Going backwards in a wagon, where much of it is beyond the rear wheels, is not an easy thing to do. Even professionally trained drivers sometimes need to pull forwards to adjust the vehicle's angle because, in reverse, you are using back-wheel steering, which does not mimic that of going forwards. And just because you cannot see something in the dark does not mean it is not there – even if it is the back of a car, sticking out from between two houses, on a bend. And so it was that my wagon crunched to a halt. I got out to discover the wagon's back end was having intimate relations with a car, which had somehow acquired two dented panels at the point of contact. Several people came to look at this, shone torches on it, and generally said things in a language I did not understand. There was one man in particular who stood out from the crowd. He was quite large and preoccupied with scratching his chin.

So, to summarise: from my perspective, things had not developed as I would have wished. Essentially, I was completely blocking a main street, wedged against a dented car, with a wagon which would not start, and surrounded by twenty or so men who spoke a language I did not understand. More worryingly, I had no special insurance, so was relying on my English policy, which only covered basic third-party claims when travelling in Europe, plus one African country (that is to say, Morocco). The most probable conclusion was that I would be returning home by hitching, while hopefully carrying a few possessions in a rucksack. From the villagers' perspective, it was necessary to involve the police in the situation.

Then a third actor emerged from the crowd. "Mechanic," he said. He then indicated that I should lift the flappy thing beneath the windscreen. This would give him access underneath the seats, where the engine lived. (Modern lorries have tilting cabs, so I have no idea what the old flappy things were called, but clearly not bonnets.) While I propped up the flappy thing, the mechanic first borrowed a torch from a resident, then returned to poke his head into the engine compartment. A moment later, he said, "Understand" and walked away.

Not much happened for the next five minutes. Then the mechanic returned with a garden hose, which he took into the engine compartment. Next he emerged, cut a precise length of hose with a pair of garden shears, and looked into a shopping bag he had brought with him. I could see from the torchlight that it contained three spanners, a screwdriver and a hammer. He returned his attention to the engine, only now tooled up with one spanner.

A minute or so later, he stood up to show me the spanner. "Bigger," he said. How much bigger it should be, he indicated with a fingernail. I went into the cab and handed him an adjustable spanner. He took it as if it was a magical, much-worshipped religious relic.

Then a policeman arrived. He spoke briefly to the man who had been scratching his chin, then turned to watch the proceedings without showing any wish to become directly involved.

After a short while, the mechanic emerged from the engine compartment. "Start," he said.

I got into the cab and, while waiting for nothing much to happen, turned the ignition key. A second later the engine burst into life. Now I was confused. (I later discovered he had bypassed a defective fuel system with the hosepipe.) *Back in England*, I thought, *any call-out repair costs at least fifty pounds*. Clearly this magical mechanic was worth every penny, but my supply of cash was based in being in Tangier by now. I only had a little money with me, because I was relying mostly on traveller's cheques. I had been told these could be exchanged for cash in banks in most major Moroccan cities. But, I reasoned, probably not here – wherever this was. "Pay," I said to the mechanic.

He smiled, nodded, then held my adjustable spanner to his chest. "Me... mine," he said.

"Yes."

He gave me the most amazing smile. Then he proudly put his second-hand adjustable spanner in his shopping bag and stepped into the background.

Next the policeman took command of the situation. With his torch pointing the way, and my wagon having a working engine, I soon reversed efficiently to a turning point. The stage now held only three actors: the policeman, the guy scratching his chin, and me.

"Follow," said the policeman.

The other man, who I assumed owned the dented car, got into the police vehicle, leaving me to follow. I reckoned that in England, replacing two dented panels would cost around six hundred pounds. If a bureaucratic insurance claim was involved, this price would be double, because that is how the garage trade works. I just accepted that my wagon was going to be impounded in a police yard while such things were sorted out. But I had always accepted that in Africa I might be reduced to public transport, so I was better off than I had been in Spain, given that I had now crossed the Mediterranean.

The police station turned out to be a run-down shack; the sort you might expect to see in a Wild West film. Just inside the entrance was an interview room, to either side of which were two prison cells. I knew this, because the doors had bars. Also, the policeman produced a massive key to open one lock. He then ushered both me and the car owner inside.

"Sort it," said the policeman. He then left the cell and, after closing the door, I heard the loud clunking of the lock being secured.

I glanced at the single small window, which also had bars. Then I looked at the man, who had returned to scratching his chin. It occurred to me that he was unsure about how to deal with a European who could not speak his language. Presently, he held up both hands to display ten outstretched fingers. I assumed he was trying to indicate one thousand pounds… or possibly one hundred? He had the build of a labourer who swung massive sledgehammers for a living, so I decided my best policy was to look really nervous. If he thought I was likely to burst into tears, it would surely embarrass him. I could imagine his workmates saying, "What, you got locked in a jail all night with a girly man? Did you do any kissing?" I had sixty pounds in the wagon, but only one ten-pound note in my pocket. I recovered this, while holding up five fingers. In response, he held up nine fingers. Well, at least the decimal point was in the right place.

And so the negotiations began. I am ashamed to say that we reached agreement at six fingers. My cellmate then went to bang on the door. But time moves very slowly in Africa. I assumed that the policeman wanted to finish whatever he was doing before being distracted by his 'guests'. Or maybe he was simply reading a good book and wanted to finish the chapter. Anyway, he eventually came to unlock the door, then entered the cell to speak a language I did not understand. I interrupted to say that my money was in the wagon. Neither man seemed worried as I walked out of the station. I suppose they knew that in this location I had nowhere to run.

After I had given the gentleman his sixty pounds, the policeman dramatically parted his hands, then waved them to either side. "Finish," he said, his voice authoritative. And that, it seemed, was how they did things in Africa.

After the gentleman had gone, I asked the policeman where I was. He knew a little basic English, so his replies included a lot of hand gestures. The combination of the two allowed me to understand a little of my situation. Apparently, I was in a Spanish enclave on the African coast called Ceuta. Its status is similar to that of Gibraltar; that is to say, a colonial outpost based largely on spurious historical claims. In consequence, the land border with Morocco has a continuous, very high fence reinforced with tangles of barbed wire, similar to those once used around concentration camps. The gate which allows passage between the two countries is controlled by a Spanish customs post. It closes at night and opens in the morning, apparently whenever an officer feels like turning up. Hardly anyone wants to leave Ceuta due to the refugee camps which surround it. In these settlements, half-starved migrants can only look through the fence with envious eyes. For them, there is no entry. The policeman told me the road journey between Ceuta and Tangier was controlled by various thugs who would expect me to pay for a safe passage through their roadblocks.

So, I thought, *just like the French motorways, which use the same highway-robbery system.*

The policeman thought the total distance was about 150 kilometres, but he had never tried it because it was too dangerous. "Best way leave here," he concluded, "is go Algeciras, then take ferry to Tangier."

Given my late night in the jail, I did not wake up until ten o'clock the following morning. Then I thought about where I was and tried to motivate myself with the exciting adventure which lay ahead.

Before leaving England, I had set myself three challenges: first, go to Casablanca, because I had seen the film of that name; second, drive south to the Sahara, park up, then walk due west until I came to the Atlantic Ocean, where I would go for a swim in what I imagined would be beautifully warm water; and third, climb Toubkal. I now had a fourth challenge: to get out of this place.

By the time I finished breakfast, it was midday and very hot. Finally, it became sensible to change into shorts and a T-shirt. A little later, on arriving at the customs post, I saw a sign in the window saying something I did not understand. Inside, a solitary customs officer was sitting back in a chair, feet up on his desk, and obviously asleep. I reasoned that if I disturbed him he could make my passage very awkward, so I parked outside his window and waited.

There was no one else wanting to enter the hostile land on the other side of the fence, and I could see why. The shanty town clustered around the far side of the gates was a sprawling mass of humanity. The dusty track through its centre was essentially a children's playground. And the policeman who had advised me about the gang-controlled checkpoints had said the total safe-passage fees were likely to be about twenty pounds. I accepted this was just part of their culture and a lot cheaper than using the horrible French motorways. But I did not have twenty pounds and, when I had informed the policeman of this, he'd responded with a worried look. Then, after a little thought, he had told me what I needed to do.

"No stop – go-go; gang probably jump away from lorry."

When the Spanish customs man emerged from his post, he looked around to discover that I was the only vehicle wanting to leave the enclave. Then he shrugged, went to unlock the gates, and waved me through. Thirty seconds later I was in a country where the official language was Arabic, including the road signs. I decided the best way to survive was to pretend I knew what I was doing.

Chapter Thirty

A bright yellow British Telecom wagon is possibly an unusual sight in Morocco. In any event it seemed to confuse the gangs who stood across the road. When they appeared to conclude I had no intention of slowing down, they acted all innocent and wandered to the verge to watch me pass. I suppose for them, extracting money from a car was a lot less complicated, especially if children were inside.

I reached the outskirts of Tangier with a gallon or so of diesel left in the tank. After parking in the suburbs, I wandered into the centre in search of a bank. This proved straightforward and I exchanged one hundred pounds of traveller's cheques for British banknotes. After leaving the bank I walked about the city, lost in wonder at all the unfamiliar sights. Of particular interest was that there seemed to be no Highway Code in force, and virtually every car had an alarming collection of dents and scratches. I even saw two buses with no surviving back panels; the passengers sitting on the adjacent seats with nothing to stop them falling onto the road if the vehicle took a bend too quickly. However, because the tyres were mostly threadbare canvas (presumably relying on the inner tube to stay inflated), turning anywhere in a hurry seemed unlikely. All of this made me feel a lot better about the man whose car I had dented. Most likely he would just pocket the sixty pounds, then drive around with the damage, advising others to keep their distance.

Anyway, while walking around Tangier I was distracted by a quiet voice saying, "Mister." Looking down, I saw a boy of about eight. With focused determination, he tugged the bottom of my T-shirt. "Follow," he said.

Obeying this instruction is often unwise but, on this occasion, it was all very innocent. After leading me to a pebble beach, he stopped outside the place where he obviously lived. It was built from driftwood, roughly fashioned in the shape of an igloo. The roof was covered with seaweed. Sitting on a driftwood log outside the open entrance was a lady, doing nothing in particular. Like the boy, she was dressed in rags held together with bits of string. On seeing me, she pointed inside her dwelling. Bending down, I could see that it contained numerous children in a very gloomy single 'room'.

"Live here," said the boy. He then held out his hand, while nervously gazing up at me with tearful eyes. (Which I suspect was a well-practised act.)

I gave him two pounds, which transformed his expression into a great beaming smile. He then ran across to his presumed mother and gave her the money. She looked at it in amazement. Then she glanced at me.

"Thank you," she said quietly.

Unknown to me at the time, I had just given the boy two days' pay for the average labourer. Taking advantage of the black-market value of sterling, it could feed her family for a week. My own homeless phase suddenly seemed to represent a comfortable middle-class existence. For though my level of physical destitution was similar to that of the lady, I had no children to look after. How she coped with the anguish of knowing that her pre-teenage son was 'going out to work', I could not comprehend. But more than this, her face showed a resigned acceptance that her life would always be like this: without hope. During my homeless phase, in my head I always believed that one day things would get better.

While wandering around the streets of Tangier, I saw a gang of men, drenched in sweat, laying a concrete base for a garage forecourt.

They did not even have a portable cement mixer; just shovels and a wheelbarrow. In Britain a foreman would have just telephoned for a cement-mixer lorry, and perhaps three men would lay such a forecourt in a couple of hours. But with the cost of labour so cheap, I guess it is more cost-effective to use the muscle power of de facto slaves.

Once on the main road south from Tangier there were no more unofficial tolls, which allowed me to relax. I had money and diesel, and my tollophobia was no longer an issue. But other things came to replace my anxiety. I witnessed several women standing by the roadside, holding out live chickens by their legs. As a vegetarian I go through life pretending that the slaughter of animals does not really happen. So, if I accidentally see a lump of dead meat in a shop window, I close my eyes to make it go away. I was now faced with the reality of poor chickens hanging upside down, flapping their wings in terror, and me knowing that they would soon be killed.

Another thing to worry me was the numerous children, generally aged about ten, sitting on the verge. Each was holding a length of rope, the other end being attached to a goat which grazed the odd patch of scrubby vegetation. An eight-hour shift would probably give their family a jug of milk. Other common sights included people living in shelters made of fertiliser bags, alongside office blocks of concrete.

I witnessed a more complicated child-labour situation in a sprawling town, where a boy asked me to follow. Again some instinct told me that this pre-teenager was honest. I also found it interesting to be guided along narrow backstreets where few tourists ever ventured. Then I was shown into a gloomy Dickensian workshop where six children sat at a long table, making intricate jewellery. They all looked well fed and their happy smiles seemed genuine. The head of the family spoke perfect, well-educated English. He told me what they were making could only be done by really tiny fingers.

"All children in this workshop," he said, "will retire at the age of eleven."

I did wonder if the juniors back in Britain, forced to sit in a classroom to learn ancient history, were using their time in the most enjoyable or productive way. The children in this workshop were learning a trade which would help them prepare for adult life. And in the meantime, they were earning money to feed their family. Certainly they knew how to sell things to foreigners, because they made me believe that buying a tiny, three-segment silver ring for five pounds was essential to my happiness. (The closing segments on a pinhead hinge represented a man and a woman coming together, often in marriage.) Bear in mind that five pounds represents a week's wage for an average adult worker, and silver is a relatively cheap metal, at least when four rings could have been made by melting down an old silver sixpence.

After returning to my wagon I continued my travels south until I happened to catch a glimpse of the Atlantic Ocean on the right. I turned onto a track and stopped before a lift barrier, beyond which lay a beach. I wondered how it could be so wide, without any vegetation encroaching from the land. I then turned my attention to a man sitting next to the barrier. I wondered how long he had been sitting there with nothing to do, and why he was doing so. I approached him, pointed to my wagon, then to the beach. He looked around as if to check no one was watching, then held out his hand. I was still unaccustomed to the cost of things in this country, so gave him a pound. This quickly disappeared into his pocket. He then manually lifted the barrier and waved me through.

I drove onto the beach, parked, and looked around. Nearby, I could see twenty or so men shovelling sand into wheelbarrows. Periodically, they took their loads to a cobbled-together wooden ramp, up which they laboriously struggled to gain the height needed to tip their cargo into an open-backed lorry. I reckoned that in Britain, one worker with a mechanical digger could load the same amount of sand in five minutes. These men, using pre-Industrial-Age tools, would probably take twenty man-hours.

After surveying the scene, I walked two hundred yards to the water's edge. Because I was wearing shorts, in theory I only needed to throw off my T-shirt to be ready for swimming. But not only is the

Atlantic Ocean very big, it is also exceptionally cold. I waded in up to my waist, then came back out, ran to my wagon, and made myself a cup of coffee.

After sitting in my kitchen for twenty minutes, I was surprised to see the view outside my open door was no longer sand, but a great swirl of water. On reflection, I realised that because the Atlantic is used for surfing, logic dictates that monster waves occasionally wash hundreds of yards up the beach. Jumping up to take a closer look, I discovered that I was surrounded by sea. Then the wave retreated, pulling the sand with it – or at least the sand which had been beneath the tyres of my five-and-a-half-ton wagon. My wheels were now comfortably settled in their own private pools. In a fit of unrealistic optimism, I raced around to the cab and tried to reverse up the beach. The wheels responded by spinning out more sand until my axles came to rest on the surface, thereby slowing down any further sinking. From my childhood at Brean, I knew what happened to cars on a beach if they were caught by the incoming tide. By the time the sea retreated, maybe the roof was still visible – or maybe not.

Within a few minutes of realising I was about to become homeless (again), I was surrounded by men. Every one of those who had previously been shovelling sand was now digging behind my wheels to make a trench through which I could reverse. But surfing waves generally come in threes, so essentially the men were trying to defeat the Atlantic with shovels. Then the man driving the sand lorry, now parked a hundred yards further up the beach, raced to my wagon with a thick rope, which he looped over the tow bar. I jumped into the cab to do the steering as the vehicle was pulled backwards. The good-natured men thought it a hilarious distraction from their toil; except for the one who had let me onto the beach in the first place, who now realised all quarrying had ceased. But my gratitude to the men who had saved my 'house' was so great that, when one held out his hand, I gave him a five-pound note – enough to keep a large family well fed for a week.

I suppose I should have been more observant of my saviours. They were all incredibly thin; their calorie intake presumably being insufficient for their hard manual work. The man holding the five-pound note was punched in the face, which sent him reeling backwards, allowing his attacker to grab the money – which he then dropped when another man hit him on the arm with a shovel. Soon it was similar to a game of rugby, only using a five-pound note for the ball and shovels to disable whoever happened to be holding it. The man who had let me onto the beach gave me a hostile glare, then pointed to the exit. As I drove away, in the mirror I could see the men still hitting each other with shovels. I suppose the last man left standing would get to keep the cash.

Casablanca is the most unromantic city in the whole world. Noisy, chaotic, and largely dominated by cars whose drivers had clearly passed their test on fairground dodgems. As I began exploring on foot, the first person to approach me was a policeman, who I imagined had noticed my relatively white skin and European-style rucksack. Initially speaking French, he blocked the pavement and gestured to me to halt. In response, I told him I was English. His attempt to reply was basic but understandable.

"Be gone six o'clock," he said. "Night not safe." He then walked on without further ado.

Well, I thought, *that comment implies it is safe in the daytime.* Anyway, first I needed to find the area where they had shot the *Casablanca* film. Would a romantic heroine see me and exclaim, "Mike, of all the places, fancy meeting you here!"?

Inspired by this, I wandered hither and thither, until a tug on my T-shirt caused me to look down to see a boy aged about ten.

"Change money?" he asked.

When I had visited the bank in Tangier, a cashier had told me in a loud voice that it was illegal for Moroccan residents to possess foreign currency. He had then whispered it was frequently used in a thriving black-market economy. Their own currency, the dirham, he said, was very weak, so the exchange rate 'on the street' for the pound and American dollar was twice that used by the official money markets. Nevertheless, while still in the bank I had exchanged a small amount of British sterling for dirham, so had both currencies to hand. How worldly-wise and organised is that?!

So, when in Casablanca, I had enough local currency for my immediate needs. Also, I thought giving pound notes to a boy I met on the street highly likely to lead to another visit to a jail. Then a much older man came to stand nervously behind the boy and rest a protective hand on his shoulder. I decided he was a grandad protecting his vulnerable grandson, so quite harmless. I was deliberately wearing the oldest clothes I possessed, and my rucksack had seen fifteen years of service, so was very tatty. I was therefore advertising to all that I was a vagabond of no financial value. And truth be told, it would be far more profitable for a bad person to mug rich Americans, who tended to advertise their wealth by wearing the latest fashion. Some even liked to display a wristwatch!

"Change money," said the grandfather. "Good rate."

I shook my head. But now the conversation had been opened, the pair seemed eager for some sort of deal to take place. And because I had been in Africa for three days, I clearly knew what I was doing: the exchange rate they offered would split the profit equally between us. Soon the disagreement focused only on how much should be exchanged. They suggested one hundred pounds, which was unnecessary for my needs so represented greed. However, exchanging twenty pounds would do no harm, and perhaps help my new friends provide a meal for the family. I pulled a twenty-pound note from my pocket and simultaneously held out my other hand to receive the agreed thousand dirham. This sent the grandfather into a right panic.

"No here," he said. He placed both hands behind his back to make them inaccessible. He then looked furtively around. "Police," he whispered. "If see, arrest us."

Everything he said made perfect sense. My extensive travel experience also meant I was accustomed to little boys tugging at my T-shirt to tell me where I needed to go. (This is obviously an incorrect statement – having my T-shirt pulled indicated where *they* wanted me to go.)

There is something reassuring about a grandad and grandson sharing a bond of mutual affection. I obviously realised they were working as a well-established team, but they would make five pounds from the deal, so everything seemed perfectly logical. Even when I found myself in a courtyard, with only one passageway leading to the street, I felt safe. I was more concerned about a middle-aged man loitering in the alley. He was pretending not to see us, but was obviously aware that some sort of deal was about to take place. I decided he was not a very good secret policeman. Then I had a strange thought. Going to a proper prison in Casablanca would give me a lot more 'street credibility' than a two-room jailhouse up north. Anyway, I was trapped, so had to go through with the deal and see where I ended up.

The grandad was very keen to assure me of his honesty. He counted out ten hundred-dirham notes, then counted them again, and again. Whenever I said it was fine, he just counted them more slowly. Then I was distracted by the little boy tugging at my shirt. "We good," he said.

"Very," I replied.

This seemed to satisfy the grandad, because when I looked back up the money exchange was done in an instant.

"Quick, quick," said the grandad, "hide money."

Well, that seemed very sensible. I pushed the dirham into my back pocket, which caused my friends to hurry away.

Then the gentleman loitering in the alleyway strode confidently across. He was dressed like my bank manager, which instinctively made me think he wanted a cut of the cash. Then he spoke using perfect English, like those who had attended elocution lessons. "Very foolish," he said. "Never go into hidden places with strangers. Those two would have been carrying knives and wanted all your money. Had I not been here as a witness, they would not have settled for so little. I will now escort you back to the street."

"Sorry," I said, thereby proving I was English… and a very foolish one at that!

Attentive readers might have noticed I am not over-fond of maps. They take all the mystery out of life, whereas I like to be surprised by things I did not know existed. But equally, in Africa knowing only that Toubkal lay somewhere east of Casablanca was a little too vague. Added to this, because my world atlas was back in Worcester, I was relying entirely on overworked brain cells to visualise everything. Truthfully, I only remembered that in my atlas Morocco was five inches long and lay next to Algeria. Hence, even a small error could represent quite a long geographical distance.

"Ah," you might say, "but Toubkal is 13,664 feet high – how can you fail to find it?"

Well, first there was the complication that many road signs were in a wriggly Arabic script. Also, the second language is overwhelmingly French. And thirdly, even a small error on a compass bearing can, after a hundred miles (or whatever it was), lead to adventures better suited to a period when 'gentleman' explorers had a private income, so could disappear into a jungle for years without facing poverty when finally discovered.

HEALTH AND SAFETY ALERT: Toubkal is nowhere near east of Casablanca; that is merely what my confused brain believed at the time.

Anyway, while wandering about the streets of Casablanca I happened to notice a large shop window which displayed touristy sorts of stuff. Closer inspection revealed this included a folded sheet map. *Buy me,* it seemed to say, *and I will tell you everything you need to know, so your exciting adventure can end here.*

Don't buy it, said a rogue thought inside my head, *and then you might have an exciting adventure that ends up in Timbuktu, wherever that might be.*

I struggled with this dilemma for some time before remembering I needed to be back at work in a month. So I entered the shop and asked the gentleman behind the counter for a map like the one in the window. He failed to understand, which suggested my decision to buy something written down, which I could study, had been sensible in this Arabic- and French-speaking nation. Presently the gentleman understood, and gave me the map I wanted – or did not want, depending on my mood. It only covered Morocco, so was much too detailed for my liking. However, I took comfort in the fact it was written entirely in Arabic script, thereby retaining some of its mystery. After refolding the map, I gave the gentleman a hundred-dirham note (recently acquired from the illegal currency transaction). Secretly, I was rather pleased that it meant this map was only costing me two pounds in English money. I almost said, "Keep the change", but that would sound rather arrogant.

Strangely, the gentleman shook his head. "More," he said, while pointing to the price on the cover.

I had not noticed it, but had paid him enough anyway. Trying to con me indeed! I held out my hand for the change.

"More, more," he said, while stabbing his finger at the price.

Then I took a closer look at the money, and realised that, in the last panicked moment of the currency deal, the grandad had, with the speed of a magician, changed the hundred-dirham notes to similar-looking tens. I was effectively trying to pay the gentleman twenty pence. I thought it funny, but had I been greedy and changed one hundred pounds, I might have looked less kindly on my Casablancan 'friends'.

After leaving the shop with my 'very expensive' map, I decided to take the advice of the policeman I had met earlier, and leave the city before dark. A little way beyond the outskirts, I therefore found a quiet park-up and went to bed. I considered that I was now poorer in cash terms, but far richer in knowing how things worked in this part of the world.

Chapter Thirty-One

The morning after my brief visit to Casablanca, I continued south and eventually reached a very opulent, semi-desert city. (Given that everything was in Arabic script, I cannot say which one, let alone pronounce it.) In this region, the heat was so overpowering I could do nothing but park on the outskirts and crawl underneath my wagon to lie in the shade. Only as the sun neared the horizon did I climb into my kitchen and prepare a meal. Then, without even a duvet to cover my sweaty body, I lay on the camp bed and went to sleep.

The following morning, wearing nothing but shorts, socks and sandals, I set off to explore the city. Here, while walking along a palm-lined boulevard, I became distracted by a lot of shy giggling. Turning, I noticed a huddled group of ladies, all dressed identically from head to toe in black robes. I know nothing about female clothes, so will merely say that I could only see their faces. Standing nearby was a gentleman who, unlike the ladies, wore a sleeved garment which showed his hands. I thought he might be guarding the ladies from heathen foreigners like myself. As I hurried by, he smiled in a way which portrayed a friendly nature. However, I kept walking for fear of spraying unpleasant perspiration around if I inadvertently shook my head. Then I changed my mind and stepped back to stand a discreet distance from the giggling ladies. Nervously I asked the gentleman if I was offending one of their customs by only wearing shorts which did not cover my knees.

"No," he replied. "In summer men undress also, but they think you funny because it is so cold."

I decided my African friends would struggle with the concept of sleeping in a snow hole.

South of the opulent city, the road reduced to a thin strip of tarmac with gravel shoulders on either side. I guessed the hard core allowed cars to pass but, because I never encountered another vehicle on this section of the journey, do not know the customs regarding who has right of way. The scenery was now more like Arizona, with dried-up riverbeds, plenty of cacti, and barren hills glowing red beneath a scorching sun. The few buildings which did exist were notable for having no roof. I have been told that residents prefer to sleep beneath the stars, and the bedroom floor stops any very occasional rain entering the main living area beneath.

Whether or not this scenery conveys a romantic image depends very much on what you think about camels. The proper desert sort have really big munching teeth and know exactly how to look down on a weedy white man in a way that says, *And where exactly would you like me to bite you?* Regarding the ladies of the area, I was told on two separate occasions that I could buy a pretty young wife for ten camels, or an older 'used' wife for just one animal. I supposed that however opulent the southern regions of Morocco might seem, survival was no easy matter, unless you owned a lot of camels. Two days after leaving Casablanca, I reached the desert settlement of Sidi Ifni. This is a significant camel-trading station, which made me realise that, if I ever found myself owning such a beast, my immediate response would be to give it away and, if that meant reluctantly acquiring a wife, then so be it.

Beyond Sidi Ifni the landscape became so barren that even the cacti were absent. I imagined the road had been laid by the French Foreign Legion during their glory days. Now, the desert was trying to remove all traces of this sad piece of colonial history. Sand drifts lay across the thin strip of tarmac in much the same way as snow gets swept across British roads in winter. Added to this hazard, I was generally steering around potholes and scraping axles along what was fast becoming a rough track. Then I came to a sand drift so extensive, I completely lost sight of the road. I decided that from this point on, the only sensible way to travel was on a camel – which, of course, was the method of transport the locals had developed centuries before.

Having brought my wagon to a halt, I went into the back intending to make myself some dinner. But the greenhouse effect created by the transparent roof had taken the temperature to fifty plus degrees centigrade. (The 'plus' indicates that the mercury had reached the top of the tube, turning the thermometer into a potentially explosive weapon.) Retreating from the kitchen, I once again crawled beneath the wagon and waited for the midday sun to drop a little in the sky. Possibly this is a good time to remind you that, thirteen days earlier, I had been struggling with near-freezing conditions as I walked into the Bristol Channel. Now I dreamed of reaching the Atlantic, in the hope it would make me colder.

It was mid afternoon before I felt able to go into my kitchen for a drink of water. Because this had been kept in a container, it was the same heat as a recently made cup of coffee. Then, dressed in shorts, T-shirt and boots, I set out on my mission, equipped with everything I would need. That is to say, a compass and a towel, which I would need after my swim. I started walking west. Purely as a fortuitous consequence of carrying a towel, I had something to drape over my head and shoulders – rather like Arab gentlemen who wrap their head in a scarf, to leave just their eyes peering out. Except my towel was blue, so less effective at reflecting the sun's radiation. Also, the towel was only three feet long, which meant as I walked it kept trying to fall off. In fact, now I think about it, the towel was nothing at all like an Arab's flowing length of skilfully wrapped white cotton.

So, how to describe walking across a desert in the late afternoon? The only word that springs to mind is 'masochistic'. However, because I only had to keep placing one foot in front of the other, it was the sort of masochism which allowed my mind to wander into romantic places. If, for instance, a lady happened to be walking towards me, would she not exclaim, "Oh my word, it's Lawrence of Arabia!"? Or would she look down, expecting to see my feet clad in exotic sandals, only to struggle with the image of my heavy mountaineering boots clumping towards her?

"Lawrence," I would say, to distract her from my footwear, "was born in Tremadog, where I have done much climbing. So I am the *real* Arabian explorer. The guy in the film was just pretend."

"But better-looking," said my imaginary friend. "And rich. Nor did he seem unduly frightened by camels…"

Realising I was on the losing side of this argument, I plodded on alone; my mind now preoccupied with the problem of how to stop a towel falling off my head. I wished I had brought a few safety pins.

Presently, I stopped to take a good look around. There was no sign of civilisation on any horizon; just sand. Even my wagon had gone! After a moment of panic, I realised the most likely explanation was that British Telecom vehicles were painted yellow, which renders them 'invisible' against a desert backdrop. And so I continued westward on a precise compass bearing, knowing that getting home would involve walking due east. Eventually I came to a rocky gully, at the bottom of which a narrow beach led to a vast, shimmering ocean. I undressed in the gully and placed my clothes in a sandy hollow to stop them blowing away in the breeze.

Walking into the Atlantic is far harder than you might imagine. One moment you are paddling in knee-deep water which has been warmed by the sand, while your upper body is still exposed to the sun's blistering heat. The next moment you see a great tumbling wave heading in your direction and know that running away is futile. After this baptism of deeper, very cold water, I waded on until a breaking wave crashed down on my head, causing me to somersault backwards. You can best visualise swimming in such conditions by watching clothes tumbling around in a washing machine. Sleeves and trouser legs simply flail around in the swirling water. I believe only a foolish person would venture beyond the breakers into the swell, unless roped to a surfboard.

WARNING: For a land-based mammal, all oceans look the same. For a creature emerging from the Atlantic, sand appears equally uniform. So possibly leave a trekking pole, or something, to identify the precise hollow where you left your clothes. Standing naked on a beach, scratching your head, is not a suitable activity for those who suffer from an anxiety complex.

I eventually found my clothes, but rather than using my towel to get dry – which I had already achieved by walking up and down the beach – I took it to the sea and drenched it. I then placed it over my head and shoulders. In this way I benefited from the evaporation on my return journey. Using my compass to head east, I eventually noticed the slight contrast between my oblong yellow wagon and the backdrop of sand. The temperature was now much cooler and the surrounding desert pleasant to look at. I therefore saw no reason to move my wagon, which had now acquired the air of a sophisticated residence. Hence, after watching the sunset, I went to bed. Here I slept soundly, knowing that the only passing traffic would be camels, which preferred walking on the sand anyway.

I awoke before daybreak and immediately got up to open my kitchen door. The view of the desert beneath the stars was most agreeable. I particularly liked the notion that I was essentially looking at my back garden. So, after making coffee, I sat to gaze across my vast kingdom and await the dawn; a spectacle which had remained constant since the beginning of human civilisation. Not that I was very civilised at that moment; more primeval, because the temperature was only satisfactory if I remained naked, allowing a slight breeze to drift across my skin. While this might seem a reckless way to behave, it was my garden and, if a lady chose to cross it, she would do so sitting on a camel, and I would hear its approaching hooves in good time to retreat.

While I am awaiting the sunrise, it is worth a mention that, three years earlier, I had been homeless and living in a way which might be described as rugged. So, to anyone reading this book who is having a tough time at the moment, I say, just keep on fighting – because the future can be a strange and mysterious place.

After breakfast, I turned my thoughts to the harsh reality of life. In five hours my thermometer would again be in danger of exploding. I therefore got dressed, and shortly after was driving towards the High Atlas mountains.

The term 'not far' is relative to the circumstances in which it is used. When growing up in Birmingham it often meant the end of the street. When living in Somerset, 'not far' could be considered as a twenty-minute walk along the beach. Africa, on the other hand, is quite big, so saying that Toubkal is close to the Atlantic beach where I went swimming has a slightly different meaning. The drive from my desert park-up to the foothills of the High Atlas was around two hundred miles, which took five hours to complete. (Toubkal is also a long way south of Casablanca.)

On my map, a thin line squiggled northwards from the Saharan fringe to a city which I later discovered was Marrakesh. Half an inch to the right of the squiggle was a triangle identified by the number 4,165. While this might sound a bit vague, the map's Arabic script meant I had to guess certain details. So, *assuming* 4,165 represented metres, I could translate this into proper language as 13,664 feet – which I knew to be the height of Toubkal. So, *according* to my map, I needed to follow the squiggle which went to Marrakesh. However, *according* to a multilingual sign at the start of the actual road, it was unsuitable for large vehicles. But the pretty orange groves nearby made everything appear less serious. Also, it was the only line which went anywhere near Toubkal, and so it was obviously the way I had to go.

An hour later I was still crawling upwards – only now ploughing through snow. The combination of a single track, hairpin bends, and overhanging rock often forced the outer edges of my wheels onto the verge of unguarded precipices. Then the gradient eased and a sign informed me that I had reached (after translating into proper language) seven thousand feet. It felt good – I could climb this mountain with the wagon doing half of the work.

As I rounded the crest, my smile weakened as the road began a steep descent. At about five thousand feet I pulled onto a roadside parking area. I believed Toubkal should now be somewhere obvious to my right. What I actually saw was a range of mountains which looked like the pictures I had seen of the Canadian Arctic. Across the skyline, some miles away, was an icy ridge which I estimated to be about nine thousand feet. The mountain I wanted *probably* lay somewhere beyond that.

You may remember that leaving England without my ice-climbing tools had not troubled me greatly because… well, I was going to Africa, where such things seemed unnecessary. Now, at the lowly height of around five thousand feet, I was actually standing in snow. Consulting my map, I followed the squiggly line further north. This took my gaze to a few dots which headed into an area dominated by triangles. (There were no contour lines.) I decided that whatever the future held, venturing into a world of ice was more than an evening's project. I therefore returned to my wagon and, in due course, went to bed in the hope of getting a good night's sleep.

Chapter Thirty-Two

I awoke on my now-familiar camp bed to discover cold air sneaking beneath the duvet. I found this very confusing because my brain was still busy trying to process images of the Sahara Desert. Then I remembered the snow outside my front door, which was also confusing because I was now sufficiently awake to remember I was in Africa, where everything should be hot.

After breakfast, I left the snowy park-up and continued downhill which, according to the general theory of my legs, meant Toubkal's summit was growing taller by the minute. As the descent continued, the fanciful part of my brain became convinced I had discovered a new kingdom which was below sea level, and probably the lowest point on the earth's surface. However, realistically I thought it more likely that I had merely crossed the High Atlas range and returned to a similar altitude to that of the Sahara. On the positive side, I had shifted a little to the east, so might have bypassed the mountains which had (I believed) previously blocked my approach to Toubkal.

Eventually I came to the settlement of Asni. Here I set about asking those I encountered on the street if they knew the way to Toubkal. Most replied in Arabic or French, but I persevered until a man responded with a careful nod. Hoping to get a higher level of commitment, I asked if he had ever climbed Toubkal.

He shook his head. "But I have been to the monastery," he said.

I knew those who climbed in the Himalayas always wrote about passing a monastery on the approach path, so concluded this was also the case here. "And what's after the monastery?" I asked.

"Never been," he replied, "but think the path goes up the valley to a refuge. It's to the right of the river, and Toubkal is on the other side, I think."

Success! On reflection, I asked if the river was very big.

"Not very," he said, "but flows very fast. Maybe there's a bridge somewhere, or maybe you cross it at the head of the valley."

Now everything made perfect sense. I knew from my map that I was roughly fifty kilometres due south of Marrakesh, so looking towards the High Atlas, Toubkal should, as the gentleman had said, be somewhere on the left. I then asked how I might find what my map recorded as a dotted line. He answered as if I had requested directions to a place near where he lived.

Following the man's directions, I soon came to the dotted line, which revealed itself to be a dusty dirt track. I bounced along this for ten miles without, annoyingly, gaining any significant height. Then the same dotted line turned into a footpath. Around this road head were a few basic houses, from where a mob of villagers emerged to surround my wagon. Some were begging for old clothes; others trying to sell useless trinkets, or pointing to themselves while saying, "Guide." I got out of the cab and hurried to my front door. Once inside my kitchen, there came a constant banging on the walls, with cries of anguish when I retreated even further to hide inside my windowless bedroom. Due to a presumed synchronised pushing from the outside, this rocked violently, which I found quite unnerving. I could not go anywhere, let alone think constructively about the forthcoming challenge – so basically panicked. I pushed a selection of warm clothes into my rucksack, then removed the cover from my duvet, believing this to be a substitute sleeping bag. Next I crawled into my kitchen, thereby keeping below window height. Reaching into a cupboard, I recovered half a loaf and a sealed pack of cheese, which I also placed in my rucksack. (Margarine would have been desirable, but this would have melted, so could only have been poured onto bread, making it soggy.) Then the banging stopped, to be replaced by three solid knocks on my door with what I assumed to be a lump of wood. After throwing the rucksack onto my back, I cautiously unbolted the door and peeped outside. A man, who I assumed to be the village elder, looked up at me.

"Guard truck, eighty pence a day," he said. It seemed a statement rather than a question. However, he conveyed the gravitas of a man who in Britain would occupy the post of a Lord Mayor. This was supported by the fact that everyone else had taken a few steps back.

I was now more aware of how things worked in this part of the world, so asked him to wait. I then retreated to my bedroom, where I got the money bag from inside a pair of underpants at the bottom of my rucksack. After removing three pounds, I returned the remaining cash to its hiding place and went back outside. Here I gave the man his 'protection' money. In response, he held up four fingers, these presumably indicating the number of days I had paid for.

"Truck safe," he said. "Where next town?"

I considered this a clever marketing strategy – he planting the idea in my mind that I was going somewhere next, thereby indicating that I would survive whatever was about to happen now I had agreed to let him guard my wagon. "Marrakesh," I said.

He nodded, then turned and walked away. Finally I was able to do a runner, though only as the leader of a pack of villagers who trotted by my side. The adults either wanted to carry my rucksack or offer me their services as a guide at ten pounds a day. I guess they thought I was a rich American. How this idea tallied with my old wagon, I had no idea. Finally I broke from the pack of adults, while the children sprinted ahead to ascend a patch of higher ground a little to the left of my path. "Money," they all chanted, as if in a chorus performing a school play. As I ran beneath their stage, they began throwing stones at me – some large enough to render me unconscious had they landed on my head. But there was no way I was going to stop to negotiate a safe passage. Restricted by a swaying rucksack, I ran in a way best described as clumsy. They were hampered by the need to pick up stones, which evened our handicaps. Then their high ground reached some obstacle which forced them to stop. Thirty seconds later, I was all alone and left to plod up the footpath at my own pace.

Presently the steep gorge I had entered opened out into an area of cultivated land. To my left I saw the river I had been told about. Higher up, the footpath crossed this by means of a narrow bridge, so taking me to the right bank. (The same side as Toubkal.) Here I sat by the water's edge to slurp its cool contents. As I hydrated, my brain began to function more logically. It was nonsense to think that the children on the ridge had been trying to stone me to death. Such an event would have been terrible publicity for a community well practised at dealing with 'rich' foreigners. Of course, I knew lone travellers occasionally met such an end in certain parts of the world. But my footpath was hardly a remote setting where a body could simply be stripped of all assets and dumped into a ravine, never to be discovered. On reflection, I realised all the stones thrown by the children had landed ahead of me; their presumed purpose merely telling me to stop. All they wanted were a few coins. I feel a wise traveller would have kept some of these in a pocket to scatter around. The children would then have descended to fight over the money between themselves, leaving the traveller to continue their journey in peace. Now I felt terribly guilty that I had not left them a few pennies to boost their families' income. But to me, throwing small change to children seemed a bit Victorian. However, those who want things to be nice and gentle should not arrive at a remote settlement in a wagon. In fact, the more I pondered the dilemma, the more I realised it was all my fault.

Continuing my journey beyond the bridge involved plodding slowly up a zigzag path. This was quite pleasant due to the romantic nature of the nearby terraced fields. Eventually the gradient of the hillside eased, allowing the path to take a direct line up to the east. In due course, I came to another bridge that recrossed the river – sadly placing me on the opposite side to Toubkal. But I had a long way to go and, having been told this would happen, was not unduly concerned. Shortly after crossing the second bridge, I came to the monastery, so knew I was still heading in the right direction. As I walked by, a man hurried across and tried to sell me a long white cotton scarf for two pounds. When I politely replied that I was fine, he wrapped it expertly around his head to leave just his eyes peeping out.

"I beg," he said, while throwing his hands together in prayer.

Being dressed like a mummy while praying for divine intervention made him look really scary, so I hurried away before he could draw me into a God-related conversation. Only when well clear of the 'danger' did I ponder why he had wanted to sell me twenty feet of cloth for so little money. But he had seemed genuinely concerned by my refusal to buy it.

Beyond the monastery, the path zigzagged up a steep hillside until it disappeared beneath a snowfield. Here I stood awhile to ponder the wisdom of my rushed departure from the wagon. In the panic I had forgotten my compass, which meant I did not know my direction, so looking at the sun, did not tell me the time. However, at least it represented consistent behaviour because I had also forgotten my torch, whistle, first aid kit... well, pretty much everything except a duvet cover, bread, and cheese.

According to my logic, if I remained in the main valley with the watercourse to my left, I could not really get lost. This was helped by being hemmed in by high mountains on both sides. These were covered in snow and ice, which made them appear very grand. I guessed the mountain on my left was Toubkal, because it was the highest I could see. Also, it occasionally sent up wisps of snow, which seemed to emphasise the rarefied air surrounding its summit.

Plodding through the melting snow made for a strenuous afternoon's work. But I battled on until it started to get dark. Well, at least I now knew the time. Given that it was early February, I estimated this to be six o'clock. Eventually I stopped to consider my options. Walking ten miles with seven thousand feet of ascent (a wild guess) would not be that arduous, if it was possible to dig a snow hole at the end of the journey and go to sleep. However, both ascending and retreating from such an altitude without a break was not something I had attempted before. On the other hand, without a snow shovel I could not even build a basic shelter, which, in any event, was likely to be cold when only using a duvet cover for a sleeping bag. And I was soaking wet, both from perspiration and from the snow clinging to my trousers. I decided to continue, hoping to find the refuge before the light faded completely… which was now quite important.

I struggled upwards until the first stars began to appear in a darkening blue sky. Then I happened to look into the valley on my left, where I saw yet another bridge crossing the river. A set of footprints came from this direction, crossed my intended path, then continued towards a slightly raised mound of the snowfield on my right. Could this be important? Out of curiosity, I followed the prints. Beyond the raised snowfield I discovered a chasm; mostly a crater in the snow, but with a small section of a man-made wall breaking the surface on its left side. In the middle was a door. I descended, pushed it open, and found myself looking into a room. Here, six men were sitting around a large wooden table, eating their supper. They seemed surprised to see me.

"Hello," I said, thereby explaining that I was English.

One of the group greeted me in English, while the other five looked on, apparently bemused. The English speaker then invited me to share their meal. I knew it was an Islamic custom to offer guests, whoever they might be, their food. Fortunately, I was also aware that many cultures believed cutlery to be a dirty Western practice. This is because it can be incorrectly cleaned, then left in a drawer to fester, with insects crawling all over it. Conversely, you know where your hands have been and when they were last washed. I was therefore not surprised to see all six men feeding from a communal bowl of meat curry, using their hands and bread. I politely declined their offer, using the excuse of being a strict vegetarian. Anyway, what I really needed was salt because, even though my body was hydrated from drinking river water, my ascent had probably extracted eight litres of sweat. And while salt deficiency is not *immediately* fatal, it can cause severe leg cramps during the night, and possibly dizzy spells when you try to stand up to reduce the pain. I dislike the taste of salt so got it over with in one go. After putting a palmful into a glass of water, I gulped it down before my mouth could reject it. The next bit was inevitable. My body demanded more water – vast quantities of it. But that was a good thing.

I am never shy about asking for directions, so after the group had eaten I asked the English speaker the way to Toubkal. He replied that reaching the summit was a straightforward trek. He then explained that few people ventured into these mountains during the winter, so taking shelter in the refuge for the night did not require any payment. He then went on to say that in summer the area was very busy with tourists, and I got the impression that the refuge turned into a moneymaking operation. As part of the service, guests could come up the footpath riding mules, and descend on hired BMX bikes. Failure to reach Toubkal's summit generally only happened for two reasons. Firstly, because it was too much like hard work for those who had been expecting a nice walk. Secondly, because altitude sickness caused some trekkers to panic after they had merely fainted. For this group, I advise returning to the refuge to spend a day resting, then starting again – you will most probably be fine.

Of the current six men in the refuge, two were rugged, Sherpa-like fellows, one of whom had learnt to speak English – probably to annoy the French. Two were extreme skiers, who insisted on exclusively speaking French, possibly to annoy Arabic speakers. The last pair, a climber and his guide, spoke a foreign tongue only they were able to understand. I imagined the refuge was similar to the early alpine huts which had existed before cable cars and helicopters brought mass tourism to isolated locations. I feared this basic hut would soon suffer the same fate and be replaced by a concrete-and-plastic monstrosity – as demanded by rich tourists, who expected five-star hotel service wherever they 'landed'. This refuge looked lived in. While I observed all of this, the English speaker finished his account of the area by telling me that the previous week a blizzard had dumped fifteen feet of snow into the valley. I thought this most surprising for Africa.

That night, as I lay in bed, I got a few twinges of leg cramp, but had consumed enough salt to stop them by pushing my feet onto the wooden plank at the end of the bunk. A far greater problem was my bladder, which objected to storing the six pints of water I had drunk before bedtime. The only toilet was the bare mountainside where, in summer, it would have been possible to do ablutions hiding behind some boulder, hopefully a reasonable distance from the door. But as soon as I went outside, a blast of icy air caused me to gasp in shock. My ears immediately sent my brain a frostbite alert. Anyone who thought they could survive out there for a night in a duvet cover must be completely insane. Even walking up the ramp to take a pee on the exposed snowfield could be considered as a mad British eccentricity.

The English-speaking Sherpa seemed to carry some authority as an unofficial hut guardian. In any event, the next morning he unlocked a large cupboard and recovered a pair of crampons, which he hired me for two pounds. After leaving the refuge, I strapped these to my boots and set out to climb a mountain which, two weeks earlier, I had only known as a dot on my world atlas.

In theory, altitude sickness only becomes an issue above ten thousand feet. So, I reasoned, it should be possible for me to sneak up an extra 3,665 feet before my body went into collapse. Sadly, the combination of heat (dehydration) and reduced oxygen both further decrease the ability to stay upright. In addition, I had not slept the previous night due to the need to keep going outside to take a pee. But I had eaten a really nice cheese sandwich for breakfast, so knew I would be fine.

After crossing the bridge, I headed east up a snow slope which narrowed between two obvious ridges. The surface was icy and sufficiently steep to make it feel precarious to balance without the aid of an axe (or trekking pole). However, after five hundred feet the gradient eased, making my ascent more of a walk than a climb.

Also, the rocky walls on either side meant there were no route-finding difficulties. I now realised that reaching the summit was just a formality.

At the top of the snowfield there was a headwall of perhaps one hundred feet. This would go easily at Grade I/II but, having climbed from sea level to twelve thousand feet in less than twenty-four hours, I lacked the enthusiasm for adding unnecessary difficulty. A snow ramp to my right led to the summit ridge, and this I climbed, getting more lethargic with each step. The summit ridge ascended to my left and, for a fit, acclimatised person, it would have been nothing more than a walk. But we have already established that this did not apply to me. I was soon on hands and knees, crawling doggedly upwards with my eyes focused entirely on the summit. Initially it did not seem to be getting any closer, but eventually I hauled myself onto a few projecting summit rocks with a graceful belly flop. As I glanced ahead in celebration, I became rather cross to discover the ridge continued upwards to a previously hidden summit in the distance. I realised that it was too far to crawl. So, overheating terribly beneath the baking sun and close to passing out, I stood up and tottered along the thin, melting snow ridge which led to the second summit. On reaching this, I shuffled my feet around to do a full 360-degree scan of the horizon. Snow-covered mountains stretched away in all directions, yet all summits were significantly lower than my present position. I had made it, and all of North Africa lay beneath my feet.

While ascending, the sun had been on my back so, even looking down, my face had been partially protected from its harmful rays by my shadow. But turning around to descend made me realise what it was like for a slice of white bread under a hot grill. My skin was turning to 'toast'. And while crawling uphill can be considered a lazy form of climbing, slithering down head first is quite likely to produce a dangerous somersault. Fortunately, the slow pace of my ascent had given my body time to acclimatise, so, after a few hundred feet of staggering descent, the danger of fainting passed. Now I could concentrate on the problem of the blistering radiation; some coming directly from the sun, the rest indirectly reflected up from the snow. I survived these rays by wrapping my anorak around my head, leaving just a small gap for my eyes to peek out. To reduce the risk of snow blindness, I held a handkerchief over this gap, and only occasionally looked up from my feet to make sure I was heading in the right direction. Truthfully, what I really needed was a twenty-foot length of white cotton scarf, together with extra-dark sunglasses.

By the time I returned to the refuge, my face was covered in blisters and scabs, mixed with salt and sweat. My lips were even worse, making it impossible to drink or eat. With nothing more to be done, and realising that I must cross the lower snowfield before sunrise, I simply went to bed. On the positive side, I was so dehydrated that I rested for the first part of the night without needing to take a pee.

After lying awake in the bunk for many hours, I got up, dressed quickly, and left the refuge to begin the long plod back to my wagon in the dark. Sometimes the icy crust held my weight; other times it gave way to leave me waist-deep in powder snow. On one occasion I ended up in the river, with a load of snow cascading onto my head. I am a bit vague as to how this happened, but strongly suspect I was so tired that I had drifted into a sleepwalk. Thus I found myself being carried downhill like a canoe, momentarily confused about what was happening. On passing a snow cliff I gave it a good punch, which effectively turned my left arm into a mooring line. As the current swirled me inwards I hit the snow again, this time with a right hook. The otherwise powdery structure had an ice-crystal bonding quality which allowed me to box my way back up to safety.

I now have a confession to make. The canoe image is a slight overdramatisation of what actually happened. But I used it only as an analogy to emphasise the need for positive thinking; in this case that going downhill in the right direction, without using my wasted leg muscles, was surely a wondrous miracle to behold! The fact it did not take me all the way to the monastery did not alter the general principle that it had aided my descent, if only by a little. Also on the positive side, I was washing away the salty sweat which had been causing my face to radiate pain. Added to this, I had become less smelly. And so, as I stood on the snow near the river, cascading water from my clothes, I realised it was clearly a case of win-win-win!

Sunrise happened beneath the range of mountains behind my back, so all I saw of daybreak were the stars fading into a clear blue sky. Then the westerly summits ahead of me became dazzling white beacons. As the sun rose higher, I could see the front edge of the shadow descending the opposite hill. It was now a race: I had to increase my speed to get off this snowfield and reach a non-reflective surface before the sun broke the horizon. My rapid descent brought my first steps onto stones and scrub just a few minutes before the shadow finally swept beneath my feet at roughly ten miles per hour. I had now descended about ten thousand feet from Toubkal's summit, so had more protective atmosphere between me and the sun. And I would soon be back at my wagon, resting in my kitchen while delicately sipping a cup of cold water. Or at least, that was what I expected to happen…

As I approached the settlement, many of the locals hurried to surround me, as if to welcome me back. By the time I reached my front door, three men were waiting outside. Then the village elder wandered across, presumably to sell me something I did not need. But all he said was, "Marrakesh, go soon." Then he turned away without even haggling for more protection money.

After I had entered my kitchen, I sat down and pondered why there were so many people queuing outside. Why were they looking at me? If I closed the door, it would become unbearably hot inside. I decided the only thing to do was obey the village elder, leave now, and drive away to somewhere I could be alone. But as soon as I got down from my kitchen, three of the queue climbed inside and sat down in what had once been a British Telecom truck canteen.

"Marrakesh, please," said one politely.

"Asni, please," said another.

From this, I understood that these people considered me a bus driver. Had I not felt so lousy, I would have considered this a trivial matter. But in any event, it was no use arguing, because a fourth man had now climbed into my kitchen and sat on the floor. He was obviously a third-class passenger, though still very polite. "Thank you," he said.

Logically, this isolated settlement did not get a bus service, so it was down to 'rich' foreigners like me to do the honours. Resigned to my fate, I opened the passenger door to my cab, and let the two remaining passengers board the 'first-class' compartment.

As things turned out, with a single exception of a zigzag to an out-of-the-way settlement, it was sort of on my way home. I just wished my new career as a bus driver had not begun while my face was burning with pain and oozing pus. It was quite hard to concentrate on the needs of my passengers when I was distracted by the possibility I could be scarred for life. Surprisingly, a few days later when my facial scabs and some flakes of dry skin started to fall off, the metamorphosis revealed a thin layer of 'baby skin'. It felt delicate and youthful. Considering this expedition had been inspired by a midlife crisis, it seemed a strange turn of events.

While driving along the approach road to the port, a man stepped in front of me, forcing me to halt. He was very well dressed and carrying an official-looking briefcase. After opening my driver's door, he spoke to me in perfect English. "Get you to Spain for eighty pounds," he said, presumably knowing an English-registered wagon would only be heading there.

"Er…" I replied.

"Customs very bad men," he said. "If they want to find drugs in your lorry, they will do so. If I am in the passenger seat, they will not."

By this stage, I couldn't be bothered with any more complications. "I'll pay you on board ship," I said.

He nodded, so I let him into the cab. The next bit was truly magical. My wagon became invisible! I drove directly through all the checkpoints in the manner of a Prime Minister going to an important diplomatic meeting. I did not need to stop or even buy a ticket. Within five minutes of my mystery passenger getting into the cab, I was bringing my wagon to a halt in a ship's hold. Here, I gave my guide eighty pounds. He nodded his appreciation, then left, presumably to walk back to select his next customer. On reflection, all of the men who had failed to see my invisible wagon appeared to be better fed than most of the local population. Once up on deck, how I had boarded the ship without a ticket became irrelevant. And even if the ferry company did (unofficially) employ burly conductors to check, there was little they could do about non-compliance without telling the captain to turn the ship around.

I found cruising up the Med through the Strait of Gibraltar a most agreeable experience. As the shimmering water slid gracefully by, my panic at passing the 'forty' age sign had been completely forgotten. Ahead, all I saw was an open highway, which was certain to lead to even more exciting places.

Chapter Thirty-Three

My journey back to England was uneventful, though I did discover it was possible to catch a ferry at Bilbao on the northern coast of Spain and dock in Portsmouth thirty-six hours later. In addition to reducing anxiety for tollophobia sufferers, it offers a dream cruise with an overnight cabin. For a single person travelling off-peak (in 1993), it was only slightly more expensive than driving through France, then taking a ferry across the English Channel.

On returning to Worcester, I parked in Grandstand Road, which runs between a racecourse and the River Severn. From here, the quay for the passenger boats where I worked was a fifty-yard walk. So, on my first day back, I went to see how my colleagues were doing. I was needed immediately, and it was late before I returned to my wagon. Quite suddenly it seemed silly to return to my houseboat for the night. After all, I had been living in my wagon for the past five weeks, so climbing into the box at the back and going to sleep on the camp bed now seemed entirely natural.

The following morning I opened my front door and looked across the racecourse, which I thought a most pleasant way to begin the day. A few hundred yards to my left, the road came to an end at the turnstiles, so effectively I was parked in a rather sophisticated cul-de-sac. Slightly to my right, a sweeping curve of Victorian archways carried a railway line to the far side of the river. A strange mixture of town and country, which seemed an excellent place to live. So, thinking logically, I never slept on my boat again, and Grandstand Road became my new home.

It took three years for me to acknowledge that my houseboat was merely a part of my youth which had now become redundant – or, more truthfully, been abandoned. Clearly, its unusual characteristics meant it was not something I could sell or even give away. It was simply twenty tons of stuff waiting to sink. But this time I faced the truth, and got a company to tow it away for demolition in their quayside yard. It cost six hundred pounds, but it meant the expensive part of my life was over, because I was now, very sensibly, living in a wagon with pleasant views across a racecourse. So going to Africa did change my life, though not in a way I had foreseen.

Having committed myself to the wagon, I got a garage to weld a two-foot overhanging extension to the rear. This allowed me to build a cosy brick fireplace with a tiled hearth extending back into the original box. Also, the extra space meant I had room to install a proper bed. So my life of domestic bliss finally arrived when I was forty-three. A bit later than I had hoped, but it coincided nicely with a good career. More importantly, I had become totally immune to falling in love. This immunity was induced by a very special lady, who increasingly came to occupy all of my relevant brain cells; thereby excluding other romantic aspirations. The difference now, as opposed to any unrealistic dreams of my foolish youth, was that I accepted this female would always be irrelevant to anything which might actually happen to me in the real world.

The lady I am talking about is my old potholing partner. I remember with great affection the first time she had to climb an underground wall of slippery rock. The beam of her head torch turned towards mine and her gentle voice floated through the darkness. "I can't do it," it said. But she trusted me, so agreed to give it a try, regardless of her instincts. I followed her up, saying reassuring words while holding her wellingtons firm against the muddy ledges. She was safe, I was happy, and between us the potholing challenge was successfully completed…

And now, many years later, she occupies my mind as a romantic but distant heroine – almost as if she were a character in a book.

While talking about heroines, I would like to reintroduce the mega-rock star Alison Hargreaves, who once smiled at me from the pages of a climbing magazine. After this spectacular introduction, her life was to have many similarities to my own: she dropped out of school to focus on her climbing and so, like me, failed her A levels, or never took them in the first place. She then spent a few years dreaming about becoming a professional mountaineer but, also like me, domestic stuff kept getting in the way. She became homeless, struggled to avoid bankruptcy, and had all sorts of emotional issues.

Her big break came when she solo-climbed the north-west face of the Eiger in her mid twenties, while seven months pregnant. Purists argue that this is a *little* easier than the true north face, but I doubt an ordinary mortal could tell the difference as they plunged thousands of feet to their death. And in any event, Alison next went on to successfully climb the Eiger's north face over a five-day period, as part of a roped team. As a man I find her account of long nights spent sitting on narrow ice-covered ledges while a baby kicked about inside her tummy mind-boggling. But climbing was just something she did, and having babies was part of being a married lady. Two months later, Alison was climbing in Derbyshire when her labour pains began. After ensuring that her partner was safe, she walked to a distant telephone box to call for an ambulance. Twelve hours later she gave birth to her healthy son, Tom. After that her career was put on hold for him and, two years later, the arrival of her daughter, Kate.

At the age of thirty-three, Alison made a second determined effort to become a professional climber. This stage of her life was launched with a solo ascent of Mount Everest, without oxygen or technical support, except for the occasional kindness of strangers. After Everest, she signed a book deal with a substantial advance. So, while she had achieved what I had once dreamed of doing, my own climbing ability had declined, and my ambition to become a published writer seemed to be going nowhere.

Having explained some of Alison's story, I would like to tell you more about Eric Jones, who, you may remember, first climbed Wyddfa after his Sunday school. Eric rose to fame through his natural ability and determination, and this resulted in him being invited to join many Himalayan expeditions. One of his Everest adventures coincided with Alison's successful ascent. Eric was very upset to see her tiny tent and basic provisions at an advanced camp. (She had to carry all of her own equipment for it to be a solo project.) Eric, who was at the same base camp as part of another team, thought that her apparently carefree life was now little more than a media fabrication. Fate had dictated that Alison was now the sole breadwinner for her two dependent children. Climbing had become a job, and the sponsors who had paid thousands of pounds for her expeditions expected results. For her, retreating from excessively dangerous situations was not an option, compared to commercial failure and being unable to feed her family.

I know exactly where I was on the 15th August 1995: sitting in my usual launderette, lazily watching a washing machine tumbling my soggy clothes back and forth. I then got up and went to the nearest newsagent to buy a paper. And there it was – a headline tucked on an inside page: 'Alison Hargreaves, dead.' The shock hit me so hard I simply wandered around the local streets in a daze. I did not return to the launderette until late in the afternoon. Alison was dead, but there were no real details because it had happened on a remote and notorious peak called K2 in the Karakoram range in Pakistan. It seemed to me that the paper was more interested in expressing moral outrage that a mother had 'abandoned' her children.

No one knows how Alison actually died, but after setting out on her lonely solo ascent, she was last spotted through binoculars on the summit. We can only assume the violent storm which engulfed the mountain a few hours later simply lifted her from the knife-edge ridge to which she clung while traversing during her descent. In the years before Alison's ascent, only five exceptional ladies had stood on the top of K2. Three had died on the way down. Climbing at that professional level has a very high death potential.

I only learnt the inside story of Alison's death when I was in my sixties. With the benefit of such hindsight I thought, *I am glad I failed in my attempt to become a proper mountaineer – and because of that, survive to muse over my own, lesser achievements in the climbing world.* Then I thought about Alison traversing the Crib Goch ridge, aged eight. I could imagine her as a child, full of wonder as she 'skipped' across the tiny footholds wearing her wellingtons. Who, on seeing such a cute infant, could have predicted how her life would develop… until it ended on a ridge in Pakistan?

Chapter Thirty-Four

It's 1998 and I'm sitting on a really posh, king-sized bed; the sort manufactured to satisfy those who like sinking into warmth and comfort. It is screwed to the floor of what had once been the workshop of my wagon. The multi-occupancy bed is nothing to do with finding a mate. The true reason for the luxurious sleeping arrangement is that, a few years earlier, I had used my wagon to clear a house of all its furniture and transported it to a boat on which the family had decided to live. But their deck hatches were too small to take the bed, so they gave it to me in lieu of payment for my removal service.

Anyway, I am sitting on the bed with a world atlas on my lap, trying to locate the highest mountains in Norway, Sweden and Finland. Next I studied my car atlas, which had six pages at the back covering Europe – very little detail, but it gave me a basic idea of how the Scandinavian Three Peaks might be reached using the road network. After all of this strategic planning, I left my front door, walked around to the cab, and drove to the port of Harwich. From there a ferry took me to the Hook of Holland.

While this proposed adventure might sound rather ordinary, there was a slight complication which, being impossible to resolve, I had been forced to overlook. It concerns the seasonal nature of my employment, which meant I had not been able to leave Worcester until early October. So the Arctic section of my travels would take place in… well, I did not know exactly, because my car atlas did not explain about the weather. However, I guessed late October in the Arctic was similar to Ben Nevis in January. I could cope with minus twenty degrees centigrade, though was slightly concerned about the limited daylight. I knew the North Pole remained in darkness for six months of the year, but had no idea how this applied to the top of Scandinavia. Naturally I had bought twenty torch batteries, which would allow me to climb the mountains by torchlight if necessary, but this was very much a case of hoping for the best while preparing for the worst.

After leaving the Hook of Holland, I drove north until I noticed a signpost for Amsterdam. Here, curiosity caused me to follow the 'arrow' and, after a short journey, I parked on the outskirts of the city. From there I walked to the centre, where something quite extraordinary happened. I encountered a lady who wanted to be my friend! *Why is she sitting in a shop window, wearing so few clothes, and waving at me while pointing to a side door?* I thought. Confused, I hurried away at such speed I almost collided with another lady, who also wanted to be my friend. Modesty prevents me from saying just how many ladies appeared to like me, beyond that I needed to scurry in a zigzag along the pavement to avoid them.

Presently, I wandered into a commercial area of the city, where I found a coffee shop which looked rather bohemian. Not that I knew what 'bohemian' actually meant, but instinct told me it was something to do with being modern and posh. Anyway, I ventured inside and found a quiet table to drink a very expensive cup of coffee. It had arrived with a single tiny biscuit on the saucer. Bohemians, I decided, liked to be very thin.

While sipping my coffee, I tried philosophising on the great mysteries of life. Previously it had taken many months to get a lady to like me, and even then a friendship only developed after I had convinced her I was 'safe' (i.e. did not believe in sex before Ben Nevis). Yet in Amsterdam, while walking along a single street it seemed I had magically transformed into a handsome hunk for about ten minutes. On reflection, I decided the ability to get a girlfriend so easily caused too many distractions. And surely being a magnet for so many projecting breasts could only result in a state of confused unhappiness. Life, I realised, is a lot more straightforward when all ladies completely ignore you.

After leaving Amsterdam, I drove northwards on toll-free roads. Even the twenty-mile causeway which crosses the 'ocean' to reach northern Holland was free. It was the same through Denmark, where I boarded another ferry in Copenhagen which took me to Oslo, the capital of Norway.

I now want to tell you about my bold assumption that Norwegians take great exception to foreigners climbing their highest mountain. This theory comes from the fact some maps claim it to be Galdhøpiggen; others Glittertind. My road map only mentions Glittertind, and gives no name to a lower summit placed half an inch (about thirty miles) to the left. However, my world atlas showed that Glittertind was eighteen metres higher than Galdhøpiggen. If all this leaves you confused, do not worry; it's just the Norwegian way of getting foreigners to climb the wrong mountain.

In Norway's defence, we must remember that England employs the same defensive strategy. I imagined a happy, bouncing Norwegian walking down the track to Wasdale Head. "I have just climbed the highest mountain in England," he proudly tells the first person he meets.

"Scafell?" questions the smug stranger.

The Norwegian nods.

"Then you have climbed England's second highest mountain. I think this very funny."

However, when it came to Norway I had now acquired the wisdom to avoid getting caught out by such basic, deceitful tricks. On reaching the area where the higher mountains might be found, I stopped at a tourist shop which sold postcards. I looked at all those on display. There were many featuring Galdhøpiggen, but not one depicted Glittertind. Leaving nothing to chance, I showed the lady behind the counter my chosen card and asked if this was their highest mountain.

"Yes," she replied.

For all I knew, she was part of the conspiracy to send climbers to the wrong mountain. "In England," I said, "people think Glittertind is the highest."

She was probably surprised to discover this to be a topic of conversation in a country so far away. She shook her head. "It used to be Glittertind," she said, "but now it is Galdhøpiggen." Then she shrugged in a way to suggest my purchase of a ten-pence postcard did not entitle me to a prolonged conversation.

Back in my wagon, I decided to visualise the correct highest mountain as a 'Gladly Hopping Pigeon'. So I can claim, with some authority, that at 8,102 feet it *is* Norway's highest peak. It is situated in the south of the country, within reasonable commuting distance of Oslo. My first challenge was to find the said mountain, which was not signposted from the main road north. In due course, my compass suggested I needed to do an emergency stop and take a sharp left turn at a T-junction. But my wagon only came to a gentle halt a few yards after passing the turning, which meant there was something slightly wrong with the brakes. I estimated they were still 80% effective, so believed it was possible to drive safely by keeping my speed below thirty miles per hour, rather than my normal cruising speed of forty miles per hour.

Arriving in the general region of the Gladly Hopping Pigeon, I discovered the road I wanted had both a weight and a width restriction, meaning my wagon had to stay on the main E55 highway. This passed within a few miles of Gladly Hopping Pigeon's summit. Then, a little further along the highway, I noticed a toll road running off to the left. This was the direction I needed to take; though my tollophobia obviously prevented it. So I parked on a nearby patch of gravel, knowing that the rest of my journey had to be on foot. (Free for pedestrians.)

After a good night's sleep, I loaded my rucksack for a two-day adventure, then walked up the toll road until I came to a bridge across a river. Having reached the far bank, I began to circumnavigate the lower slopes of a mountain to my right. This kept me on mossy ground, rather than fighting unpleasant-looking vegetation higher up. Eventually I came to a stream, across which I 'boulder-hopped' to reach a slight path on its far side. When this ascended into low cloud I checked my compass, which told me I should be heading slightly left. But the ground in that direction looked better suited to animals with hooves, so I followed the path to the right just to see where I ended up. This happened to be a gorge on my right, which soon curved back around to the left – the direction I needed. On both sides of the gorge, cliffs disappeared into a ceiling of cloud, but I had no particular need to climb them. More useful was a wall of ice which stretched between these cliffs. This obviously represented the lower edge of a glacier. After climbing the ice wall, the continuing ascent proved a most pleasing way to spend an afternoon. There were ice-climbing problems to amuse and, if I so wished, crevasses to leap. But I could avoid all of these by taking a zigzag walk uphill. Truthfully, '*I wandered lonely as a cloud*' and toyed with various problems as the fancy took me, but this made me lose track of time. So it also became an enjoyable way to spend an evening.

At the top of the glacier I turned left to scramble up thirty feet of rock and scree to reach a narrow ridge. Looking ahead, I could see nothing but freezing fog, which meant I had gained a lot of height. Whatever lay below was irrelevant, unless I wanted to use it for descent. The ridge to my right continued upwards, where it quickly vanished into cloud. But it was obviously the direction I needed to go. I thought it might even take me directly up to the Gladly Hopping Pigeon summit itself.

We now come to one of those embarrassing incidents which sneak up on me occasionally. After some entertaining climbing on the crest of the ridge, I was forced onto the rock face on my left. I was now a bit cold and particularly remember my freezing fingers clinging to a knobble of rock, while my crampons tried to maintain scratching placements on steeply sloping ice. I found it a surreal experience because the cloud had changed to drifting fog, which reduced visibility to about ten feet. I had no idea what the drop below me was like, and the near-vertical wall to which I was clinging felt very precarious. In such an exposed situation, and with fifteen hours of darkness looming, my situation was fairly serious. It was almost as if the mountain was telling me to go away.

"Okay," I grumbled reluctantly, "but I'll be back."

By the time I had retreated from the ridge, it was dark. My descent of the glacier therefore required great care, because the torchlight reflecting from the fog made crevasses far more difficult to locate. Then my even later retreat down the hillside gave me time to have a good think about things. I realised a repeat attempt on the Gladly Hopping Pigeon would introduce a significant delay into my schedule. And that was before I factored in my wagon's new top speed of thirty miles per hour. The remaining two summits in Sweden and Finland, both of which were a long way above the Arctic Circle, would effectively be in winter conditions and continuous darkness. So, I decided to head back to Britain the following day – and that is where things started to go wrong…

Within ten miles of leaving my park-up, the wagon's brakes had deteriorated to a highly dangerous level. When I pulled onto a remote garage forecourt and requested assistance with spanners and things, the mechanic looked at my wagon, then shook his head.

"Parts will be impossible to get," he said.

True. Even in England the vehicle would be considered of pensionable age. In modern Norway it was likely to be regarded as a museum exhibit. In any event, the mechanic did not want it on his forecourt. My only focus in life then became getting my wagon back to Grandstand Road in Worcester – over one thousand miles away.

I left the garage in the direction of the nearest seaport. Everything was uphill, so braking became less of an issue. Only when the road levelled out on the crest of a high pass did I need to slow to a walking pace to approach whatever lay ahead. But nothing happened. I stamped on the brake pedal. From beneath the chassis came a horrendous clunking noise, then the screeching of tyres. I managed to skid off the tarmac onto a patch of gravel to the right of the road. Here I juddered onwards until the engine stalled and I stopped. After some experimenting, it became apparent the rear wheel on my driver's side was locked solid. This greatly upset me. Indeed, that night I went to bed feeling quite depressed.

The following morning, I emerged from my front door to discover fate had brought me to a most pleasant lay-by with pretty views across a vast mountainous landscape. Indeed, it seemed likely that I had stopped at an observation point where summer tourists gathered to gaze across the valleys which lay far below. This idea was backed up by a precipitous drop into a gorge, and the fact that, without mountaineering skills, the only way to reach this place was by the zigzag road cut into rock by which I had arrived; the way ahead being equally steep, but going downwards. Less pleasing to the eye were the snow poles placed along roadside verges so the ploughs knew where to go. These particular poles were fifteen feet high and, because my residence was on a lay-by, I was on the wrong side of them. In a month's time it seemed likely that my home would be nothing but a slight dome in the snow, or it might simply disappear completely until the spring.

After breakfast, I left my home and began walking down the hill in search of a garage with a sympathetic mechanic. However, the road had no buildings of any description. So, after ten miles or so, I turned around to trudge back up.

That night I lay in bed to contemplate my misfortune. In addition to the practical details, my 'house' held an awful lot of emotional memories. Like the time I was in Africa, gazing out of my front door to watch a sunrise over the Sahara. I had even used my future home to provide a bus service to Marrakesh. And that thought held two key words: 'future home'. In Africa, the wagon had essentially been a mobile workshop with a camp bed screwed to the floor. Back then, I had considered home to be a houseboat, where nearly all of my possessions remained. At that stage, if the worst happened I could have just given the wagon away, jumped on a bus, and eventually been reunited with my living room. But now my houseboat had gone, and home was here: on a deserted mountain pass, miles from anywhere. If I returned to Worcester on a bus now, my new residence would be an open-sided railway arch near Grandstand Road. Eventually I decided that becoming homeless once, after my houseboat sank, could be considered a misfortune. To abandon this replacement house in Norway suggested a hint of carelessness.

So the following day, after breakfast, I took my office chair to the roadside and sat to ponder my place in the world. After about an hour, I heard a car approaching. It was heading in the direction I needed, so I leapt up to wave my arms around in a way to indicate panic. Given this, I think it lucky the driver did not simply speed by. Anyway, after telling him of my misfortune, he said he was turning off thirty-five kilometres down the road. Then he felt remorse.

"But it's not inconvenient to take you all the way to the next garage," he added.

This unspecified distance troubled me, but I had little choice other than to get in the car and see where I ended up. Not wishing to sit in silence for however many hours the journey was going to take, I remarked upon his ability to speak perfect English. In response he explained that it was taught as a second language in all Scandinavian schools.

"Were it not for this," he added, "we would have to learn Swedish, Finnish and Danish. Germany and the Netherlands also have English as a second language, but there it is only normally used for cross-border communication. Though many of us like watching American films."

"Bet that upsets the French," I said. "I expect they just shout louder and wave their arms about rather a lot."

"A little like you as you leapt up from your chair, I think. But you are two days' walk from the nearest town, so most drivers would have stopped had you simply put up your thumb."

Two days of walking, I thought. *It's nearly November, so I wonder how much of that would have been in darkness?*

After forty miles, my saviour pulled onto a forecourt which had both petrol pumps and wide workshop doors. A mechanic came out to greet me, and when I explained my situation he responded with a casual nod. I got the impression that he was accustomed to doing breakdown recovery from 'the pass'. Indeed, his rescue truck turned out to be the most monstrous thing I had ever seen. But I suppose pulling articulated lorries up very steep hills needs an engine the size of a killer whale. (Slight exaggeration, but that's the image it gave.) I thanked the car driver, then waved as he drove away.

My ride back into the mountains was very manly. The truck was so wide it totally dominated the road. But, as implied earlier, the pass saw about one vehicle every hour, so oncoming traffic was unlikely to be an issue. The negative side of this manly activity was that I calculated each mile travelled was costing me the equivalent of two hours' pay. But my house needed to be rescued, so whether my actions were logical or not was irrelevant. The sentimental attachment our shared memories had generated was far more important.

On reaching the lay-by, the breakdown truck treated my home as a toy. Within five minutes its back end was hanging from the crane; the front wheels locked in place. Then we were off, returning to the garage about an hour later. Here, the owner came out to look at my house, then shook his head. However, it was now on his forecourt and so, to a certain extent, also his problem.

For this trip I had brought the cash needed to deal with all expected outcomes. That is to say, seven hundred pounds. In addition, for emergencies I had fixed an envelope containing five hundred pounds beneath my bed. However, after I had paid six hundred pounds for the recovery, I was clearly facing financial embarrassment. This was exacerbated when the mechanic dismantled the back-wheel assembly and reported his findings to the owner. Apparently the brake drum and associated fixings had completely disintegrated.

"We will never get the parts," said the owner. "Not in Norway."

Such a statement would never have been made in Africa, I thought. Indeed, the garden-hose repair the 'proper' mechanic had inserted into the fuel system was still in place and working perfectly. An African mechanic would never have shaken his head on seeing my wagon, but merely said something like "I've just dismantled an old lawnmower, so have just the part to sort it." But in Norway they do things differently.

I explained about it being my home, but the garage owner failed to grasp the concept. I think it was because Norwegians have such a high standard of living that even driving a five-year-old motorhome would be considered a symbol of poverty. However, my house was on his garage forecourt so, in my view, the term 'impossible to repair' lacked substance. Soon, he also came to see it this way. In fact, I could almost see him completing a risk-assessment form in his head. This probably included the idea of me running away and leaving my immobile house on his forecourt.

"I suppose we could," he said, eventually and somewhat nervously, "remove the brake drum and seal off the hydraulic pipework, so brake fluid does not squirt all over the road. But we cannot let you drive it away on a public road. We can tow you to the port in the fjord where a ferry will take you out of the mountainous area. When you arrive in the lowlands, you still cannot drive it on the road, because it is unsafe."

Bet I could, I thought, *so long as I do not go above ten miles per hour, and only drive in the middle of the night to save queues of traffic following.* "I understand," I said.

"Once the back wheel is unlocked," continued the garage owner, "you should be able to get a normal tow truck to take you to the main ferry which sails to England, where you can buy parts... I suppose."

"I'm sure I can," I said. *Though it would be better if your garage bill was not going to cost me one thousand pounds.*

Having thought all this, I remembered that my finances had recovered substantially since my homeless phase, so I was far from destitute – just separated from my bank account by the North Sea. I gave the garage the go-ahead and walked to the town centre, where I found a local bank with friendly staff. After I explained my situation, they replied that because my money was in a deposit account, a transfer was more complicated. I do not really understand what went on behind the scenes, beyond the fact it was something to do with international monetary exchange. Essentially, I opened a Norwegian bank account, then had the money transferred to it. This took four days, which was fine, because living on a garage forecourt surrounded by beautiful mountains was a most relaxing experience.

After paying the garage a further four hundred pounds, they towed my house to a port, where they dropped it off – very much like a shipping container, which, given my wagon's misfortune, I suppose it was. However, it still had 75% of its designated braking power, so I was able to drive up a loading ramp to the ferry deck without the indignity of using a crane. Once on board the ferry, I began a conversation with a crew member, who told me how they operated. According to him, the locals treated it like a bus service. Indeed, given all the fjords, it generally offered the shortest and cheapest way to get around.

The sailing was most scenic, allowing me to gaze romantically over the rail at all the mountains rising directly from the water. What I remember most was the vessel edging towards a wooden walkway; the sort to which you would normally tie a small rowing boat. I imagine the vessel had some sort of doorway and ramp from a lower deck, because an old lady soon began walking along the narrow jetty towards the shore. She was pushing an overloaded shopping trolley! Nobody else got off, leaving me to watch in fascination as the lady began to push her presumed weekly shop up a footpath to wherever she lived in the mountains. From the surrounding scenery it was obvious she had no other access route. In the old days, I reasoned, this jetty would have been built to moor a small craft so she could get to town.

Eventually I reached Bergen, a major port on the south-west coast of Norway. Here my memory fades; a bit like in a film when the director wishes to wash over events which cannot be depicted.

HEALTH AND SAFETY ALERT: Losing the brake from one side of any vehicle causes it to swerve if hard braking is required. My personal opinion is that it is quite safe for 'shunting' operations around a goods yard at less than ten miles per hour. This can be done legally on private land. Such an operation from Norway to Worcester is obviously illegal in all circumstances.

Seven days later I was back in Grandstand Road, Worcester. After sorting myself out – like a chicken rustles its feathers after escaping a difficult situation – I boarded a bus to a nearby town. According to a trade magazine, here a steel stockholder was selling a Mercedes 814 flatbed lorry. My plan was to transfer the house part of my old wagon onto this new foundation. Not so posh as it sounds because, with five hundred thousand kilometres on the clock, the Mercedes had come to the end of its useful commercial life. It therefore cost me 1,600 pounds – on the understanding that I just drove it away from the factory yard, sold as seen.

In practice, I found the 'drive it away' bit really scary. I climbed into the cab, thinking, *Am I really allowed to take this thing out of the gates, based on my little car licence?* Legally, perhaps, but the morals of it were far more questionable. However, my 'house' needed good foundations, so I drove many miles before I let the speedometer edge above thirty kilometres an hour. Anyway, with the help of two forklift trucks I lifted my 'residential box' fifteen inches off its chassis, then drove the old wagon forwards and away to a waiting scrap dealer. Next, I reversed the replacement seven-and-a-half-ton lorry underneath. I then dropped the box onto the flatbed and bolted it down.

The only hiccup with my new lorry was that it had nearly forty square feet of exposed flatbed planking behind the residential box. This meant it was still able to carry commercial goods, so was governed by HGV regulations, which are rather bureaucratic. Only after I built a house extension over the back planking could it be reclassified as a 'camper van' and therefore something a normal garage could MOT. This also gave me an end room, in which I built a normal single bed. Where the old king-sized bed had been became a dedicated living room. Having no need of electric or fancy modern gadgets, my home was now complete in the way a Victorian gentleman would have understood. (Except for the modern shower-room – a bath tub being impractical due to its high water use.)

Chapter Thirty-Five

In the summer of 1999 I abandoned all work-related activities to begin a second Scandinavian Three Peaks adventure. This time I sensibly decided to do the Arctic section first, then travel back down to the Gladly Hopping Pigeon in September.

To get to the Arctic, I first drove to the small port of Helsingør on the eastern coast of Denmark. From here a very short ferry crossing took me to Helsingborg in Sweden. (The two countries were later linked by a road bridge.) From Helsingborg I drove across Sweden to Stockholm on the Baltic coast. There were two reasons for choosing this route. Firstly, the further you travel north, Scandinavia bends towards Russia. The highest mountain in Finland, Halti, is near the top of the continent, so it is even further east than Stockholm. Secondly, and more importantly, Norway is a terrible place for those who suffer from tollophobia. In Sweden, virtually all roads are free to use.

Sweden is a very friendly country, whose residents take pride in helping each other. Following this philosophy, while driving north from Stockholm I was joined by two lady hitch-hikers. (Natural waist-length hair, no make-up, and both sufficiently fit to carry enormous rucksacks – essentially a male fantasy, times two.) Naturally, I kept my eyes on the road, but their gentle words settled softly on my ears. It even crossed my mind that I was living the 'American dream'; a notion helped by the fact I was driving a Mercedes lorry with a luxurious cab, and cruising along a wide highway with two charming ladies sitting beside me. Of course, my 'house' was bolted onto the back, but that just gave it an air of mystery. I was quite disappointed when my new friends said they lived only ten miles along the road. However, whenever I asked where they would like to be dropped, they kept saying, "Further."

"Ah," said one presently, "I think English miles are not the same as Swedish ones."

"Yes," said the other. "Our mile is about twelve kilometres."

"Ours," I said mournfully, "are not much longer than a kilometre." *Because*, I thought, *my country is very small, and so densely packed with people there are no great wilderness areas left*. "I am going to Arctic Finland," I said, thereby announcing my manly credentials.

My passengers thought this quite normal. "Up there," said one, "the Sami people use a distance based on how far a reindeer can run without taking a pee. It's about five kilometres. This is essential knowledge for a reindeer herder or wolf following their scent marks, I think."

But I only really heard the word 'wolf', which awakened a lost memory of childhood storybooks, which sometimes included bears. "Are wolves and bears going to want to eat me?" I asked.

This very English question caused my passengers to laugh. "Wolves do not think we taste very nice," said one. "They much prefer reindeer, and bears are mostly vegetarian."

"But," said the other, "you need to be careful of musk ox. If they feel threatened, they will charge and kill on contact. They weigh nearly half a tonne and can run at thirty-five kilometres an hour."

Their words now seemed less delightful than they had earlier. In particular, they made me think about something I had previously noticed while studying my car atlas. In both Sweden and Finland it is possible to walk directly away from a road and not reach another for two hundred miles. Now, being told that such a vast area might be inhabited by bears, wolves and musk ox gave a new meaning to the concept of wilderness. I suddenly realised this was to be my first adventure in such a place. I no longer felt so manly, for even in the High Atlas I had only been two days' trek away from a village.

At the end of the eight Swedish miles, I diverted to the town where the ladies lived. On reaching a pleasant residential street, my passengers pointed to their front door. After climbing from my cab, they said, "*Hay*" twice, which, confusingly, means 'goodbye'.

I said, "*Hay*" once, which means 'hello'.

It all makes it very difficult to know if you are coming or going; though in this case, I fear 'going' was the correct interpretation. After leaving the ladies, I drove to a car park overlooking a vast expanse of water. Some distance from the shore was an impressive array of diving boards. They were of a height not generally allowed in England, unless as part of a supervised Olympic training programme. These Swedish boards were reached by floating walkways, presumably because the water surrounding them had to be at least sixteen feet deep. I left my lorry to take a closer look and so became aware that a lot of children were diving from the top board, or jumping carefree from the lower ones. There were no lifeguards; nor namby-pamby grown-ups having panic attacks on the shore. All I saw was children having fun in a way which even to me looked less than entirely safe.

Having recently rescued two damsels in distress, my manly instincts took control of my brain, making me believe I was a James Bond doppelganger. I therefore imagined myself going for a swim in what I suspected was a northern arm of the Baltic Sea. Not that I owned a pair of the bottom-hugging trunks which a real special agent might wear. I was more in disguise, because I always wore old-fashioned tennis shorts for public swimming. Anyway, I returned home, changed, and fifteen minutes later strode purposefully back to the shore, then straight into the water. It was freezing! As it reached the tops of my legs, all I could do was stand there, shivering, terrified that my next step might send the water up to my tummy. Then I heard giggling from a nearby walkway. I looked around to see a group of children, who seemed to think my 'English' behaviour hilarious. Then one of the teenage boys decided to make friends with me in the way all children are prone to do. He introduced himself by leaping from the walkway, tucking into a bomb position, and landing beside me. There must have been something about my involuntary "Arggghh!" scream which implied I was mostly harmless and possibly funny, because the other children also decided to be my friend. Back in England, even 'bombing' gets you banned from the public swimming pool; here it was an expected part of the fun.

HEALTH AND SAFETY ALERT: The water temperature in an English swimming pool is typically twenty-eight degrees centigrade. If it falls below twenty-seven degrees centigrade, the pool is closed on health and safety grounds. The water in the northern arm of the Baltic is literally close to freezing.

Here, all the children surrounded me while splashing their hands in joyous gestures of greeting. This was their swimming pool and those who ventured into its depths were expected to play by their rules. I particularly remember a girl, aged about eight, giggling uncontrollably as she patted her hands on the water towards me as if I were her favourite grandpa. Defending myself was pointless. I swam away... for maybe two minutes. That was as much as I could take. I returned to the shore, ran to my lorry, and lit the fire. Next I shivered my way to the gas stove to boil milk for a mug of drinking chocolate. Now my only mission in life was to sit in my fireside armchair and get warm. Any masculine Bond ideas I may have previously held were history.

So this aquatic episode explains how the happy, friendly children of northern Sweden have adapted to an environment where winter icebergs float around their outdoor swimming pool. Hence, their definition of a gentle summer playtime is completely different to those of people living nearer the equator.

After completing my drive up the east coast of Sweden, I entered Finland at the northern end of the Gulf of Bothnia. From here I followed the E8, which would take me six hundred miles to the mountainous region where I expected to find Halti. It is located 220 miles above the Arctic Circle, which means in summer it never gets dark. Its height of 4,360 feet makes it lower than Ben Nevis, which I imagine Finnish people find most embarrassing. Or possibly its diminutive height is a clever ploy to stop foreigners finding it?

According to my car atlas, on the Finnish side Halti is twenty-five miles from the nearest road. However, the summit lies so close to Norway that the atlas does not differentiate between the border and the little triangle representing the mountain. On the Norwegian side, the E8 trunk road passes within twenty miles of Halti. Because Norway is not politically in Europe, some sort of border fence might be imagined; but if such a thing exists, it is clearly the sort of fence which needs to be climbed.

In Arctic Scandinavia, main roads have little resemblance to those in Britain. Imagine travelling a hundred miles without passing a settlement or a petrol station. In the rush hour, maybe you will meet another vehicle every fifteen minutes. The road surface is likely to be compacted gravel. The greatest hazard is wandering moose, who have no understanding of the Highway Code, and hard braking on a loose surface has unpredictable consequences. My recommended speed is forty miles per hour, but I suppose boy racers, who do not worry about having a dead moose crashing onto their bonnet, might go a little faster.

The accurate 'yacht' compass fixed to my lorry's dashboard, together with the milometer, let me know roughly where I was at any given time. The same principle was used by ancient mariners, who sailed all over the world. Of course, for sailors this was backed up by occasional sightings of useful things such as a lighthouse or an island. In my case, I fixed my location on reaching the settlement of Kaaresuvanto, 150 miles (by road) above the Arctic Circle. From here I headed north-west for two hundred miles, which took me into Norway. Shortly after this, the E8 headed north for a few miles, after which it veered north-west – a direction in which I did not want to go. So, when my course headed north I knew I was about to make the closest approach to Halti, which lay to the north-east. On this due-north section, my voyage of discovery came across a narrow lane leading off to starboard (the right). I stopped to investigate. Importantly, the lane did not have a toll barrier and, though not recorded on my road map, seemed to be heading in the right direction. My new course along this narrow backwater caused my elevated lorry cab to sway gently like the wheelhouse of a boat. This, together with the compass, gave my journey a romantic, nautical feel as I navigated at a slow-ahead – roughly four knots or six miles an hour.

After a couple of miles, the tarmac came to an end; the way ahead being rough gravel unsuited to lorries. Thankfully, there was an area of flat land to starboard; a safe harbour, about the size of five tennis courts. After making certain it was free to use, I entered with my lorry, and so established base camp. Why no other vehicles were using the car park was a mystery. However, my arrival was slightly outside the main summer season and, I guess, beyond the school holidays.

With the sun going around in a continuous circle, the word 'tomorrow' has no meaning. So I can only say that I spent some time in bed, and the first meal after getting up might still be called 'breakfast'. After this, I left my front door with a full tummy and walked back to look up the lane. I realised that, with all this permanent daylight, climbing Halti was going to be easy. I would not even need to pack a torch.

Chapter Thirty-Six

The rough gravel track beyond the car park soon became steep with many interesting features, such as a few planks resting on opposing banks of a ravine. Crossing these in my lorry would have been suicidal, but on foot seemed less so. Of equal importance, I was heading in the direction my compass required me to go.

I was still congratulating myself on all my common sense when I came to a type of geological formation I had never seen before. Ahead, as far as the eye could see, the land had been concertinaed into giant folds, with each dip perhaps a hundred feet below the following crest. Even ten of these involved one thousand feet of ascent and descent. Plus, this 'giant corrugated-iron' landscape meant that walking a mile did not represent a mile as the crow flies.

As I continued the up-and-down military-style march, I became increasingly convinced that it would last for all eternity, so was astonished when I climbed yet another mound and saw a level surface – or, more precisely, a lake. From the far shore, a mountain rose into a ceiling of cloud. In scale, compared to what we have in England, both features could be considered spectacular. After surveying the scene for a short while, I realised the mountain was too far north to be Halti; also, a bit big for something less mighty than Ben Nevis.

Next I turned my attention to the swampy area around the lake. I obviously needed to circle around this and so reach the big mountain, which would allow me to walk south-west without being swallowed up by mud. The track I had been following continued by taking a wide circle around the bog on my left; a route which included a substantial detour up an adjacent hillside. It had clearly been designed for tractors with large fuel tanks, rather than humans who relied on porridge stored in the tummy. However, not wishing to get my boots muddy, I initially followed the 'recommended' route, until realising how silly it was. I then took a shortcut... where I quickly found myself knee-deep in bog, while waving my arms about to maintain balance on unpredictable footings. I squelched back up to the track, and sat on a boulder to survey the scenery. From this lofty position overlooking the water, I could place everything I saw in reasonable order. I decided that, given the extent of the bog, the only way to reach Halti was to ascend the big mountain first and then, from its summit (estimated due to the clouds), head south-east for about three miles. Something like that, anyway.

My legs were aching and my knees up to their old creaky tricks of making my brain repeatedly think, *Ouch* as I walked. However, I understood that returning to my house would achieve nothing. I would only have to repeat the trek after the sun had done another circle of the sky. I had taken two ibuprofen tablets on the way up. Now, for the first time in my life, I decided to go beyond the recommended dose for this once-in-a-lifetime opportunity. So I popped two more tablets and continued my long plod along the track.

Eventually, this descended until it became a lakeside walk; that is to say, the same height as I had been an hour earlier. Then my path came to a sudden end beneath the foot of the big mountain. I knew this could not be Halti because I had not yet encountered a border fence. The mountain before me had nothing resembling a path. It was just a great pile of boulders towering above me until they disappeared into a ceiling of cloud. In ancient England, I reasoned, such a thing would have once supported moss, then vegetation, and finally become the green and pleasant hillside we know today. But I was now in a place where everything would be covered by snow for most of the year, meaning no vegetation was hardy enough to begin the process of providing a foothold for grassy hillsides.

Climbing the boulders was not technically difficult, but it was very time-consuming and hazardous, because any slip would likely 'swallow' my leg and wedge it in place. I popped two more ibuprofen to reduce the knee pain and continued upwards. After perhaps five hundred feet of ascent, it started to snow; gently at first, and with no wind this merely added to the Arctic experience. My heavy cotton trousers and two woolly jumpers began to get damp, then increasingly wet as I clambered upwards. Wrapping myself in waterproofs at this stage would only trap water next to my skin. However, I was still producing more heat than I was losing, and knew my clothing would soon dry out when the snow flurries ceased. The snow now reduced visibility to my immediate surroundings but, because I only had to keep heading upwards until reaching the summit, this was not an issue.

But sadly, on cresting the top I discovered it to be a massive, broad plateau scattered with individual boulder summits. However, my compass bearing was also approximate, so hopefully any navigational errors would cancel each other out. Eventually I set off on my chosen compass bearing, until I dropped beneath the cloud, where the snow turned to rain. Here I beheld a magical vision. Below, in a wide valley, a high chain-link fence stretched in both directions for as far as the eye could see. At the far side of this was another mountain, which I realised must be Halti, because my compass and walking distance calculations meant I knew my position to within the nearest mile or so, and my atlas had placed the summit so close to the border that it did differentiate between them.

As I descended towards the fence, I noticed a man-sized hole cut through the wire at the bottom. So, I reasoned, someone had ventured this way before with a pair of bolt croppers. Because it was the sort of fence which would be very awkward to climb over, I thought this a very necessary act of kindness. Crawling through such a hole is an excellent way to enter a new country, because it involves wriggling, then lying prostrate on the ground as if to kiss the earth – or in this case, a patch of slushy snow which covered it. Having shown respect to the Finnish nation in general, I gazed up to look at their highest mountain – or at least, the snow now falling from the sky, which reduced visibility to about a hundred feet. I decided Finland was very keen on snow. Then I had a more profound thought. Aged ten, I had learnt all about going out of bounds at boarding school – to a new 'country' which lay on the other side of the fence. Now, thirty-six years later, I was merely doing a grown-up version of those great escapes.

Anyway, from the hole in the Finnish border fence I climbed Halti without any technical or endurance challenges getting in the way. Then, on reaching the top, it became obvious why no one had bothered to produce a postcard of the summit. It was just a vast, virtually level plateau without any impressive features. I spent half an hour wandering around to visit every bump which could conceivably be the highest place. However, better this than the abomination of building a cafe on the top. On my third visit to a stone-built cairn painted yellow around its base, I decided this represented the 'roof of Finland'.

By the time I crawled back through the fence to Norway, the wind was making it difficult to remain upright. *I want to go home!* I thought. Reaching my comfortable house, situated fifteen miles away as the legs walk, now became my overriding desire. This raised the question of how I might achieve it. Should I go back over the top of the big mountain, where conditions might be serious, or circumnavigate it at my present height? If I kept the upper slope on my right, I could eventually begin walking directly down on the compass bearing along which I had arrived.

Presently, I decided to circumnavigate the mountain. This offered no respite from the boulders or the blizzard, which reduced visibility to my immediate surroundings. I cannot say how long this took, other than, given the ever-present danger of an accidental slip, every move required careful thought. But eventually I was able to look straight down the mountain on the correct compass bearing. I gave myself an imaginary pat on the back because, as I dropped lower, the falling snow turned to rain, which allowed me to see that I was within a quarter of a mile of where I needed to be. But I was now very wet and cold. Also, I was overloaded with ibuprofen – the known side effect of which is water retention. My cells had expanded with fluid, making my skin all bloated and squishy like a soggy balloon. On reaching the track around the lake, the rain became torrential. I took two more ibuprofen and continued walking by swinging my legs at the hips, minimising the need to bend my seized-up knees. This results in a human walking like a monster, with legs swinging outwards, across a film set. Then came all those peak-and-trough sections… and the realisation of a great truth.

The fact it never gets dark up here in the summer does not mean a human body is magically redesigned to keep on going endlessly until the autumn arrives. Also, once progress slows to a crawl, five miles takes an awfully long time to complete. Next thing I knew, I collapsed in the middle of the track, very cold, half-conscious, and without functioning legs. I crawled a little way on all fours, then lay unmoving. I had not seen another human since leaving my house, so slowly the truth of the situation came to me. Lying here, in torrential, near-freezing rain, I would soon lose consciousness and be discovered as a dead body sometime in the future. But the desire to survive can have a remarkable effect on the brain. Semi-comatose, I somehow managed to crawl and slither onwards through the puddles, mud and stones of the rough track.

Eventually I looked up to see my house towering above me. Because it is built on a flatbed lorry, even when standing I have to reach up to undo the padlock on the front door. Then I climb a three-rung ladder to step inside. But my legs had now stopped working altogether. I was also lying flat on my back. Fortunately my arms, which had only been used to climb the big mountain, plus a little crawling, had some muscle power remaining. So, using my hands, I hauled myself upwards, unlocked the door and, now in the kitchen, lit the gas stove. Realising the immediate danger had passed, my brain finally shut down.

I remember nothing more until I became aware of convulsive shivering more akin to an epileptic fit. Then I realised I was lying on the slate floor of my kitchen. My skin was quite warm, which gave rise to the curious notion that, had the box of matches not been lying next to the gas stove, I would probably have died of hypothermia. But now my depleted muscles had recovered sufficient energy from the warm air to start extreme shivering and so produce internal heat. While still lying down, I struggled from my soggy clothes; then, after reaching up to turn off the stove, slithered along the floor to my bedroom. Though my skin was still wet, I soon had a soft mattress beneath and a duvet above, both of which would eventually absorb the water. Now completely safe, I once again lost consciousness.

How long this mental state lasted, I cannot say. I only know that I came round when agonising cramps seized my legs; the normal cure for which is to stand and walk around a little. However, on this occasion my muscles lacked the strength to do so. All I could do was wiggle my feet and wait for the 'leg torture' to fade. Eventually I drifted to sleep, but with frequent interruptions of cramp. More awkwardly, the fluid which had accumulated in my cells due to the ibuprofen overdose began returning to my bloodstream, then to my bladder. I just had to take a pee…

I have no memory of what happened next; only that I emerged from a state of unconsciousness to discover I was sprawled naked on a floor, with my limbs in contorted positions. A pool of urine surrounded me. (I assume I had tried to stand and passed out.) I crawled back into bed, very cold, and probably a bit smelly.

With the sun going around in a circle, I had no idea how long my recovery took. Instinct tells me I was able to stagger into the kitchen to make a hot drink about forty hours after returning home. Maybe sixty hours passed before I was well enough to take an ultra-hot shower, get dressed, and sit to eat lots of porridge with sweetened condensed milk. Only then could I change the bedding, and return to hide beneath the duvet for a conventional sleep. Later still, I emerged from my front door to amble around the car park, using a long-shafted ice axe as a walking stick.

HEALTH AND SAFETY ALERT: *I am in no way overstating the medical emergency I suffered from my complete exhaustion, while overdosed on ibuprofen. I believe that while I was lying unconscious on my kitchen floor, my vital organs were struggling to survive. That is to say, I was struggling to survive.*

Having said all this, my recovery sent my level of fitness in the opposite direction. My legs, possibly fearing for the future, put on a mass of muscle, while my knees gave the impression of having been oiled with ibuprofen. Any obvious fat reserves had vanished.

As stated earlier, topics covered in this book are limited to projects which ordinary people can complete on ordinary wages, without facing anything unduly dangerous – subject to avoiding my occasional mistakes. However, for Halti, I suggest those with dodgy knees take a tent in order to have a period of rest beneath the big mountain. (It is a very open landscape with no obvious nooks or crannies where you can snuggle up in a bivvy bag.) Regarding finances, my time in the mountains cost nothing. Indeed, short of tearing up ten-pound notes, spending any money was impossible.

For Halti, I need to offer a special word of caution. Norway, feeling sorry for flat Finland, is considering changing the border to encircle the big mountain mentioned earlier. So, unless you are happy just to climb what might become Finland's second highest mountain, I suggest you also do the 'big mountain' at the same time. Because of this, I have researched the subject and can state the big mountain is called Ráisduottarháldi, its height being 4,465 feet.

Chapter Thirty-Seven

The highest mountain in Sweden is Kebnekaise. At 6,926 feet it is also the highest in Arctic Scandinavia. Because it is a long way from the nearest road, for normal people an ascent requires periods of rest every ten hours or so. Given such planned stops, any unfortunate occurrences are clearly unlikely.

The nearest town to Kebnekaise is Kiruna, from where a road heads into wilderness for forty miles. (Lakes, mountains, a few moose wandering around, that sort of thing.) After this distance, the road terminates abruptly at a car park. This has a souvenir shop and a cafe, but no other building. Yet on my visit, the car park had hundreds of people buzzing around in ways which showed their determination to hike places. This was my first indication that Swedish people have an obsessional love of extreme outdoor adventures; this being evident from their massive rucksacks and boots, the sort you did not bother putting on for anything less than a fifty-mile trek. After enjoying a reasonably priced mug of coffee in the cafe, I loaded my rucksack with everything I needed for a multi-day expedition, then marched up a well-trodden path which looked to be heading in the correct direction. All those coming towards me said, "*Hi*," and I replied likewise.

Later, higher in the mountains, I passed many wigwam-like shelters made of sticks and covered with turf. So, I reasoned, the car park was also an area of flat land where the nomadic reindeer herders retreated to live in winter. (I later learnt that the road head had the local name of Nikkaluokta, which suggests its origins began with Sami culture – the term 'Laplander' being considered derogatory.) After a few miles I came across a wigwam which had a sign outside saying, 'Cola'. Sitting on a stool outside the small entrance was a man in full nomadic dress. The only English he knew was a friendly smile of greeting. Accordingly, as I approached he pointed to the sign, which also displayed the price of his drinks. A can of Coke cost much the same as one purchased from an upmarket shop in England. And, I assume, he had to carry them up from the car park.

After a short refreshment break, I walked on and eventually came to a vast lake. The path around this kept close to its shore and so followed level ground. Climbing Kebnekaise, I realised, was going to be a lot easier than Halti. This was confirmed when, after walking about thirteen miles from the car park, I came across a youth hostel. However, it was too expensive for ordinary people to use, which explained the fifty or so tents pitched in the surrounding area. (Wild camping is normal in Scandinavia.) Presently, I found a bit of flat grassland, laid out my bivvy bag and sat, Buddha-like, to contemplate the harmonious setting. I could still visualise the sun as something which circled around the horizon, thereby representing a giant clock face with a compass needle acting as the little hand. Hence, I know that at 2200 hours I crawled into my sleeping bag and drifted serenely into a world of pleasant dreams.

After ten hours' rest, I sat up and, without leaving my sleeping bag, made a cheese sandwich. Then a family group consisting of a man, a woman and a small boy came across to say, "*Hi.*"

I announced my nationality by saying, "Hello." I reckoned the boy to be about eight yet, like his presumed parents, he was carrying a massive rucksack. I commented on this, but was further discombobulated by his response. In perfect English, he told me that they were on a seven-day hike covering two hundred kilometres, so needed to carry a lot of food. The presumed father then explained they had left the wilderness to replenish their supplies from the shop. It all made me feel very inferior.

After this small talk, I asked the family for directions to Kebnekaise. Their response sounded very straightforward. The family then added that Kebnekaise had a variable-height ice pyramid on the summit, which this year had added fifty metres. This took any successful climber above seven thousand feet, which pleased me greatly. More worryingly, they mentioned the restaurant and shop were supplied with goods brought up by a regular helicopter service. This travelled back without a commercial payload, so generally had passenger places available for less than one hundred pounds. I thought this cheating, but supposed that those who stayed in the hostel/hotel might like it. Personally, I had enjoyed waking up in the open air while gazing up at a clear blue sky, so had every intention of returning to my house using my own muscle power.

After getting up, I went to the shop to do something which, for me, was very unusual. I purchased two 'tourist' T-shirts with 'Kebnekaise' written above a mountaineering-rope logo. Well, it was just that sort of mountain: considered wild by those who had not been there, but friendly by those who knew it to be a gentle experience, at least when taken by the normal route.

After repacking my rucksack, I set off along an obvious path which went deeper into the mountains. The family I had spoken to said I had to follow this for around three kilometres to where a right turn led to a mountain composed mostly of boulders, so it was not possible to deviate from the gravel track. They had then explained that, after this mountain, the path descended to a valley with Kebnekaise straight ahead. This could be ascended by a path or well-trodden track through the snow, depending on circumstances.

Carrying a heavy rucksack uphill for three kilometres would normally take me about an hour. However, thanks to the Halti experience, my super-manly legs had no need of rest. Also, even without ibuprofen my knees made no complaint about my power-walking. Because of this, I marched onwards; my gaze admiring the scenery with all the critical awareness of Wordsworth being distracted by daffodils. Then I became aware of vegetation brushing against my legs. I looked down to realise the previously good path had become narrow and uneven. Ahead, it became indistinct and wandering; the sort of thing a reindeer herd might create. Looking right, I saw a gently rising valley, up which a slightly more obvious 'path' could be identified. Thinking logically, I forced my way through the intervening vegetation to rejoin what had to be the normal tourist route up the mountain. Shortly after reaching the proper path, it entered an increasingly narrow gorge. This came to an end when the cliffs joined to become a headwall, from the top of which cascaded a spectacular, free-falling waterfall. Here, I expect, tourists might stand to admire the torrent thundering onto the boulders which marked the beginning of a river. Where the path went next was more of a mystery.

Presently, I noticed the cliff to my right had a fault line which included a narrow, rising ledge. I was surprised my Swedish friends had underplayed this feature, but supposed, given their outdoor lifestyle, to them it was all rather routine. Only halfway up the traverse, when the drifting spray from the waterfall was showering both me and the rock with water, did I stop to admire the scene. I thought it odd there were no human skeletons scattered across the boulders below, because the ledge on this section was only a few inches of scree balancing precariously on the lip of a precipice. However, there were some good, easily reachable handholds on the wall, and this 'handrail' had obviously prevented any slips.

After reaching the top of the gorge, I was confused to find myself gazing into another valley containing two lakes, which the Swedish family had forgotten to mention. I walked down to the first, which allowed me to appreciate the scale of the second. It was wide enough to have waves rippling up the shore! After accidentally exploring a bog, I stood to contemplate the surrounding wilderness. *I must have missed the path*, I thought. So, I reasoned, if I had been walking at four miles per hour, without a pain alert from my knees requesting a rest period, I might have daydreamed away two pleasant hours and so now, most probably, was in the wrong place. According to my compass, the big mountain towering above me was in the vague direction of the youth hostel. *I bet the path the family told me about goes over the top of it*, I thought.

The next bit of the journey was remarkably similar to the experience of going out of bounds when I was at boarding school. I found myself crossing streams which flowed over smooth rock, only to arrive at a scrambling section where 30% of the ice-damaged holds detached from the surrounding rock with ease. Basically, I was back to discovering a new world with a childlike urge to conquer anything which got in my way. I escaped my unfavourable circumstances by ascending a steep, scree-filled gully; the handholds on its left wall compensating for the loose stones beneath my boots. As these cascaded down the mountain, a few larger rocks which had lost their precarious foundations rolled down from above. While all of this could be considered as a fun regression to childhood adventure, I eventually came to a serious grown-up problem. While still standing on unstable scree, I could only reach one hold on the left-hand wall. I needed to fantasise about lunging upwards for a higher handhold, then using the momentum to power-reach the one above that. Why I have a photographic memory of this position I cannot say, but I expect it's something to do with knowing the jump would most likely send my feet flying into space as the scree avalanched three hundred feet down the mountain, with me following close behind. Eventually, I realised that if facing this problem while tied to a rope, I would make the lunge without concern, and most probably succeed. But a rope is only a psychological prop. It does not actually make a difference to the difficulty of the move. As Simon from the mountaineering club would say, "Just do it", because going back down was impractical. As it happened, the move was quite challenging, but no harder than some of the problems I had completed on the indoor climbing wall.

And so I escaped the gully, after which the climb became less steep with many escape routes. I headed left, where a rising valley gave me a pleasant snow-plod to a col between two distinct mountains. Many hikers were marching down from my left before ascending the hillside on my right. An equally happy column of people were heading in the opposite direction. On reaching this surging mass of humanity, I asked someone the way to Kebnekaise. He said it was the mountain on my left.

The track up Kebnekaise was a deep trench in the snow which zigzagged upwards to lessen its gradient. In both scale and nature it was remarkably like doing a winter ascent up the broad flank of Ben Nevis. (Except on the Ben the broad dome is on the right and the climbing face on the left. On Kebnekaise it is the opposite.) After the slope became more gentle, the zigzags stopped to take a more direct route. Then I came across a building to the left of the path. Opening the door, I discovered a luxurious cabin fitted out with raised platforms for sleeping. I reckoned it would accommodate fifty people in comfort. A sign informed me that it was owned by a local mountaineering club, with additional information stating that anyone could use it. Shortly after passing the hut, I came to a spectacular ice pyramid. It had children sledging down it on their bottoms, which seemed a little dangerous. However, pre-teenagers are quite light, so could crash into the legs of an adult trying to climb upwards without causing an incident.

The summit was marked by a piece of cloth tied to a rough stick. More notable was the wider view. In whichever direction I looked, snow-covered mountains seemed to go on forever. After descending to the club hut, I climbed onto a raised platform and snuggled inside my sleeping bag to contemplate the beauty of my recent experiences. Next, checking my thermometer, I noted that it recorded a temperature a fraction above freezing. Because of the twenty-four-hour daylight, I did not expect this to change. And so, effortlessly, I drifted to sleep, awaking much later feeling warm and invigorated.

After breakfast, I followed the path of hard-trodden snow to the valley, and then upwards to the summit of the 'in-the-way' mountain; that is to say, the normal tourist route. I found this both dangerously boring and pointless, given there is such a pleasant way to avoid it by climbing up by the side of an idyllic waterfall. However, for those who enjoy walking across the hills of the English Lake District, the normal footpath to the summit of Kebnekaise provides three days of gentle exercise. But remember: in winter there is continuous darkness, with temperatures in the region of minus forty degrees centigrade. My original plan of 1998 – to visit the Arctic in October – might have proved quite challenging.

After Kebnekaise, I descended to the car park, where my house awaited my return. I made myself a nice bowl of porridge, then, looking out of the kitchen window at all the beautiful scenery, I thought it a pleasant place to live. So why leave? Swedish culture is so relaxed about such things. When the Sami came down from the high mountains to build their wigwams, I would blend into their community quite well. Except I don't know the first thing about reindeer, and sooner or later I would run out of money, and die of starvation. So I took a compromise of living happily on the car park for a few days. Then it started to get gloomy around the midnight hour, so I accepted the inevitable and began heading south. My next date was with the Gladly Hopping Pigeon…

Chapter Thirty-Eight

The headlights of my posh Mercedes lorry swept gracefully onto the lay-by, from where an ascent of the Gladly Hopping Pigeon might begin. With power steering and air brakes, I manfully came to a halt on the gravel where my old wagon had parked eleven months earlier. Now, on this more organised arrival, I climbed from the cab and stared into darkness where I knew the Gladly Hopping Pigeon was hiding.

"Well," I said, "I'm back, and this time let's see who's the boss."

Fortunately the car park was deserted, otherwise an eavesdropper might have thought I was talking to myself.

My second attempt began with a good night's sleep followed by a lazy morning of doing nothing in particular. Then, after a healthy meal of boiled potatoes, margarine (for calories), and tomato sauce (for salt), I stepped outside to sample the air. For late September it was relatively mild, but cooler than it would have been had my love for Sweden postponed my arrival by two weeks.

After dinner, I took a gentle wander into the mountains. Later, while plodding up the path beside the stream (which originated from the glacier), I saw two men swaggering towards me. Both wore excessively posh clothes which made them look like fashion models training for a catwalk parade. My own view of fashion had changed due to my proper 1920s mountaineering attire having been lost when my boat sank. Now the most expensive anorak I owned had cost ten pounds from a charity shop. Where clothing was concerned, I treated climbing very much like posh people undertook their gardening: wear anything old, but too good to throw away. As we got closer, I could see one of the men had a neatly coiled rope around his shoulder. When I had first seen this fashion accessory on the summit of Wyddfa, I had been very impressed and determined to copy the charisma it created. Now seeing a perfectly coiled, rarely used rope reminded me of my earlier pretentious vanity. When the men were a few feet away, they stood side by side to completely block the path. Then one said something in Norwegian.

"Sorry, English," I replied.

They instantly began speaking perfect English. "Where are you going?" asked one.

"Gladly Hopping Pigeon," I replied.

They frowned, as if confused about something. Then their expressions registered horror. "Impossible!" they exclaimed. "You need to go back to the road, then—"

"It's fine," I interrupted. "I'm going up the glacier that's just around the corner."

"The Heimre Illåbrean?" they gasped. (For ease, in future I will simply refer to this as 'the first glacier'.)

"Don't know," I replied. "It's the one where this stream comes from."

"Certain death," said one of the men.

Suddenly I understood what these men were doing in this part of the world. I imagined their smart rucksacks to be full of the completed risk-assessment forms so beloved by Norwegian society.

"And it does not lead to Galdhøpiggen," said the other. "You need to start at the ski centre."

"At the top of the glacier," I replied confidently, "there is a ridge to climb up—"

"That only leads to the Svellnosbreen glacier," they said smugly. (In future, I will refer to this as 'the second glacier'.) "It has hundreds of hidden crevasses," they added.

"I did not see any when I was there last time," I replied truthfully.

"Certain death," they both repeated.

Worryingly, I noticed their arms beginning to twitch. I just knew they wanted to grab hold of me and carry me back to the road, where they would no doubt inform the health and safety police of my intentions. Without giving any warning, I jumped to the side, ran past them, rejoined the path, then sprinted upwards. I could hear them shouting for me to come back. But I reckoned they could only give chase once they had filled out a risk-assessment form – for surely running uphill beside a stream is somewhat unsafe. After a few hundred yards I looked back and saw they were now walking downwards.

I continued plodding upwards until I came to the ice wall which represented the termination of the first glacier. From my previous attempt I knew this was a good place to rest so, after unpacking my rucksack, I placed my sleeping mat on the gravel, then set about preparing my supper. I had all the kitchen equipment available to an SAS military unit. That is to say, a spoon, a tin mug, fire pellets, and waterproof matches. The mug could be used to prepare both porridge and coffee, though not at the same time. Essential to my logistical planning was the stream which emerged from the base of the glacier. This provided me with the sort of mineral water which costs a fortune if bought in a bottle from a warm supermarket shelf. After supper, I settled into my sleeping bag, then relaxed to the gentle sounds of the gurgling stream. With the pretty ice wall a few yards to my right, it was a perfect place to drift into a world of beautiful dreams…

Waking up with a cold, flattened bottom quickly alerts the brain to the notion that the body is in a sitting position. Any experienced mountaineer will immediately understand that some sort of bivvy is taking place. If the back is cushioned by a rucksack resting against a wall, and there is no shivering, it is reasonable to assume that everything is in good order. Hence, the brain considers it safe to cautiously open one eye, and so establish a more precise location which, in this instance, proved most satisfactory. After admiring the ice wall, I collected water from the stream and made porridge, followed by two mugs of coffee. As expected, this used the last of my fire pellets, allowing me to continue the adventure without any complicated kitchen stuff to carry. From now on, my food would be sweetened condensed-milk sandwiches.

The ascent of the first glacier passed without incident. At the top, I scrambled up the ridge on my left. When I had reached this place the previous year, conditions had reduced my visibility to about ten feet. So, on this second attempt I had been totally honest with the men who had tried to block my approach path. I had not seen any hidden crevasses on the second glacier because freezing fog had prevented me from even knowing it was there. On my first attempt on the mountain I had believed this ridge to be a feature of the Gladly Hopping Pigeon itself, so had turned right to continue climbing upwards. Now, beneath a clear blue sky, I could see this approach was not entirely correct. (It ultimately led to the mountain I wanted, but only in a circle which represented the headwall of the second glacier.)

Ignoring the great sweep of ridge, I looked down to study the glacier directly below. It was obviously the one the men who had tried to block my approach had told me about. It was about one and a half miles across, the upper section forming a relatively level snowfield without any obvious signs of hidden crevasses. Only well to the left, where the glacier tumbled into its descent gorge, did the ice break apart to suggest that it contained mysterious depths. Rising from the far side of the glacier was a triangular peak which looked exactly like the one on my postcard. Its summit was around one thousand feet above my current position, which confirmed I had achieved most of my height gain by ascending the first glacier. Climbing up the triangular face direct did not appear that difficult but, being one and a half miles away, it was hard to be certain. Anyway, it all looked amazingly pretty.

The descent to the second glacier was easy. Walking across it made me feel like an insignificant ant slowly crawling across a vast white stage. Then, somewhere in the middle, I came across a line of boot prints – a party of three, heading directly towards a difficult-looking rock wall to the left of my previously intended line. I examined the prints in the manner of Sherlock Holmes. One set were pressed by large boots, advancing with long, confident strides. The others were shorter and left much shallower imprints. One of the group had either a walker's ice axe or an alpenstock; the other two, ski poles. My elementary conclusion was that they were ill-equipped to tackle anything too technical. Looking up, I saw the footprints came from the direction of the gap in the ridge I have previously mentioned. But now they were turning and heading towards an apparently featureless wall to the left of the Gladly Hopping Pigeon. However, they advanced without apparent hesitation or deviation. I decided these footprints represented both obscure local knowledge and, if they suddenly came to an end, a good way of finding hidden crevasses. So, believing this to be a family group, including a child, I concluded my 'easy way' was an optical illusion. I changed direction to follow the footprints.

Presently, the snow dipped steeply into a deep, narrow trench, the far side of which was a wall of rock. And that was where the footprints came to an abrupt end. *A child went up that!* I immediately realised this observation made me feel really old. Children are born to climb like monkeys, their little fingers and low body weight ideally suited to gaining height quickly. It is only 'responsible' grown-ups who panic when they see the child they were supposed to be minding now in the upper branches of a really tall tree. Having got things into perspective, I decided the child probably had parents who fed the young mountaineer with a breakfast of condensed-milk sandwiches. I had recently made my porridge with condensed milk so was likewise overflowing with calories. With all of this energy, if I gave the climb a try, what could possibly go wrong? Even if I fell, there was a safe, snowy landing zone below.

The first awkward move was overcome by bridging up with my left crampon on the rock; the other buried in the snow on my right. From here I could lunge for the next handhold, then progress with ease until I reached a wide foot ledge. Looking up, I saw a rising fault line which contained a sequence of layback holds at convenient intervals. This allowed for a series of momentum-powered ape swings, which compensated for the decreasing quality of the foot placements. As I advanced I kept catching glimpses of old, rotting rope which had clearly once been used for protection. There were also many pitons; these rarely used since the 1960s, so I knew this was a route of historic importance which was unlikely to come to a dead end. (Unless there had been a major rockfall.) It was a pleasant rising traverse, which soon led to a flat ledge onto which I gracefully stepped. This gave me an opportunity to take my first proper look around. Wow! The awesome-looking rock face I had first seen from a distance was, in truth, detached from the mountain as a free-standing tower. Between the two was a parallel gap with a boulder base which could be described as a staircase. This led me to a ridge above, where I sat down to prepare a sandwich.

After lunch, my attention turned to a substantial abseil peg on the far side of my 'kitchen' floor. Given that I did not have a rope with me, I thought this a bad omen. After crawling to the peg, I poked my head over the edge, expecting to look down a sheer wall... Oh! A third glacier. However, curving snow lapped upwards to within a few inches of the rim. It was very thin at the top, but falling would only result in a harmless slide to a soft landing below. Or, as the locals might say, a death-defying glacier fall, with a lot of screaming as a mysterious crevasse appeared from nowhere to swallow me in one gulp. To the right of the glacier, an impressive cliff towered towards the skyline, which culminated in the summit of the Gladly Hopping Pigeon, now immediately on my right. Whether this skyline was a ridge or the edge of a plateau, I could not say. But that was unimportant, because it fell away from the summit at such a gentle angle it could only represent a walk. Perhaps half a mile in the distance, the height reduced enough for snow ramps to reach up, so joining ridge and glacier together.

I walked across the 'third glacier' until I reached the first snow ramp which went all the way to the ridge. This proved to be well consolidated, so I ascended with ease. On reaching the vertical section just below the top, I cut a normal trench, which allowed my head to emerge from the snow about two feet from the edge. When doing this I became caked in snow, so possibly appeared rather 'Yetified' with an icy pyramid on top of my head. On this occasion, having secured two good axe placements on the ridge, I looked ahead to see whatever lay beyond. It was horrendous. There were two deep, parallel trenches; the sort made when many people use the same route. So many walkers had done this, the mountain needed a dual carriageway! Then I noticed a lady and a gentleman standing between the trenches, so allowing the pedestrian traffic to progress unhindered. Both were staring at me, their mouths open, faces white with a shock equal to my own on discovering this mountain highway. Then they partially closed their mouths, briefly, to mumble something in German.

"Have you got the time, please?" I replied, this being the most efficient way of saying I was English, while also discovering how long I had to locate a comfortable place to sleep.

The Germans effortlessly changed to my language. "We have been watching you cross the glacier," said the man.

Unable to see what relevance this might have to his life, or how it related to my question regarding the time, I frowned. Then I pulled myself around the edge and wriggled forwards until it was safe to stand.

"You should be dead!" exclaimed the lady. "There are signs down there to warn about all the crevasses."

"It's fine," I said.

"But you were on your own," said the man.

Did that obvious statement require an answer? Not wishing to commit myself, I brushed the snow from my clothes and hair.

"Without a guide," said the man.

Well, that certainly seemed like 'on my own'.

"There are signs down there to say this ridge should only be attempted with a guide, due to all the crevasses," said the woman.

I glanced up the ridge. "You do not need a guide," I said, "because it is a simple walk."

"No," said the man. "The signs said we must…"

While they tried to explain about all the ways a person could die in the mountains, I thought about my teenage attempt to learn German at night school. I had found it so confusing I'd stopped going after one lesson, but that had covered how to ask the time. "*Vass ist da hur?*" I asked, while pointing to my wrist, which clearly lacked a watch.

Strangely, the absence of a timepiece seemed to hypnotise them. Not wishing to get involved in their back-to-front logic, I told them there was no need to rush because they were only fifteen minutes from the top. Then, having failed to discover the time – despite asking in two languages – I plodded up the right-hand trench to the summit… where there was a cafe!

Readers should be warned that what comes next is truly horrendous. Descending the ridge – keeping to the right-hand trench to avoid head-on collisions with those still ascending – brought me to the signs the Germans had mentioned. Some merely warned, others spoke of death, and one even stated, 'Those venturing beyond this point will need to employ a guide.' Then, perhaps a hundred yards further on, I was in the midst of a hideous ski centre, where visitors paraded in their fashion clothes. After scurrying through the centre, I began a long plod down the only escape road. It was obviously taking me to the E55 at the junction which had the vehicle restriction signs at the bottom. I felt so lucky to have arrived in the area driving a lorry. The ascent of Gladly Hopping Pigeon by the tourist route is surely the most boring, pointless thing a person can do. I reckoned by following tarmac roads my walk home would be about twelve miles. I therefore anticipated having a comfortable bivvy in some forest or other en route.

However, before I reached the treeline, a car stopped beside me. It was the Germans I had met earlier, and they still seemed to believe that I was intent on killing myself – now by being run over by a vehicle whizzing around a blind bend, perhaps? They offered me a lift, which introduced a complex moral dilemma into my brain: is it bending the truth to say, "I climbed the Gladly Hopping Pigeon" without adding the disclaimer, "but got a lift back down"? Well, the ethics of descent are a controversial subject in the world of mountaineering. For example, some purists believe that if after climbing the north face of the Eiger a person gets a lift back down in a helicopter, the phrase 'I climbed the mountain' is invalid. Others say the climbing-up bit is sufficient to claim victory. Fortunately, this book is only about what normal people can reasonably do, on an average wage, without expecting to die in the process. So, I never need to worry about all of the Eiger stuff; merely the ethics of accepting a lift home when you have reached a public highway. Normally I consider getting into a car, or even the back of a pickup vehicle with a couple of pigs, most acceptable. The problem with this road was that it goes nearly to the top of the mountain. But walking down it would be the same as being confined to a treadmill in a gloomy Victorian jail. So I got in the car and immediately began telling the Germans more about my recent ascent. Then I paced the drama so that my 'death-defying' rock climb above the second glacier coincided with them reaching the E55.

"I live just the other side of Lom," I said, interrupting my story. "It's no problem to walk home from here."

The word 'live' was clearly misleading, because it implied a permanent residence. The correct word was obviously 'living', because that suggested a current, possibly temporary address. But I had acquired a liking for residing on the outskirts of a posh Norwegian town, so did not correct myself. I am pleased to say my devious plan worked: the Germans could not leave the drama while I was on a cliff face. They turned left onto the E55, which allowed me to conclude my story when I climbed up to their 'ridge of death'. Then, when my house came into view, I asked them to park on the patch of gravel which represented my garden. They looked at my house, then back and forth at each other, seemingly confused, but followed my request.

"Thanks," I said, getting out of the car. "That is so kind." Then, as far as my bewildered German friends were concerned, I walked to my front door and disappeared into a house bolted onto the back of a lorry. I heard them drive away, presumably to tell their family and friends that, while on holiday, they had met a real Yeti who lived in a lorry!

Anyway, thanks to my free 'taxi' ride, the following morning my legs were okay to explore the second glacier properly without delay. After walking directly up to its termination, I found it an enjoyable way to spend a couple of hours. (It is slightly more technical than the first glacier, and requires an ice axe in each hand – crampons essential. However, compared to most Alpine glaciers, it's very easy and safe.) At the top of the glacier I joined my original route, where I was pleased to find my previous footprints still in place. Later, while descending the glacier I located a detached snow/ice tower with a flat top measuring about eight feet by six. After jumping onto this, I snuggled up in my sleeping bag and lay on my back to gaze upwards. As day gave way to a clear, starlit sky, it became exceedingly peaceful and the icy air made my face tingle. Then, when the first rays of dawn chased away the stars, I got up, jumped back to the rest of the glacier, and so returned home in time for dinner. I was no longer a Yeti in search of a mate, but a man who had found contentment in solitude, uncomplicated by the terrible dark pains of unrequited love.

Chapter Thirty-Nine

After my Scandinavian adventure, I returned to work for the Worcester Steamer Company as a part-time training officer, plus relief captain. Domestic bliss was provided by my house on wheels parked next to the racecourse. More importantly, for my climbing there was a new piece of equipment called a Petzl Shunt. In one direction it slides up a rope, but in the other automatically locks under load. For solo climbing – assuming you have easy access to the top of the crag – it is only necessary to attach a rope above your route and dangle it over the side. The bottom end is then tied to a rucksack to weigh it down. The taut rope is then inserted into the shunt, which you also attach to your harness. If you fall, *in theory*, the shunt will lock, leaving you swinging from the rope.

> *HEALTH AND SAFETY ALERT: This is not the intended purpose of a shunt, and I am certain the manufacturers would advise against using it as a belay which slides up the rope beside the climber. But I have seen someone else using it in this way, and he said it had held a number of his falls. In any event, it is probably better than tying loops into the climbing rope, as was my earlier practice.*

It is also a lot easier than trying to get a lady to go climbing with me.

For some people, moving house means carrying all their belongings to an intermediate wagon, then expensively paying someone to drive it to another place so that their heavy furniture can be carried into a cold, empty building, where it might not match the decor. What a ridiculous idea! When I move house, I just do it. So, after living in Grandstand Road for seven years, I left Worcester to go somewhere else… yet to be decided.

Four months later, my house was nicely situated in a rural lay-by set a little way back from the main Criccieth–Porthmadog road in North Wales. Only much later did I learn that my existence had generated lots of curiosity within the surrounding towns and villages. The three most commonly asked questions about the nature of my residence, I will now answer…

Question one: Why has it got a dinghy hanging on the back? Answer: When I was twenty-seven, I happened to meet an elderly gentleman on Ben Nevis, who suggested I learn to sail. "You cannot continuously do mountaineering when you suffer from arthritic joints," he had explained. "I now spend half my time sailing, which is more relaxing." Whether this information was a subconscious factor in helping me decide to row a play dinghy around Brean Down, I cannot say. But in any event, that had been a voyage of discovery so, aged forty-seven, I developed the idea by purchasing a proper eight-foot dinghy made of really tough plastic. The mast and sails (racing rig) were kept in my bedroom, together with a life jacket. My best seagoing adventures are briefly covered in *Yeti Seeks Mate*, so I do not repeat them here. The important thing is the advice I now offer: take up sailing, preferably using a boat you can keep at home to avoid mooring fees. It needs to be small enough to carry on whatever vehicle you happen to own, possibly using a roof rack. Throwing yourself about the bottom of a dinghy like moving ballast to stop it capsizing is a fun thing to do, and nicely complements an otherwise wonderful life of mountaineering.

Question two: Why is there a lamp post sticking from the top of your lorry? (It's just the post; the lamp part having been removed.)

Answer: People often telephone the fire brigade when they see smoke coming from the back of a lorry. The chimney needs to be really high to indicate that the 'house' is not actually on fire, and everything is as it should be.

Question three: Why are there plants growing from your roof? Answer: They are nice to look at. Others are good to eat. You cannot dig up a lay-by to achieve a garden, so the roof is all I have. (Note: bridges over roads occasionally reduce total headroom to fourteen feet, so avoid planting sunflowers.)

After living in the lay-by for eighteen months, I was offered a patch of land on a posh business park in Porthmadog. The only condition was that the landowner wanted to stick 'site security' signs on my residence. Apparently, not only did my house intrigue people, but the mysterious man who lived inside it had a reputation for being a bit scary.

My lorry finally stopped its occasional wanderings in 2010, when it fortuitously broke down in its site-security location. Since then it has been like any other house, except for the minor detail that its foundations are six lorry-sized wheels. So I have been living in the most pleasant business park on the outskirts of the lovely coastal town of Porthmadog for over twenty years. With its wonderful mix of friendly residents, summer visitors, and famous attractions such as the Cob sea barrier, Portmeirion Italianate village, and the Ffestiniog & Welsh Highland Railways, it suits me very well indeed.

My dream of living near some mountains and being a professional writer began after I had returned from Mont Blanc in 1980. My first book was published forty-one years later in 2021 – I do not like being defeated in any project I undertake.

Chapter Forty

When I first came to Wyddfa, aged twenty-four, I gave no thought as to how this might affect my old age – which I then believed would begin at thirty. This was because I could never imagine a life without climbing, or being so old as to be classified as a thirty-something. Then, as each year passed, mostly without notice, I carried on climbing pretty much as before. I solved my fortieth-birthday midlife crisis by going to Africa. Aged forty-seven, I moved to North Wales, so my adventurous activities actually increased. At fifty, I had four hobbies: rock climbing, mountaineering, potholing, and sailing. In my head I was still a teenager. Ten years later, it was much the same, except I had a free bus pass, so my lorry breaking down was not an issue.

When I was sixty-seven I met Eric Jones, who lives in the next village to Porthmadog. (He was the first British person to solo-climb the north face of the Eiger, but is such a modest gentleman that he avoids talking about his youthful achievements.) He is still climbing in his eighties and, for relaxation, enjoys mountain biking, parachuting, and bungee-jumping from suspension bridges.

So where is this old age I had been dreading? It seems not to exist. The only effect it has on my life is that I can visit the mountains using a bus pass. And if I miss the last bus back to town, I can bivvy under a hedge or walk home, depending on my mood and/or physical condition.

Anyway, returning to Eric. After our first meeting, I read his autobiography *A Life on the Edge*, which I now recommend to all those wanting to learn more about hardcore adventures far beyond my ordinary, sentimental wanderings. In his book, he also mentions Alison Hargreaves, which made me very curious about her true personality rather than her climbing credentials. After finishing his book, I asked Eric if he had indeed met Alison on one of his five Himalayan expeditions.

His normal happy expression immediately faded. "Yes," he said quietly.

"Was she really as nice as I believe?" I asked.

"Lovely girl; always kind and considerate. Tragic way for her to die."

"I remember exactly where I was when I read about it," I said. "At the launderette. I roamed the streets for two hours before I could return to transfer my washing to the dryers."

"I also remember where I was…"

And then he told me more about her story. As he continued, I became really upset. He went quiet, then decided to lighten our mood.

"I remember when she was seventeen," he said, "and coming into my cafe after climbing the local crags."

"What?! She was here, then. I was also here the same year." *Had I known this, I would have set up camp outside your doorway, perchance we should 'accidentally' meet.*

I got upset again by what he told me next. Apparently, hardly anyone could climb at her grade, and the few who did would struggle with the idea of being led by a 'girl'. So, while I had failed to get a girlfriend because I was (relative to her grade) a rubbish climber, she had experienced boyfriend issues because she was too amazing. Because of this, we had both mostly climbed solo. If only I had laid siege to Eric's cafe…

The what-ifs are too sad to think about. Or at least, that is what men are supposed to say. But the night after my talk with Eric, as I sat before my warm fireside with a mug of drinking chocolate, I thought back to the time I was on the iced-up wall near the Gladly Hopping Pigeon. Like Alison on her K2 trip, I had also been completely alone, deciding whether to make the next difficult move. The fog, the cold, and not knowing my precise location were all against me. So I had retreated – because I could. Okay, let's say it straight: I retreated because I was a coward and a failure. But how had it been for Alison on her last mountain? Obviously vastly harder than my Norwegian effort, but the principle was the same. I had passed the sensible limit of my ability. Alison, however, had a manager to satisfy, so felt she had to continue, no matter what. Also, like Alison, had I continued and fallen, I would have disappeared into the fog on the way down to the second glacier, never to be seen again. But nobody cared much about me one way or the other, so I could retreat. Alison went on, in temperatures of around minus fifty degrees centigrade, until torn from the ridge by winds in excess of 150 miles per hour. No one knows where she landed and, in any event, that mountain range has many shattered bodies scattered around; their recovery being impractical. So, frozen in time, Alison will always be thirty-three, though I only really remember the photograph I had seen when she was seventeen. Weirdly, this means I now only view her as the granddaughter figure who I wanted to tell off for doing exceedingly dangerous things.

Anyway, returning to this 'old age' nonsense. In considering this, it is necessary to differentiate between the 'arbitrary age number' and the probability of a specific illness randomly occurring over an increasing length of time. In my case, this principally concerns the damage done to my knees when I was twenty-seven. But miraculously they have shown some improvement in recent years, which I believe is a beneficial side effect of potholing.

I am currently exploring a cave system which begins with a long walk through a thigh-deep underground river. This maintains gentle pressure on the knee joints, while also taking a little weight off my legs. I could probably enjoy the same effect by walking back and forth across the shallow end of a swimming pool – but such strange behaviour would annoy family groups, who use it as a play area.

Obviously I have never attempted this swimming pool experiment, but assume it would also be extremely boring. Back down the pothole, after walking through cold water for half an hour I emerge onto mud which sucks on my wellingtons. I am then presented with a delightful rock climb of two hundred feet. And that is only the start of the fun!

A different pothole I recently explored involved wriggling through a tiny tunnel created by the fallen boulders of a collapsed roof. The intricate sequence of gaps only just allowed my shoulders and hips to pass. But no gaps lined up, which meant doing twisting moves, often while upside down, with my arms and legs forced into extreme, yoga-like positions. Then I came to a downward shaft, across which the boulders had wedged in place. This meant curling my body up and getting my feet onto the wall. Like I said, all amazing good fun and, after such workouts, my knees generally remain pain-free for the following week.

Naturally I buy the bimonthly glossy potholing magazine, which confirms my fellowship with like-minded, sensible people. The magazine is called *Descent*, and is such a good read I am baffled as to why all shops do not sell it. But according to my local newsagents, they do not even keep it beneath the counter as an 'underground' magazine! However, you can order it direct from the publishers, whose address is online.

At the age of sixty-eight I was descending the relatively isolated south ridge of Wyddfa when I saw something strange emerging through the mist. Coming up a steep section were three men, all wearing shorts and T-shirts. What struck me as odd was that two of them were carrying a telegraph pole on their shoulders, while the third appeared to be supervising. I stopped my descent to observe their approach, while thoughtfully scratching my chin. When the men were about six feet away I said hello; this being the etiquette for an encounter in a remote setting.

"'Old yer 'orses," said the supervisor in a broad northern accent, real friendly, like.

I thought this a most appropriate comment, given that all three had the bulging muscles of a carthorse. I imagined they worked in a shipyard, carrying the steel girders which were too heavy for forklift trucks. And now the men stood idling, apparently forgetting they had a massive pole on their shoulders.

"What are you doing?" I asked.

"Snowdon," answered the supervisor.

"Not the easiest route when you are… er… well, carrying a telegraph pole. And is it to be used on the top?"

"Nah."

"So you are… er…?"

He gave me a look which suggested sympathy towards a man of limited intelligence. I reckoned he was thinking, *Surely it is obvious that we are climbing Snowdon with a telegraph pole. Why else would we be here?*

"Ah! For charity," I exclaimed.

"Nah."

I was perplexed. "And you do this often?" I asked.

"At this min't we're doin' t' Three Peaks."

"Including Ben Nevis?!"

This established me as a simpleton who was unsure as to what the highest mountain in Scotland might be. The men, apparently bored with my childlike interrogation, decided to continue their upwards march without further ado. I watched them disappear into the mist, then stood awhile to ponder their unusual activity. Finally I decided that it was merely an extreme form of tossing the caber, a sport which Scottish people who roamed Ben Nevis would appreciate.

On completing my descent to the col where the south ridge levels out, before rising again to the summit of Yr Aran, I noticed another three men crowding around a large sheet map. As I deviated slightly to get past the trio, I said the normal polite hello and walked on for another two paces.

"Do you know these parts well?" called a voice from behind.

Since moving to Wales I had visited every area in central Snowdonia, and knew what led to where, together with the places better suited to goats. "I've been coming here over forty years," I replied.

"Our first time," said one of them. He then handed me the map. "Are we here?" he asked, while pointing to a specific place.

This was the first time I had seen an Ordnance Survey map of the area, and initially all the wriggly lines confused me. "Give me a moment," I said. "I only work in three dimensions, so where you are pointing is just a splodge of orange ink to me." After a couple of minutes I looked away from the map. "What you are pointing to is the Crib Goch ridge," I said.

"Yes," said the man. "Is this it?"

Before committing myself, I asked the men to tell me about their route that day. They had parked in the Pen-y-Pass car park, intending to do the Crib Goch, but had, I deduced, gone up the Miners' Track to reach Wyddfa's summit. On their second attempt to find the ridge they had somehow circumnavigated Wyddfa, using rough animal tracks, to end up here, completely on the opposite side to where they thought. "What time did you leave the car park," I asked, "and what time is it now?"

"We left at nine o'clock; now it's… 5.30."

Even if I run, I thought, *I'll miss the last bus home* (the S4). "So you've been walking for eight and a half hours," I said.

"Climbing," said the man. "We've been to the very top of Snowdon itself."

I looked them up and down. Their clothes appeared brand new, which gave me a dilemma. Truthfully, I knew that the only practical way to get from here to where their car was parked was back over the summit of Wyddfa. It would be dark in four hours and, after already walking for over eight, climbing the south ridge as an encore would be exhausting. Also, their eight-and-a-half-hour adventure told me that they had been a bit more lost than they admitted. A map in their hands was a lethal weapon. I made a decision on their behalf to send them a way which, though less practical than going back over the top, would have a lower death potential. "Go down that scrambly path there," I said, "then bear left. That will take you to the Watkin Path. Keep heading down this, and you will come to a road. Turn left—"

"Sounds a long way. Can't we take a shortcut across the mountains?" one interrupted.

"It's better suited to goats," I said, "and it will be dark in four hours. Reaching the road is downhill all the way. You'll be there in an hour."

After some debate, I watched the men tramp away in the direction I had indicated. But I knew they would eventually try to take a shortcut across the mountains, because even though I had not mentioned the four hours of road walking ahead of them, I expected the tangled hillside vegetation would eventually force them back onto the safer tarmac option.

After they were out of sight, I stood to ponder my situation. On my first visit to Wyddfa, I too had come this way in a desperate bid to reach the Pen-y-Pass car park. I could almost see my younger self trudging by, exhausted and with ragged pumps. And what had I done then? Got myself stranded on the top of Lliwedd after attempting a shortcut. That particular experience had inspired me, and so changed my life – I was now back on the same spot forty-four years later. Then I remembered what the men had said about the time. I turned on my heels and hurried down the track I had first ascended aged twenty-four. My only panic now was trying to reach Rhyd Ddu in half an hour, when the last bus would leave for Caernarfon, with a later express service heading to Porthmadog. Using these, I would be home and tucked up in bed within five hours – such a different end to this day than that of my first visit, when I had arrived on a glorified moped with a Woolworths tent for accommodation.

Epilogue

A Day in the Life of Me, Aged Seventy

It began on a Saturday morning in late January. After getting out of bed, I lit a candle, then quickly dressed. Next I made my way to the kitchen where, the previous night, I had a prepared a kettle of water and a pan of milk. In winter this is essential because, if both liquids freeze in plastic containers, my morning mug of cappuccino is delayed, possibly by an hour. (Heating plastic containers on a gas ring is impractical.) Anyway, on this day my foresight was correct because all water within my home had turned to ice. After leaving the kettle and milk pan on the stove to melt their contents, I turned my thoughts to lighting the fire. However, on re-entering the living room I held the candle near the wall thermometer which, to my surprise, was reading minus five degrees centigrade! The coastal town of Porthmadog rarely has such a low temperature. I returned to the kitchen. Here, because the windows were covered with curtains of ice, I opened the door to look outside. The frost was all sparkly and pretty. I decided that, for the first time in many years, Wyddfa might be in condition. Panic! All my ice-climbing tools were somewhere under the bed. The bus to the Pen-y-Pass car park would leave Porthmadog in forty minutes. Within that time I had to get everything I needed into a rucksack and race to the nearest bus stop, from where the S4 would take me to a longed-for winter paradise.

Thirty-five minutes later I emerged from a footpath in sight of the bus stop, but still two hundred yards from it. Running with a rucksack, while carrying ice axes and crampons, is hard. Yet I knew if the bus came, it would appear briefly from behind a row of houses, then whizz past the stop and be gone. Thankfully, I got there first, but only with a few seconds to spare. It was the most disorganised start to any trip I had ever 'achieved'. Perspiring after my run, I sat down, while telling the friendly driver that my various ice-climbing fangs would not damage the seat. Then I took off my recently acquired boots to adjust my crampons to their shape. But the fixing bolts had corroded in place and, however hard I tried with the spanner, they remained stuck. Then I discovered I had picked up a torch with flat batteries. As well as this inconvenience, the list of things I had forgotten to pack was too long to mention, but at least it distracted me from the corroded crampons. On the positive side, this was going to be a really good diet day because, in my haste to leave home, I had needed to abandon all thoughts of breakfast or cappuccino.

After half an hour or so, the bus climbed to the Pen-y-Pass car park, which acts as a public transport hub. So this is a good time to mention essential knowledge for first-time visitors to the area. A Wyddfa experience in 2024 will bear little resemblance to my solitary wanderings of forty years earlier. Ascending one of the main paths is now about socialising with like-minded folk who might otherwise be working out in a gym. The summit itself is packed with people, the queue to the trig point sometimes taking half an hour, as those reaching it pose to have their photograph taken, many times over. When I first came here, the summit cafe was little more than a glorified shed which almost – but not quite – fitted in. That has now been replaced by a 'monstrous alien spacecraft' which seems to have landed in a place where it could best dominate the surrounding landscape.

For those who wish to avoid the crowds, there are many (rarely used) scrambling routes up Wyddfa, but I only recommend using them once you are familiar with the area and have achieved a basic climbing technique. The Pen-y-Pass car park – where once I was *unreasonably* charged for tying a Woolworths tent to my moped – is now impractical to use for 'camping'. It is highly regulated, needs to be booked in advance, and if you have to ask the price then, like a Rolls-Royce, you can't afford it. The National Park Authority prefer all but disabled visitors to park at the bottom of the pass, which is a fraction of the cost. A newly laid path allows a fit person to reach the higher car park in about twenty minutes. Police patrols tow away any vehicle they consider to be causing an obstruction.

Anyway, back to me, aged seventy. The setting is a narrow waterfall which, before freezing, had cut a channel through well-consolidated snow. For my ascent I needed to place both axes on a band of ice no more than nine inches wide, while my crampon-less boots bridged across to the walls of snow. At the very top the ice became vertical, which meant a long reach to plant the shaft of my walker's axe into the snow above. Using the axe as a handhold, I carefully pulled myself up and over. It was a very delicate balancing act, which eventually allowed me to stand on the steep snowfield above. As I turned to survey the winter wonderland I thought, *That's just the sort of thing I would have done in my youth, before acquiring all the fancy equipment, like crampons.* Playtime then continued – quite forgetting that I had a bus to catch.

After retreating from my near-vertical solitude, I rejoined a snowfield which lay above the main footpath. It was so crowded, it caused me to blink – twice. There were snowball fights, improvised slides, and hundreds of people taking photographs. Looking up to Wyddfa's summit, I saw a swarming splodge of humanity in brightly coloured clothes. On my first winter visit to the summit, there had been no one else present. I was pleased to see so many people enjoying themselves – but glad not to be part of it. Turning away, I began the gentle plod back to the car park, knowing that unless something very unusual happened, I would be home in time for tea…

In rural Wales, a pessimist might believe the public transport system starts shutting down at five o'clock and ceases to exist two hours later. Those who look on the positive side know in their heart that, on major roads, a bus will be going somewhere until at least six in the evening... perhaps. An optimist also knows if they stare at a timetable long enough, it will eventually reveal more favourable information. The idea of the last bus to Porthmadog leaving at 3.30 was just too silly to be believed.

Presently, I stepped aside so two other visitors could study the bus schedule. (Being observed by three people was certain to make the timetable behave differently.) Then one of the men checked his wristwatch.

"3.40," he said. "Reckon we missed it."

"No," I contradicted firmly, "there must be another bus because..." *Because from this side of the mountain, my walk home is eighteen miles.*

The men, not being privy to my thoughts, were unconcerned by this. Apparently, they had only wanted to use the bus to reach their car at the bottom of the pass. I explained my predicament – or more correctly, hinted they might be able to help me. They responded by saying they were staying in Llanberis.

"But we'll be coming back this way in half an hour," said one of the men. "Is a lift to Llanberis any good?"

Snap decisions are often unwise, but there seemed very little to lose by accepting their kind offer. It would take me down to sea level, where it might be above freezing, so allowing the snow inside my boots to thaw. Also, Llanberis is a major town, which meant buses would be going to both Caernarfon and Bangor, where I could pick up a coastal service until around eight o'clock.

Anyway, the promised lift eventually arrived and took me to a bus stop in Llanberis High Street. I went to look at the timetable; my plan being to get cake and coffee if my transport was more than half an hour away. (This would be my first food and drink of the day.) But the timetable was covered by a sign stating that the stop was out of use. I walked to the next, passing many warm cafes en route. Maybe, if my bus was not imminent, I could nip in and get a hot drink, but the next stop was also out of service. However, it had a poster advising of a temporary stop on the bypass. This turned out to be a rusty sign fixed to a scaffold post, nicely hidden between two bushes. There was no timetable, which meant I could not leave this dark, windy, unlit bypass for fear of unknowingly missing an important bus.

To prevent my well-used muscles seizing up due to cold inactivity, I began walking back and forth as if on sentry duty, always staying within twenty paces of the post. This went on for so long it melted the snow from my boots, allowing the water to squelch in my socks. Later still, I began to consider the possibility of bus drivers forgetting they were supposed to be coming along the bypass, or simply preferring their familiar High Street route instead.

Finally a bus appeared – as expected, whizzing along at a reckless speed. I jumped up and down, waved my arms, and generally panicked that the driver would fail to see me in the darkness. In response, he flashed a message on his electronic destination display. In Welsh, it said the equivalent of 'Sorry, out of service.' As I watched its rear lights disappearing into the night, I decided it was the last bus leaving this town until the morning. It seemed my only option was to walk towards Caernarfon with my thumb out.

Paradoxically, my saviour was the rough verge of the bypass, which was used as a fly-tipping area. This caused me to stagger through uneven mud until I tripped over a shopping trolley. Then a car screeched to a halt by my side.

"You are going to kill yourself," shouted an angry voice from inside.

"The buses did not come..." I whined.

"I'm going to Bangor, any good?"

Anywhere was better than here, so I got in. Then I noticed the time on the dashboard clock: 7.15. I had been patrolling the pretend bus stop for three hours. Then the driver redirected his panic attack regarding my personal safety to my rucksack with its attached axes and crampons. I admit they did seem out of place so near the car's upholstery. Also, I was very wet and soggy, and the heater was causing steam to rise from my clothes. This made the man less kind.

"I'm going to the other side of Bangor," he said, "one and a half miles from the centre."

"Long way from the bus station," I hinted.

"Don't know; never use buses," he replied crossly, obviously insulted by my slanderous accusation. "I'm going around the bypass; where would you like to be dropped?"

Even running, I could not make the last bus leaving Bangor city centre, especially with a rucksack bouncing up and down on my back.

"It would be best," said the man forcefully, "if you got out of my car at the next traffic island. From there a road goes down the hill to a bus route, I think. But I don't know for certain, because I never use them!"

"Understand," I replied, while secretly waiting for him to introduce a radical new idea like driving through Bangor, because it would shorten his journey. But he stopped a few yards past the island. I thanked him, got out, then thought, *I have no idea where I am.* The only answer I could think of was, *Much further away from home than when my journey began.*

Following the man's instructions, I soon found myself staggering through a tunnel of trees, the overhanging branches so densely interwoven not even starlight could penetrate. Sometimes I walked on the uneven, muddy verge until unseen, spiky twigs attacked me, forcing me backwards to the road. Down this I blindly zigzagged, using my walker's ice axe to tap my way forwards – until a car whizzed around one of the many hairpin bends. Then I used its headlights to fix my position and so leap to the nearest verge, turning quickly to see where the tail lights were heading.

After a fairly unpleasant, mostly blind plod, I came to a settlement with a local service bus stop. The timetable showed that the next bus to Caernarfon was due at 8pm. Well, that sounded positive. Shortly afterwards it arrived and took me to Caernarfon; arriving at the central bus station a mere ten minutes after the last bus to Porthmadog had departed.

The best place to stay the night in Caernarfon is beneath the old railway arches, which span a very pretty nature reserve on the outskirts. (Not official council policy.) How ironic that, until falling victim to the substantial destruction of the rail network in the 1960s, this viaduct had carried a branch line that went directly to Llanberis. Back then, when they had proper steam locomotives, I could have boarded at Llanberis and travelled to Porthmadog on the main coast line, now also decommissioned. So the railways could no longer get me where I wanted to go; only offer me a place to sleep. However, I still had one slight hope of getting home that night. A sign told me there would be a final bus heading south-west to Pwllheli in ten minutes' time. This was still eighteen miles from my house, but many locals knew me and it only needed one to stop and offer me a lift.

While still weighing up my limited options, the bus to Pwllheli arrived; its doors sliding open to entice weary travellers onto its warm, soft seats. My need for instant gratification made me accept its invitation. Hence, the bus dropped me at Pwllheli at about nine. I knew all public transport to Porthmadog had long departed, so began a weary plod. An hour later, I modified this prediction to a *very long* plod. This caused me to start looking around for a place to sleep. Then a car stopped, reversed, and wound down a window.

"I'm going to Criccieth," said a man's voice from inside.

Criccieth is where the posh people live. So, the fact the car looked a bit like a Rolls-Royce did not surprise me. Okay, it might have been a BMW, but so long as it had wheels and an engine, I did not really care. I sank into the soft upholstery of the rear seat and marvelled at the computer display on the dashboard. It seemed surreal that ten hours earlier I had been hanging from ice axes with fresh air beneath my feet; then found myself staggering blindly along a road-cum-racetrack; and now had a chauffeur-driven ride in a car which appeared to be floating upon its suspension system.

For my part, I provided what I hoped might be entertaining conversation about my day and my current attempt to reach Porthmadog, where I lived. The driver's lady passenger remained silent, possibly thinking, *This man sounds really interesting; if we take him to his house in Porthmadog, I might learn more about his life.*

Normally, I have no problem walking the four miles home from Criccieth, but tonight I was less enthusiastic about it. And so I said something very naughty. As I told the man about myself, I 'accidentally' mentioned that I had recently passed my seventieth birthday.

"Seventy?!" he exclaimed. (I imagine my tale about hanging from ice axes had made him think I was younger.)

The lady gave a little cough, like royalty when they expect something more to happen.

"It's no problem taking you home," said the man.

"I could not possibly impose…"

"But I insist."

As we approached Porthmadog, he asked where I lived, so he might take me to my door – like you do with old people.

"A lorry on the business park," I said. "If you could drop me at the corner by the builders' merchants, I would be very grateful."

"A lorry?" he said.

"Yes, but I can easily walk from the corner."

The kindness of strangers often goes unrecorded, so I want to tell everyone about this couple who went out of their way for maybe twenty minutes – yet saved me from having to choose between a night in the bushes or a long walk home. Because of them, I was in my soft, warm bed by eleven.

The following morning I got up and walked around my living room to test my knees. They were fine. Then I stood on my bathroom scales to discover that my previous adventure had reduced my weight by 1.8 kilograms. After giving my flatter tummy a congratulatory pat, I dressed quickly and hurried to Porthmadog's leisure centre to play a table tennis match. After that I had snooker booked at a local village hall, followed by a meeting with my agent and publicist Ian Spindley to discuss how my fourth book (a third novel) might best be promoted.

So to all you young people out there, I say: having survived an unnatural upbringing in a city, and later suffered terribly from the dark torments of unrequited love, at the age of forty-six I awoke on a Norwegian glacier, knowing that I had found complete serenity in a perfect world, and without needing a girlfriend. A year later, after emigrating to Wales I became overwhelmed with happiness, which still lasts now.

In conclusion, I can say that old age is like a bus which you always expect to arrive, but which never does. Though it is quite useful to pretend otherwise if you want a lift home.

NORK FROM NOWHERE

Upper-class teen Sara flees her parents' middle-England mansion after a disastrous party. She happens upon Nork, a mysterious, young, orphan boy seemingly from nowhere.

Together they go on the run. Evading the authorities and becoming ever more inter-dependent during their long journey, they finally end up in the Scottish wilderness.

They find themselves in a small loch-side town, but will they become the victims of the ruthless, hotel owner McTavish – or can they discover a new life and purpose there?

This is a coming-of-age story with comedy, romance and sexual references, that is both amusing and thought-provoking.

THE ICE CREAM TERRORIST

Two forcibly segregated, separate-sex and rurally isolated schools are inhabited by malevolent masters, petrified pupils, more kindly matrons and a handful of true heroes – including The Ice Cream Terrorist.

This titanic tale of redemption shows how pupils and staff – blighted by dysfunctional, post-war, orphanage schools in Britain – escape and reform the brutal system.

Join their journey through school suffering, then on a road trip to a coastal idyll full of kindness, safety and real-life skills, and eventually different lives. Free from oppression with more enlightened care, they create progressive futures.

YETI SEEKS MATE

Yeti (male 28) seeks mate. Can be seen Christmas/Easter roaming Ben Nevis, Snowdon some weekends in between. Migrates to Alps around June. Very friendly, generally harmless, except on ski-slopes. Very safe experienced motorcyclist Britain and abroad – would get sidecar, if nagged. Please write…
(Personal ad published in a national mountaineering magazine.)

From an asthmatic childhood spent on post-war Birmingham bomb sites, Mike Leaver escaped from cruel state boarding schools to careers as a lab technician, accountant, pleasure-boat captain and local builder.

Mike has also been:
A homeless hermit inhabiting a derelict boat surrounded by drug addicts;
An adventurer/mountaineer in the UK, Scandinavia, and North Africa; and

A semi-retired handyman writing books while enjoying an ideal life off-grid in a converted lorry in a pretty coastal town.

Embark on an extraordinary journey of an eccentric pursuing dreams of love, writing and the path to happiness in a memoir that's as charming as it is quirky.

NEWSPAPER CURTAINS

Two teenage girls from opposite sides of the tracks in 1960s Midlands England are forced into prostitution in this engrossing tale of loss, liberty, and love.

Weep at the relationship between clever Janet and spoiled Priscilla, as their handsome, young English teacher, Mr Edwards – and his corrupting father – become embroiled in their tortuous journeys.

But then a smart heroine Tara fatefully enters the fray on a secret detective mission.

Dramatic and topical events include a city-slum killing, police malfeasance, newspaper-business bribery, emotional blackmail, destitute homelessness, and a mountaineering adventure.

This saga combines a socio-political struggle by the under-privileged against repression, with both feminine and asexual insights into love, to produce a thought-provoking, yet stylishly old-fashioned, romantic rollercoaster.

Mike Leaver, 71, lives off-grid in a converted, static truck on a business park in Snowdonia. Like Alan Bennett's the Lady in the Van, Mike has become a well-known eccentric around his adopted home of Gwynedd. He is the author of three saga novels – *Nork from Nowhere*, *The Ice Cream Terrorist*, and *Newspaper Curtains*, and his *Yeti Seeks Mate* autobiography. As well as writing 'Yeti' and his first three modern fictions – almost 500,000 words on a battery-powered laptop often by candlelight in his lorry – this book is the second part of his intriguing life story.

Mike is a single, vegetarian, animal-loving pensioner, who writes and plays chess for pleasure. Aspects of his own personal experience feature – and are sometimes exaggerated – in the travails and adventures of his fictional characters! His books explore the themes of: power, perversion, and coercion versus loyalty, friendliness and collaboration; adult, teenage and child relationships; destitute homelessness, unrequited love and wider social mores.